Due

Measuring and Controlling Interest Rate Risk

Frank J. Fabozzi, CFA
Adjunct Professor of Finance
Yale University
and
Editor
Journal of Portfolio Management

Published by Frank J. Fabozzi Associates

© 1996 By Frank J. Fabozzi Associates
New Hope, Pennsylvania

This publication is designed to provide accurate and authoritative information in regard to the subject matter covered. It is sold with the understanding that the publisher is not engaged in rendering legal, accounting, or other professional services.

ISBN: 1-883249-09-0

Printed in the United States of America
1 2 3 4 5 6 7 8 9 0

To my son,
Francesco Alfonso

TABLE OF CONTENTS

ACKNOWLEDGEMENTS

I am grateful to the following individuals who assisted me in various ways:

Anand Bhattacharya	Prudential Securities
David Canuel	Aeltus Investment Management
John Carlson	Fidelity Management and Research
Martin Czigler	Andrew Kalotay Associates
Ravi Dattatreya	Sumitomo Bank Capital Markets
Richard Ellson	ITT Hartford Life
Michael Ferri	George Mason University
Gifford Fong	Gifford Fong Associates
Joseph Guagliardo, Jr.	FNX Limited
Frank Jones	The Guardian
Andrew Kalotay	Andrew Kalotay Associates
Clinton Lively	Bankers Trust
Jacques Longerstaey	Morgan Guaranty Trust Company
Jan Mayl	TIPS
Mark Pitts	White Oak Capital Management
Frank Ramirez	Structured Capital Management
Chuck Ramsey	Structured Capital Management
Scott Richard	Miller, Anderson & Sherrerd
Ron Ryan	Ryan Labs
George Williams	Andrew Kalotay Associates
David Yuen	Structured Capital Management
Paul Zhao	TIAA

Special thanks to Haitao Li, a doctoral student at Yale University and my teaching assistant, for reading the entire manuscript and providing me with valuable comments.

The two consultants to this project, Megan McAuliffe who provided editorial assistance and Scott Riether who prepared the artwork, greatly facilitated the production process.

Finally, I wish to thank the advertisers for supporting this venture.

Frank J. Fabozzi

INDEX OF ADVERTISERS

Chapter 1
Overview of Measurement and Control of Interest Rate Risk

The goal of this book is to describe how to measure and control the interest rate risk of a bond portfolio or trading position. In this chapter we provide an overview of these two critical areas of risk management. This overview will provide a roadmap for the chapters to follow.

The objectives of this chapter are to:

1. explain two approaches to measuring interest rate risk — the full valuation approach and the duration approach;

2. explain what is meant by the duration of a bond or bond portfolio;

3. explain why the measurement of yield volatility is important in measuring interest rate risk;

4. briefly describe what the value at risk approach is; and,

5. describe what is involved in controlling interest rate risk.

MEASURING INTEREST RATE RISK

The value of a bond changes in the opposite direction to the change in interest rates. For a long bond position, the position's value will decline if interest rates rise, resulting in a loss. For a short bond position, a loss will be realized if interest rates fall.

A manager wants to know more than simply when a position will realize a loss. To control interest rate risk, a manager must be able to quantify what will result. The fundamental relationship is that the *potential dollar loss of a position* resulting from an adverse interest rate change is:

> potential dollar loss of a position
> = value of position after adverse rate change
> − current market value of position

1

Full Valuation Approach to Risk Measurement

The key to measuring the potential dollar loss of a position is how good the estimate is of the value of the position after an adverse rate change. A *valuation model* is used to determine the value of a position after an adverse rate move. Consequently, if a reliable valuation model is not used, there is no way to measure the potential dollar loss. Because valuation models are essential in the measurement of risk, we describe the principles of valuation and two commonly used valuation models in Chapter 2.

The approach to measuring the potential dollar loss whereby the value of the position after the adverse rate change is estimated from a valuation model is referred to as the *full valuation model.*[1] Given a valuation model, the dollar loss for specific scenarios can be determined. Analyzing interest rate risk in this manner is referred to as *scenario analysis.* The manager can then assess the likelihood or probability of each scenario occurring and any unacceptable outcomes can be modified by using the tools described in this book.

Duration Approach to Risk Measurement

An alternate approach is to estimate the potential dollar loss for any rate change by approximating the sensitivity of a position to a rate change. For example, suppose that a trader has a $20 million long position in a bond whose value changes by approximately 4% for a 100 basis point change in rates. Then the manager knows that for a 100 basis point increase in rates, the value of the position will decline by approximately $800,000 ($20 million × 0.04). For a 25 basis point rise in rates, the position will change in value by approximately 1% or $200,000.

Duration is a measure of the approximate sensitivity of a bond's value to rate changes. More specifically, it is the approximate percentage change in value for a 100 basis point change in rates.[2] Consequently, duration can be used to approximate the potential dollar loss. For example, if the market value of a bond held is $20 million and if its duration is 4, then the potential dollar loss for a 25 basis point (0.0025) change in rates is:

$$\$20,000,000 \times 4 \times 0.0025 \ = \ \$200,000$$

For a 5 basis point (0.0005) change in rates, the potential dollar loss is:

$$\$20,000,000 \times 4 \times 0.0005 \ = \ \$40,000$$

Using duration to approximate the potential dollar loss is referred to as the *duration approach to risk management.* The advantage of the duration approach over the full valuation approach is that the latter requires more compu-

---

[1] *RiskMetrics™ — Technical Document*, JP Morgan, Third Edition, 1995, p. 14.
[2] Similarly, the duration of a liability is the approximate percentage change in the value of the liability for a 100 basis point change in rates.

tational time to obtain the new value under each scenario analyzed. The duration approach allows the manager to quickly estimate the effect of an adverse rate change on the potential dollar loss.

A drawback of the duration approach is that duration is only a first approximation as to how sensitive the value of a bond or bond portfolio is to rate changes. Thus, the potential dollar loss of a position is only an approximation, whereas the full valuation approach provides the precise amount of the loss. However, for both approaches, it is essential to have a good valuation model. The duration measure is obtained from a valuation model, so if the valuation model does not do a good job of valuing a security, the duration measure will not be useful. Consequently, when we say that the full valuation approach gives a precise amount of the potential dollar loss, we mean precise given the valuation model used.

In Chapter 3, we take a close look at duration. We will see how it is measured and its limitations. We will see that the approximation provided by duration can be improved by introducing another parameter called convexity. Together, duration and convexity do a more effective job of estimating the sensitivity of a position to adverse rate changes. Both duration and convexity are referred to as parameters of a valuation model. Consequently, estimating the sensitivity of the value of a portfolio or position to adverse rate changes is referred to as the *parametric approach*. Since the full valuation approach does not use parameters, it is also sometimes called the *nonparametric approach*.

Our discussion of the limitations of duration and convexity in Chapter 3 will lead us to the conclusion that the duration and convexity of a portfolio of bonds with different maturities does not tell the whole story about interest rate risk. Another important source of interest rate risk for a portfolio of bonds is how the yield curve changes. In Chapter 2 we describe the yield curve and its role in valuation. In Chapter 4, we discuss several measures of yield curve risk.

Yield Volatility

What we have not considered thus far is how volatile rates are. For example, as we will explain in Chapter 3, all other factors equal, the higher the coupon rate, the lower the duration. Thus, a 10-year junk (high-yield) bond has a lower duration than a current coupon 10-year Treasury note since the former has a higher coupon rate. Does this mean that a 10-year junk bond has less interest rate risk than a current coupon 10-year Treasury note? Consider also that a 10-year Swiss government bond has a lower coupon rate than a current coupon 10-year U.S. Treasury note and therefore a higher duration. Does this mean that a 10-year Swiss government bond has greater interest rate risk than a current coupon 10-year U.S. Treasury note? The missing link is the relative volatility of rates which we shall refer to as *yield volatility*.

The greater the expected yield volatility, the greater the interest rate risk for a given duration and current value of a position. In the case of junk bonds, while their durations are less than current coupon Treasuries of the same maturity, the yield volatility on junk bonds is greater than that of current coupon Treasuries. For the 10-year Swiss government bond, while the duration is greater than for a current coupon 10-year U.S. Treasury, the yield volatility of 10-year Swiss bonds is considerably less than that of 10-year Treasury U.S. bonds.

Consequently, to measure the exposure of a portfolio or position to rate changes it is necessary to measure yield volatility. This requires an understanding of the fundamental principles of probability distributions. This topic is covered in Chapter 5. The measure of yield volatility is the standard deviation of yield changes. In Chapter 6, we show how to estimate yield volatility. As we will see, depending on the underlying assumptions, there could be a wide range for the yield volatility estimate.

Value at Risk

A framework that ties together the price sensitivity of a bond position to rate changes and yield volatility is the *value at risk* (VaR) framework. Risk in this framework is defined as the maximum estimated loss in market value of a given position that is expected to happen a certain percentage of times. JP Morgan has been the major force in promoting VaR.[3,4]

We will discuss the VaR framework further in Chapter 5 after we have discussed duration, yield volatility, and probability distributions. What is critical to understand is that measures of duration and yield volatility are not precise, therefore, there could be considerable variation in the VaR of a position.

---

[3] *RiskMetrics™ — Technical Document*, JP Morgan, May 26, 1995.

[4] Other banks and dealers have developed similar approaches to measuring risk. Most notable is the risk-adjusted return on capital (RAROC™) system developed by Bankers Trust for measuring risk. This system was originally developed and implemented by Bankers Trust in the bond and currency trading department in 1978. In the early 1980s it was applied as a measure of credit risk using the volatility of corporate bond yield premia as proxies for the risk of loss in economic value of credit exposures. The RAROC system is essentially a VaR method scaled very conservatively. The description of RAROC capital provided in Bankers Trust's 1995 annual report is as follows:

> ... the amount of funds required 99 percent of the time to cover a potential after-tax loss over a one year holding period. Specifically, if the Corporation maintained an absolutely static portfolio for one year, there would be less than a 1 percent chance that the portfolio would decline in value by more than the RAROC^{TM} risk capital amount after adjusting for taxes.

Bankers Trust created the first Risk management function in finance in 1987. This group formally monitors and evaluates each day the market risks taken by the firm worldwide. In 1988 this group implemented internally a VaR measure scaled to 99% confidence, 1-day holding period. This measure is known as Daily Price Volatility (DPV) and is used by Bankers Trust as its primary market risk disclosure measure.

A VaR measure can be computed for a single bond position or a bond portfolio. Measurement of the risk of a portfolio of bonds or the risk of several trading positions in different assets is more complicated. This measurement involves the correlation between the yields or prices of these assets. For this reason, we describe correlation analysis in Chapter 7 and explain how correlation affects the risk of a portfolio.

CONTROLLING INTEREST RATE RISK

Once the interest rate risk of a bond portfolio or position is measured, the next step in risk management is to alter the risk exposure to an acceptable level. This is the control phase of risk management.

To control the interest rate risk of a position or portfolio, a position must be taken in another instrument or instruments. We shall refer to an instrument that is used to control the risk of a position as a *risk control instrument*. These instruments include derivative instruments and cash market instruments. The former includes futures, forwards, options, swaps, caps, and floors. They are referred to as derivative instruments because their value is derived from some underlying price, index, or interest rate.

Typically, when cash market instruments are used the instruments of choice are Treasury securities or stripped Treasuries (i.e., zero-coupon Treasuries). In the case of positions in mortgage-backed securities, certain types of mortgage strips (i.e., interest-only and principal-only securities) and certain collateralized mortgage obligation (CMO) products are used. Typically, these products are created from mortgage passthrough securities. These mortgage products are referred to as *mortgage derivative products* because they derive their value from mortgage passthrough securities.

With the advent of derivative instruments, risk management, in its broadest sense, assumes a new dimension. Risk managers can achieve new degrees of freedom. It is now possible to alter the interest rate sensitivity of a bond portfolio, bond position, or asset/liability position economically and quickly. Derivative instruments offer risk and return patterns that previously were either unavailable or too costly to achieve.

In Chapters 8, 9, 10, and 11 we describe these derivative instruments. Chapter 8 describes futures and forward contracts. Chapter 10 describes interest rate swaps. Chapters 10 and 11 cover interest rate options and related products. Chapter 10 focuses on exchange-traded options; Chapter 11 looks at over-the-counter options, interest caps, and interest rate floors.

The selection of the specific instrument or instruments to use involves determining which risk control instruments are the most appropriate to employ given the investment objectives. A key factor in this decision is the correlation between the yield movement of a potential risk control instrument and the yield movement of the bonds whose interest rate risk the manager seeks to control. In addition, it may be necessary to estimate the relationship between yield movements using regression analysis. Correlation and regression analyses are covered in Chapter 7.

Once the appropriate risk control instrument or instruments are selected, the appropriate position (i.e., long or short) and the amount of the position must be determined. The potential outcome of the risk control strategy can then be assessed prior to its implementation. We will explain how this is done in Chapters 12 and 13 using derivative instruments.

KEY POINTS

1. *To control interest rate risk, a manager must be able to quantify the potential dollar loss of a position resulting from an adverse interest rate change.*

2. *The key to measuring the potential dollar loss of a position is having a good valuation model that can be used to determine what the value of a position is after an adverse rate change.*

3. *The full valuation approach to measuring the potential dollar loss of a position after the adverse rate change uses a valuation model.*

4. *Scenario analysis is used to estimate the dollar loss for various interest rate scenarios.*

5. *The duration approach is an alternative approach for estimating the potential dollar loss for any adverse rate change.*

6. *The duration of a position is the approximate percentage change in the position's value for a 100 basis point change in rates.*

7. *A good valuation model is needed to obtain the duration estimate.*

8. *The advantage of the duration approach over the full valuation approach is that it allows the manager to quickly estimate the effect of an adverse rate change on the potential dollar loss.*

9. *A drawback of the duration approach is that duration is only a first approximation of how sensitive the value of a bond or bond portfolio is to rate changes.*

10. *The duration approach to risk management is referred to as the parametric approach while the full valuation approach is called the nonparametric approach.*

11. *Measurement of the interest rate risk of a position must take into account expected yield volatility.*

12. *The greater the expected yield volatility, the greater the interest rate risk of a position for a given duration and current value of a position.*

13. *Yield volatility is measured by the standard deviation of yield changes.*

14. *The value at risk framework ties together the price sensitivity of a bond position to rate changes and yield volatility.*

15. *In the value at risk framework, risk is defined as the maximum estimated loss in market value of a given position that is expected to happen a certain percentage of times.*

16. *The control phase of risk management involves altering the risk exposure to an acceptable level.*

17. *To control the interest rate risk of a position or portfolio, a position must be taken in one or more risk control instruments.*

18. *Risk control instruments include derivative instruments (futures, forwards, options, swaps, caps, and floors) and cash market instruments.*

19. *Derivative instruments allow a risk manager to alter the interest rate sensitivity of a bond portfolio or position or an asset/liability position economically and quickly.*

20. *A key factor in selecting the risk control instrument to employ is the correlation between the yield movements of the bond whose risk is sought to be controlled and the candidate risk control instrument.*

21. *Once the appropriate risk control instrument or instruments are selected, the appropriate position (i.e., long or short) and the amount of the position must be determined.*

Chapter 2

Valuation

Valuation is the process of determining the fair value of a financial asset. The fundamental principle of valuation is that the value of any financial asset is the present value of the expected cash flow. This principle applies regardless of the financial asset. In this chapter, we will explain the general principles of bond valuation and discuss two valuation methodologies.

The objectives of this chapter are to:

1. discuss the process involved in valuing a bond;

2. explain the situations in which determination of a bond's cash flow is complex;

3. explain why a bond should be viewed as a package of zero-coupon securities;

4. explain the difference between the Treasury yield curve and the Treasury spot rate curve and how the theoretical spot rate curve for Treasury securities can be constructed from the Treasury yield curve;

5. demonstrate how the Treasury spot rate curve can be used to value any Treasury security;

6. explain how credit risk should be introduced into the term structure;

7. describe what is meant by the option-adjusted spread;

8. explain why the volatility assumption is critical in the valuation of bonds with embedded options;

9. explain the binomial method for valuation; and,

10. explain the Monte Carlo method for valuing mortgage-backed securities.

ESTIMATING CASH FLOW

Cash flow is simply the cash that is expected to be received each period from an investment. In the case of a bond, it does not make any difference whether the cash flow is interest income or repayment of principal.

The cash flow for only a few types of bonds are simple to project. Non-callable Treasury securities have a known cash flow. For a Treasury coupon security, the cash flow is the coupon interest payments every six months up to the maturity date and the principal payment at the maturity date. For any bond in which neither the issuer nor the investor can alter the repayment of the principal before its contractual due date, the cash flow can easily be determined assuming that the issuer does not default. The difficulty in determining the cash flow for bonds arises under the following circumstances: (1) either the issuer or the investor has the option to change the contractual due date of the repayment of the principal; (2) the coupon payment is reset periodically based on some reference rate; or, (3) the investor has an option to convert the bond to common stock.

Most non-Treasury securities include a provision in the indenture that grants the issuer or the bondholder the right to change the scheduled date or dates when the principal repayment is due. Assuming that the issuer does not default, the investor knows that the principal amount will be repaid, but does not know when that principal will be received. Because of this, the cash flow is not known with certainty.

A key factor determining whether either the issuer of the bond or the investor would exercise an option is the level of interest rates in the future relative to the bond's coupon rate. Specifically, for a callable bond, if the prevailing market rate at which the issuer can refund an issue is sufficiently below the issue's coupon rate to justify the costs associated with refunding the issue, the issuer is likely to call the issue. Similarly, for a mortgage loan, if the prevailing refinancing rate available in the mortgage market is sufficiently below the loan's mortgage rate so that there will be savings by refinancing after considering the associated refinancing costs, then the homeowner has an incentive to refinance. For a putable bond, if the rate on comparable securities rises such that the value of the putable bond falls below the value at which it must be repurchased by the issuer, then the investor will put the issue.

What this means is that to properly estimate the cash flow of a bond it is necessary to incorporate into the analysis how interest rates can change in the future and how such changes affect the cash flow. As we will see later, this is done in valuation models by introducing a parameter that reflects the volatility of interest rates.

DISCOUNTING THE CASH FLOW

Once the cash flow for a bond is estimated, the next step is to determine the appropriate interest rate to use to discount the cash flow. The minimum interest rate that an investor should require is the yield available in the marketplace on a default-free cash flow. In the United States this is the yield on a U.S. Treasury security. The premium over the yield on a Treasury security that the investor should require should reflect the risks associated with realizing the estimated cash flow.

The traditional practice in valuation has been to discount every cash flow of a bond by the same interest rate (or discount rate). For example, consider the following three hypothetical 10-year Treasury securities: a 12% coupon bond, an 8% coupon bond, and a zero-coupon bond. Since the cash flow of all three securities is viewed as default free, the traditional practice is to use the same discount rate to calculate the present value of all three securities and the same discount rate for the cash flow for each period.

The fundamental flaw of the traditional approach is that it views each security as the same package of cash flows. The proper way to view a bond is as a package of zero-coupon instruments. Each cash flow should be considered a zero-coupon instrument whose maturity value is the amount of the cash flow and whose maturity date is the date of the cash flow. Thus, a 10-year 8% coupon bond should be viewed as 20 zero-coupon instruments. The reason that this is the proper way is because it does not allow a market participant to realize an arbitrage profit. This will be made clearer later in this chapter.

By viewing any financial asset in this way, a consistent valuation framework can be developed. For example, under the traditional approach to the valuation of bonds, a 10-year zero-coupon bond would be viewed as the same financial asset as a 10-year 8% coupon bond. Viewing a financial asset as a package of zero-coupon instruments means that these two bonds would be viewed as different packages of zero-coupon instruments and valued accordingly.

To properly value a bond it is necessary to determine the theoretical rate that the U.S. Treasury would have to pay to issue a zero-coupon instrument for each maturity. Another name used for the zero-coupon rate is the *spot rate*. As explained later, the spot rate can be estimated from the Treasury yield curve.

SPOT RATES AND THEIR ROLE IN VALUATION

The key to the valuation of any security is the estimation of its cash flow and the discounting of each cash flow by an appropriate rate. The starting point for the determination of the appropriate rate is the theoretical spot rate on default-free securities. Since Treasury securities are viewed as default-free securities, the theoretical spot rates on these securities are the benchmark rates.

The Treasury Yield Curve

The graphical depiction of the relationship between the yield on Treasury securities of different maturities is known as the *yield curve*. The Treasury yield curve is typically constructed from on-the-run Treasury issues. Treasury bills are zero-coupon securities. Treasury notes and bonds are coupon securities. Consequently, the Treasury yield curve is a combination of zero-coupon securities and coupon securities.

In the valuation of securities what is needed is the rate on zero-coupon default-free securities or, equivalently, the rate on zero-coupon Treasury securities. However, there are no zero-coupon Treasury securities issued by the U.S. Department of the Treasury with a maturity greater than one year. The goal is to construct a theoretical rate that the U.S. government would have to offer if it issued zero-coupon securities with a maturity greater than one year.

There are zero-coupon Treasury securities with a maturity greater than one year that are created by government dealer firms — Treasury STRIPS. It would seem logical that the observed yield on Treasury STRIPS could be used to construct an actual spot rate curve rather than go through the procedure we will describe. There are three problems with using the observed rates on Treasury STRIPS. First, the liquidity of the Treasury STRIPS market is not as great as that of the Treasury coupon market. Thus, the observed rates on Treasury STRIPS reflect a premium for liquidity. Second, there are maturity sectors of the Treasury STRIPS market that attract specific investors who may be willing to trade off yield in exchange for an attractive feature associated with that particular maturity sector, thereby distorting the term structure relationship. For example, certain foreign governments may grant investors preferential tax treatment on zero-coupon bonds. As a result, these foreign investors invest heavily in long-maturity Treasury STRIPS, driving down yields in that maturity sector. Finally, the tax treatment of stripped Treasury securities is different from that of Treasury coupon securities. Specifically, the accrued interest on Treasury STRIPS is taxed even though no cash is received by the investor. Thus they are negative cash flow securities to taxable entities, and, as a result, their yield reflects this tax disadvantage.

Constructing the Theoretical Spot Rate Curve for Treasuries

A default-free theoretical spot rate curve can be constructed from the observed Treasury yield curve. There are several approaches that are used in practice. The approach that we describe below for creating a theoretical spot rate curve is called *bootstrapping*. To explain this approach, we use the price, annualized yield (yield to maturity), and maturity for the 20 hypothetical Treasury securities shown in Exhibit 1.

Throughout the analysis and illustrations to come, it is important to remember that the basic principle is that the value of the Treasury coupon security should be equal to the value of the package of zero-coupon Treasury securities that duplicates the coupon bond's cash flow.

Consider the 6-month Treasury bill in Exhibit 1. Since a Treasury bill is a zero-coupon instrument, its annualized yield of 3.00% is equal to the spot rate. Similarly, for the 1-year Treasury, the cited yield of 3.30% is the 1-year spot rate. Given these two spot rates, we can compute the spot rate for a theoretical 1.5-year zero-coupon Treasury. The price of a theoretical 1.5-year Treasury should equal the present value of the three cash flows from the 1.5-year coupon Treasury, where the yield used for discounting is the spot rate corresponding to the cash flow. Since all the coupon bonds are selling at par, the yield to maturity for each bond is the coupon rate. Using $100 as par, the cash flow for the 1.5-year coupon Treasury is:

Exhibit 1: Maturity and Yield to Maturity
for 20 Hypothetical Treasury Securities

Period	Years	Yield to maturity (%)	Price ($)	Spot rate (%)	Discount function
1	0.5	3.00	—	3.0000	0.9852
2	1.0	3.30	—	3.3000	0.9678
3	1.5	3.50	100.00	3.5053	0.9492
4	2.0	3.90	100.00	3.9164	0.9254
5	2.5	4.40	100.00	4.4376	0.8961
6	3.0	4.70	100.00	4.7520	0.8686
7	3.5	4.90	100.00	4.9622	0.8424
8	4.0	5.00	100.00	5.0650	0.8187
9	4.5	5.10	100.00	5.1701	0.7948
10	5.0	5.20	100.00	5.2772	0.7707
11	5.5	5.30	100.00	5.3864	0.7465
12	6.0	5.40	100.00	5.4976	0.7222
13	6.5	5.50	100.00	5.6108	0.6979
14	7.0	5.55	100.00	5.6643	0.6764
15	7.5	5.60	100.00	5.7193	0.6551
16	8.0	5.65	100.00	5.7755	0.6341
17	8.5	5.70	100.00	5.8331	0.6134
18	9.0	5.80	100.00	5.9584	0.5895
19	9.5	5.90	100.00	6.0863	0.5658
20	10.0	6.00	100.00	6.2169	0.5421

$$
\begin{aligned}
0.5 \text{ years} \quad & 0.035 \times \$100 \times 0.5 = \$1.75 \\
1.0 \text{ years} \quad & 0.035 \times \$100 \times 0.5 = \$1.75 \\
1.5 \text{ years} \quad & 0.035 \times \$100 \times 0.5 + \$100 = \$101.75
\end{aligned}
$$

The present value of the cash flow is then:

$$
\frac{1.75}{(1+z_1)^1} + \frac{1.75}{(1+z_2)^2} + \frac{101.75}{(1+z_3)^3}
$$

where

z_1 = one-half the annualized 6-month theoretical spot rate
z_2 = one-half the 1-year theoretical spot rate
z_3 = one-half the 1.5-year theoretical spot rate

Since the 6-month spot rate and 1-year spot rate are 3.00% and 3.30%, respectively, we know that z_1 is 0.0150 and z_2 is 0.0165. We can compute the present value of the 1.5-year coupon Treasury security as follows:

$$
\frac{1.75}{(1+z_1)^1} + \frac{1.75}{(1+z_2)^2} + \frac{101.75}{(1+z_3)^3} = \frac{1.75}{(1.015)^1} + \frac{1.75}{(1.0165)^2} + \frac{101.75}{(1+z_3)^3}
$$

Since the price of the 1.5-year coupon Treasury security is par, the following relationship must hold:

$$\frac{1.75}{(1.015)^1} + \frac{1.75}{(1.0165)^2} + \frac{101.75}{(1+z_3)^3} = 100$$

We can solve for the theoretical 1.5-year spot rate to find that z_3 is 1.75265%. Doubling this yield we obtain 3.5053%, which is the theoretical 1.5-year spot rate. That rate is the rate that the market would apply to a 1.5-year zero-coupon Treasury security if, in fact, such a security existed.

Given the theoretical 1.5-year spot rate, we can obtain the theoretical 2-year spot rate. The present value of the cash flow of the 2-year Treasury is:

$$\frac{1.95}{(1+z_1)^1} + \frac{1.95}{(1+z_2)^2} + \frac{1.95}{(1+z_3)^3} + \frac{101.95}{(1+z_4)^4}$$

where z_4 is one-half the 2-year theoretical spot rate. Since the 6-month spot rate, 1-year spot rate, and 1.5-year spot rate are 3.00%, 3.30%, and 3.5053%, respectively, then z_1 is 0.0150, z_2 is 0.0165, and z_3 is 0.0175265. Therefore, the present value of the 2-year coupon Treasury security is:

$$\frac{1.95}{(1.015)^1} + \frac{1.95}{(1.0165)^2} + \frac{1.95}{(1.0175265)^3} + \frac{101.95}{(1+z_4)^4}$$

Since the price of the 2-year coupon Treasury security is par, the following relationship must hold:

$$\frac{1.95}{(1.015)^1} + \frac{1.95}{(1.0165)^2} + \frac{1.95}{(1.0175265)^3} + \frac{101.95}{(1+z_4)^4} = 100$$

Solving for the theoretical 2-year spot rate, we find that z_4 is 1.9582%. Doubling this yield, we obtain the theoretical 2-year spot rate of 3.9164%.

One can follow this approach sequentially to derive the theoretical 2.5-year spot rate from the calculated values of z_1, z_2, z_3, and z_4 (the 6-month, 1-year, 1.5-year, and 2-year rates), and the price and coupon of the bond with a maturity of 2.5 years. Further, one could derive theoretical spot rates for the remaining 15 semi-annual rates. The spot rates thus obtained are shown in the next-to-the-last column of Exhibit 1. They represent the term structure of default-free spot rate for maturities up to ten years at the particular time to which the bond price quotations refer.

The Discount Function

The term structure is represented by the spot rate curve. We also know that the present value of $1 to be received n periods from now when discounted at the spot rate for period n is:

$$\frac{\$1}{\left[1 + \left(\frac{\text{Spot rate for period n}}{2}\right)\right]^n}$$

For example, the present value of $1 five years from now using the spot rate for 10 periods in Exhibit 3, 5.2772%, is

$$\frac{\$1}{\left[1 + \left(\frac{0.052772}{2}\right)\right]^{10}} = 0.7707$$

This value can be viewed as the time value of $1 for a default-free cash flow to be received in five years. Equivalently, it shows the price of a zero-coupon default-free security with a maturity of five years and a maturity value of $1.

The last column of Exhibit 1 shows the time value of $1 for each period. The set of time values for all periods is called the *discount function*.

Applying the Spot Rates to Value a Treasury Coupon Security

To demonstrate how to use the spot rate curve, suppose that we want to price an 8% 10-year Treasury security. The price of this issue is the present value of the cash flow where each cash flow is discounted at the corresponding spot rate. This is illustrated in Exhibit 2.

The third column shows the cash flow for each period. The fourth column shows the spot rate curve. The discount function is shown in the next-to-the-last column. Multiplying the value in the discount function column by the cash flow gives the present value of the cash flow. The sum of the present values is equal to $115.2619. This is the theoretical price of this issue.

Why Treasuries Must be Valued Based on Spot Rates

The value of a Treasury security is determined by the spot rates, not the yield-to-maturity of a Treasury coupon security of the same maturity. We will use an illustration to demonstrate the economic forces that will assure that the actual market price of a Treasury coupon security will not depart significantly from its theoretical price.

To demonstrate this, consider the 8% 10-year Treasury security. Suppose that this Treasury security is priced based on the 6% yield to maturity of the 10-year maturity Treasury coupon security in Exhibit 1. Discounting each cash flow of the 8% 10-year Treasury security at 6% gives a present value of $114.88.

The question is, could this security trade at $114.88 in the market? Let's see what would happen if the 8% 10-year Treasury traded at $114.88. Suppose that a dealer firm buys this issue at $114.88 and strips it. By stripping this issue, the dealer firm creates 20 zero-coupon instruments guaranteed by the U.S. Treasury. How much can the 20 zero-coupon instruments be sold for by the dealer firm? Expressed equivalently, at what yield can each of the zero-coupon instruments be sold? The answer is in Exhibit 1. The yield at which each zero-coupon instrument can be sold is the spot rate shown in the next-to-the-last column.

Exhibit 2: Determination of the Theoretical Price of an 8% 10-Year Treasury

Period	Years	Cash flow ($)	Spot rate (%)	Discount function	Present Value ($)
1	0.5	4.00	3.0000	0.9852	3.9409
2	1.0	4.00	3.3000	0.9678	3.8712
3	1.5	4.00	3.5053	0.9492	3.7968
4	2.0	4.00	3.9164	0.9254	3.7014
5	2.5	4.00	4.4376	0.8961	3.5843
6	3.0	4.00	4.7520	0.8686	3.4743
7	3.5	4.00	4.9622	0.8424	3.3694
8	4.0	4.00	5.0650	0.8187	3.2747
9	4.5	4.00	5.1701	0.7948	3.1791
10	5.0	4.00	5.2772	0.7707	3.0828
11	5.5	4.00	5.3864	0.7465	2.9861
12	6.0	4.00	5.4976	0.7222	2.8889
13	6.5	4.00	5.6108	0.6979	2.7916
14	7.0	4.00	5.6643	0.6764	2.7055
15	7.5	4.00	5.7193	0.6551	2.6205
16	8.0	4.00	5.7755	0.6341	2.5365
17	8.5	4.00	5.8331	0.6134	2.4536
18	9.0	4.00	5.9584	0.5895	2.3581
19	9.5	4.00	6.0863	0.5658	2.2631
20	10.0	104.00	6.2169	0.5421	56.3828
				Total	115.2619

We can use Exhibit 2 to determine the proceeds that would be received per $100 of par value of the 8% 10-year issue stripped. The last column shows how much would be received for each coupon sold as a zero-coupon instrument. The total proceeds received from selling the zero-coupon Treasury securities created would be $115.2619 per $100 of par value of the Treasury issue purchased by the dealer. Since the dealer purchased the issue for $114.88, this would result in an arbitrage profit of $0.3819 per $100 of the 8% 10-year Treasury issue purchased.

To understand why the dealer has the opportunity to realize this arbitrage profit, consider the $4 coupon payment in four years. By buying the 10-year Treasury bond priced to yield 6%, the dealer effectively pays a price based on 6% (3% semiannual) for that coupon payment, or, equivalently, $3.1577.[1] Under the assumptions of this illustration, however, investors were willing to accept a lower yield to maturity (the 4-year spot rate), 5.065% (2.5325% semiannual), to purchase a zero-coupon Treasury security with four years to maturity. Thus investors

---

[1] This is determined as follows: $\$1/(1.03)^8$.

were willing to pay $3.2747. (See Exhibit 2.) On this one coupon payment, the dealer realizes a profit equal to the difference between $3.2747 and $3.1577 (or $0.117). From all the cash flows, the total profit is $0.3819. In this instance, coupon stripping results in the sum of the parts being greater than the whole.

Suppose that, instead of the observed yield to maturity from Exhibit 1, the yields that investors want are the same as the theoretical spot rates that are shown in the exhibit. As can be seen in Exhibit 2, if we use these spot rates to discount the cash flows, the total proceeds from the sale of the zero-coupon Treasury securities would be equal to $115.2619, making coupon stripping uneconomic since the proceeds from stripping would be the same as the cost of purchasing the issue.

In our illustration of coupon stripping, the price of the Treasury security is less than its theoretical price. Suppose instead that the price of the Treasury coupon security is greater than its theoretical price. In this case, investors can create a portfolio of zero-coupon Treasury securities such that the cash flow of the portfolio replicates the cash flow of the mispriced Treasury coupon security. By doing so, the investor will realize a yield higher than the yield on the Treasury coupon security. For example, suppose that the market price of the 10-year Treasury coupon security we used in our illustration is $116. An investor could buy 20 outstanding zero-coupon stripped Treasury securities with a maturity value identical to the cash flow shown in the third column of Exhibit 2. The cost of purchasing this portfolio of stripped Treasury securities would be $115.1880. Thus, an investor is effectively purchasing a portfolio of stripped Treasury securities that has the same cash flow as an 8% 10-year Treasury coupon security at a cost of $115.1880 instead of $116.

It is the process of coupon stripping (when the market price is less than the theoretical price) and reconstituting (when the market price is greater than the theoretical price) that will prevent the market price of Treasury securities from departing significantly from their theoretical price.

THE TERM STRUCTURE OF CREDIT SPREADS

For a non-Treasury bond, the theoretical value is not as easy to determine. The value of a non-Treasury bond must reflect not only the spot rate for default-free bonds, but also a risk premium to reflect default risk and any options embedded in the issue.

In practice, the spot rate that has been used to discount the cash flow of a non-Treasury bond is the Treasury spot rate plus a constant credit spread. For example, if the 6-month Treasury spot rate is 3%, and the 10-year Treasury spot rate is 6%, and a suitable credit spread is deemed to be 100 basis points, then a 4% spot rate is used to discount a 6-month cash flow of a non-Treasury bond and a 7% discount rate to discount a 10-year cash flow.

The drawback of this approach is that there is no reason to expect the credit spread to be the same regardless of when the cash flow is expected to be received. Instead, it might be expected that the credit spread increases with the maturity of the bond.[2] That is, there is a term structure for credit spreads.

When the generic zero spreads for a given credit quality and in a given industry are added to the default-free spot rates, the resulting term structure is used to value bonds of issuers of the same credit quality in the industry sector. This term structure is referred to as the *benchmark spot rate curve* or *benchmark zero-coupon rate curve*.

VALUATION METHODOLOGIES

Our discussion of bond valuation has thus far been limited to bonds in which neither the issuer nor the bondholder has the option to alter a bond's cash flows. Now we look at how to value bonds with embedded options. The methodology described here is used to value options, caps, and floors in Chapter 11.

There are two main approaches to the valuation of bonds with embedded options: (1) the binomial lattice method, or simply, binomial method and (2) the Monte Carlo simulation method. There are two things that are common to both methods. First, each begins with an assumption as to the statistical process that is assumed to generate the term structure of interest rates. Second, each method is based on the principle that arbitrage profits cannot be generated. By this it is meant that the model will correctly price the on-the-run issues; or, equivalently, the model is calibrated to the market.

It is important to understand that the user of any valuation model is exposed to *modeling risk*. This is the risk that the output of the model is incorrect because the assumptions upon which it is based are incorrect. Consequently, it is imperative that the results of a valuation model be stress-tested for modeling risk by altering the assumptions.

Option-Adjusted Spread
What an investor seeks to do is to buy securities whose value is greater than their price. A valuation model allows an investor to estimate the theoretical value of a security, which at this point would be sufficient to determine the fairness of the price of the security. That is, the investor can say that a particular bond is 1 point cheap or 2 points cheap, and so on.

---

[2] Theoretical reasons for this relationship are given in Robert C. Merton, "On the Pricing of Corporate Debt: The Risk Structure of Interest Rates," *Journal of Finance* (May 1974), pp. 449-470. For empirical evidence, see O. Sarig and Arthur D. Warga, "Bond Price Data and Bond Market Liquidity," *Journal of Financial and Quantitative Analysis* (September 1989), pp. 1351-1360; and, Jerome S. Fons, "Using Default Rates to Model the Term Structure of Credit Risk," *Financial Analysts Journal* (September/October 1994), pp. 25-32.

Exhibit 3: On-the-Run Yield Curve and Spot Rates for an Issuer

Maturity (yrs)	Yield to maturity (%)	Market Price ($)	Spot Rate (%)
1	3.5	100	3.5000
2	4.2	100	4.2147
3	4.7	100	4.7345
4	5.2	100	5.2707

A valuation model need not stop here, however. Instead, it can convert the divergence between the price observed in the market for the security and the theoretical value derived from the valuation model into a yield spread measure. This step is necessary since many market participants find it more convenient to think about yield spreads than price differences.

The *option-adjusted spread* (OAS) was developed as a measure of the yield spread that can be used to convert dollar differences between value and price. Thus, basically, the OAS is used to reconcile value with market price. But what is it a "spread" over? As we shall see when we describe the two valuation methodologies, the OAS is a spread over the issuer's spot rate curve or benchmark. The spot rate curve itself is not a single curve, but a series of spot rate curves that allow for changes in rates and cash flows. The reason that the resulting spread is referred to as "option-adjusted" is because the cash flows of the security whose value is sought are adjusted to reflect any embedded options.

Binomial Method[3]

The binomial method is a popular technique for valuing callable and putable bonds. To illustrate this, we start with the on-the-run yield curve for the particular issuer whose bonds we want to value. The starting point is the Treasury's on-the-run yield curve. To obtain a particular issuer's on-the-run yield curve, an appropriate credit spread is added to each on-the-run Treasury issue. The credit spread need not be constant for all maturities. For example, the credit spread may increase with maturity.

In our illustration, we use the hypothetical on-the-run issues for an issuer shown in Exhibit 3. Each bond is trading at par value (100) so the coupon rate is equal to the yield to maturity. We will simplify the illustration by assuming annual-pay bonds. Using the bootstrapping methodology, the spot rates are those shown in the last column of Exhibit 3.

Binomial Interest Rate Tree Once we allow for embedded options, consideration must be given to interest rate volatility. This can be done by introducing a *binomial interest rate tree*. This tree is nothing more than a graphical depiction of the 1-period or short rates over time based on some assumption about interest rate volatility. How this tree is constructed is illustrated below.

---

[3] The model described in this section was presented in Andrew J. Kalotay, George O. Williams, and Frank J. Fabozzi, "A Model for the Valuation of Bonds and Embedded Options," *Financial Analysts Journal* (May-June 1993), pp. 35-46.

Exhibit 4: Four-Year Binomial Interest Rate Tree

| Today | 1 Year | 2 Years | 3 Years | 4 Years |

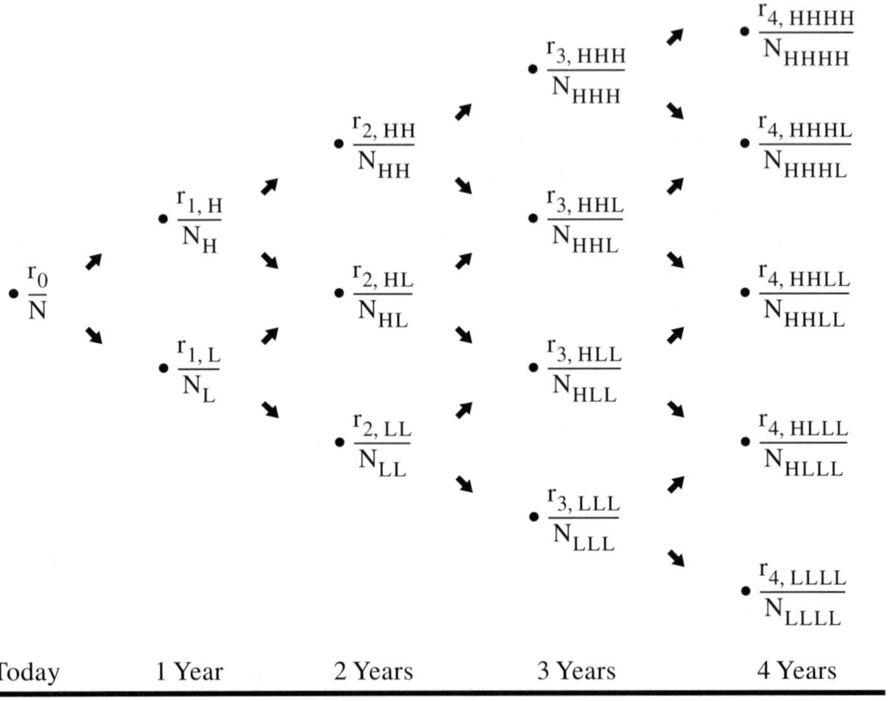

Exhibit 4 shows an example of a binomial interest rate tree. In this tree, each node (bold circle) represents a time period that is equal to one year from the node to its left. Each node is labeled with an N, representing node, and a subscript that indicates the path that the 1-year rate took to get to that node. L represents the lower of the two 1-year rates and H represents the higher of the two 1-year rates. For example, node N_{HH} means to get to that node the following path for 1-year rates occurred: the 1-year rate realized is the higher of the two rates in the first year and then the higher of the 1-year rates in the second year.[4]

Look first at the point denoted by just N in Exhibit 4. This is the root of the tree and is nothing more than the current 1-year spot rate, or equivalently the current 1-year rate, which we denote by r_0. What we have assumed in creating this tree is that the 1-year rate can take on two possible values the next period and the two rates have the same probability of occurring. One rate will be higher than the other. It is assumed that the 1-year rate can evolve over time based on a random process called a lognormal random walk with a certain volatility.

---

[4] Note that N_{HL} is equivalent to N_{LH} in the second year and that in the third year N_{HHL} is equivalent to N_{HLH} and N_{LHH} and that N_{HLL} is equivalent to N_{LLH}. We have simply selected one label for a node rather than clutter up the figure with unnecessary information.

We use the following notation to describe the tree in the first year. Let

σ = assumed volatility of the 1-year rate

$r_{1,L}$ = lower 1-year rate one year from now

$r_{1,H}$ = higher 1-year rate one year from now

The relationship between $r_{1,L}$ and $r_{1,H}$ is as follows:

$$r_{1,H} = r_{1,L}(e^{2\sigma})$$

where e is the base of the natural logarithm 2.71828.

For example, suppose that $r_{1,L}$ is 4.4448% and σ is 10% per year, then:

$$r_{1,H} = 4.4448\%(e^{2\times 0.10}) = 5.4289\%$$

In the second year, there are three possible values for the 1-year rate, which we will denote as follows:

$r_{2,LL}$ = 1-year rate in second year assuming the lower rate in the first year and the lower rate in the second year

$r_{2,HH}$ = 1-year rate in second year assuming the higher rate in the first year and the higher rate in the second year

$r_{2,HL}$ = 1-year rate in second year assuming the higher rate in the first year and the lower rate in the second year or equivalently the lower rate in the first year and the higher rate in the second year.

The relationship between $r_{2,LL}$ and the other two 1-year rates is as follows: $r_{2,HH} = r_{2,LL}(e^{4\sigma})$ and $r_{2,HL} = r_{2,LL}(e^{2\sigma})$. So, for example, if $r_{2,LL}$ is 4.6958% and assuming once again that σ is 10%, then

$$r_{2,HH} = 4.6958\%(e^{4\times 0.10}) = 7.0053\%$$

and

$$r_{2,HL} = 4.6958\%(e^{2\times 0.10}) = 5.7354\%$$

In the third year there are four possible values for the 1-year rate, which are denoted as follows: $r_{3,HHH}$, $r_{3,HHL}$, $r_{3,HLL}$, and $r_{3,LLL}$, and whose first three values are related to the last as follows:

$$r_{3,HHH} = r_{3,LLL}(e^{6\sigma})$$
$$r_{3,HHL} = r_{3,LLL}(e^{4\sigma})$$
$$r_{3,HLL} = r_{3,LLL}(e^{2\sigma})$$

Exhibit 5: Four-Year Binomial Interest Rate Tree with 1-Year Rates*

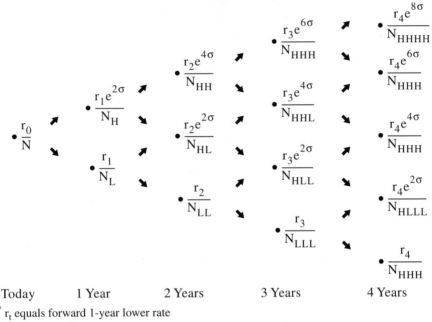

| Today | 1 Year | 2 Years | 3 Years | 4 Years |

* r_t equals forward 1-year lower rate

Exhibit 4 shows the notation for a 4-year binomial interest rate tree. We can simplify the notation by letting r_t be the 1-year rate t years from now for the lower rate since all the other short rates t years from now depend on that rate. Exhibit 5 shows the interest rate tree using this simplified notation.

It can be shown that the standard deviation of the 1-year rate is equal to $r_0\sigma$. The standard deviation is a statistical measure of volatility and we will discuss this measure and its estimation in Chapters 5 and 6. It is important to understand that the process that we assumed generates the binomial interest rate tree (or equivalently the short rates), implies that volatility is measured relative to the current level of rates. For example, if σ is 10% and the 1-year rate (r_0) is 4%, then the standard deviation of the 1-year rate is 4% × 10% = 0.4% or 40 basis points. However, if the current 1-year rate is 12%, the standard deviation of the 1-year rate would be 12% × 10% or 120 basis points.

Determining the Value at a Node To find the value of the bond at a node, we first calculate the bond's value at the two nodes to the right of the node we are interested in. For example, in Exhibit 5, suppose we want to determine the bond's value at node N_H. The bond's value at nodes N_{HH} and N_{HL} must be determined. Hold aside for now how we get these two values because as we will see, the process involves starting from the last year in the tree and working backwards to get the final solution we want, so these two values will be known.

Effectively what we are saying is that if we are at some node, then the value at that node will depend on the future cash flows. In turn, the future cash flows depend on (1) the bond's value one year from now and (2) the coupon payment one year from now. The latter is known. The former depends on whether the 1-year rate is the higher or lower rate. The bond's value depending on whether the rate is the higher or lower rate is reported at the two nodes to the right of the node that is the focus of our attention. So, the cash flow at a node will be either (1) the bond's value if the short rate is the higher rate plus the coupon payment, or (2) the bond's value if the short rate is the lower rate plus the coupon payment. For example, suppose that we are interested in the bond's value at N_H. The cash flow will be either the bond's value at N_{HH} plus the coupon payment, or the bond's value at N_{HL} plus the coupon payment.

To get the bond's value at a node we follow the fundamental rule for valuation: the value is the present value of the expected cash flows. The appropriate discount rate to use is the 1-year rate at the node. Now there are two present values in this case: the present value if the 1-year rate is the higher rate and one if it is the lower rate. Since it is assumed that the probability of both outcomes is equal, an average of the two present values is computed. This is illustrated in Exhibit 6 for any node assuming that the 1-year rate is r_* at the node where the valuation is sought and letting:

$$V_H = \text{bond's value for the higher 1-year rate}$$
$$V_L = \text{bond's value for the lower 1-year rate}$$
$$C = \text{coupon payment}$$

Using our notation, the cash flow at a node is either:

$$V_H + C \text{ for the higher 1-year rate}$$
$$V_L + C \text{ for the lower 1-year rate}$$

The present value of these two cash flows using the 1-year rate at the node, r_*, is:

$$\frac{V_H + C}{(1 + r_*)} = \text{present value for the higher 1-year rate}$$

$$\frac{V_L + C}{(1 + r_*)} = \text{present value for the lower 1-year rate}$$

Then, the value of the bond at the node is found as follows:

$$\text{Value at a node} = \frac{1}{2}\left[\frac{V_H + C}{(1 + r_*)} + \frac{V_L + C}{(1 + r_*)}\right]$$

Exhibit 6: Calculating a Value at a Node

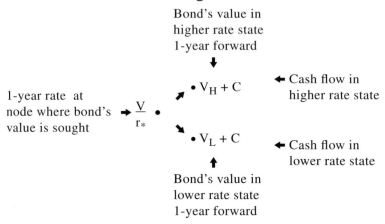

Bond's value in
higher rate state
1-year forward

1-year rate at
node where bond's
value is sought

$\dfrac{V}{r_*}$

• $V_H + C$ ← Cash flow in
higher rate state

• $V_L + C$ ← Cash flow in
lower rate state

Bond's value in
lower rate state
1-year forward

Constructing The Binomial Interest Rate Tree To see how to construct the binomial interest rate tree, let's use the assumed on-the-run yields we used earlier. We will assume that volatility, σ, is 10% and construct a 2-year tree using the 2-year bond with a coupon rate of 4.2%.

Exhibit 7 shows a more detailed binomial interest rate tree with the cash flow shown at each node. We'll see how all the values reported in the exhibit are obtained. The root rate for the tree, r_0, is simply the current 1-year rate, 3.5%.

In the first year there are two possible 1-year rates, the higher rate and the lower rate. What we want to find is the two 1-year rates that will be consistent with the volatility assumption, the process that is assumed to generate the short rates, and the observed market value of the bond. There is no simple formula for this. It must be found by an iterative process (i.e., trial-and-error). The steps are described and illustrated below.

Step 1: Select a value for r_1. Recall that r_1 is the lower 1-year rate. In this first trial, we *arbitrarily* selected a value of 4.75%.

Step 2: Determine the corresponding value for the higher 1-year rate. As explained earlier, this rate is related to the lower 1-year rate as follows: $r_1 e^{2\sigma}$. Since r_1 is 4.75%, the higher 1-year rate is 5.8017% (= 4.75% $e^{2 \times 0.10}$). This value is reported in Exhibit 7 at node N_H.

Step 3: Compute the bond value's one year from now. This value is determined as follows:

> *3a.* Determine the bond's value two years from now. In our example, this is simple. Since we are using a 2-year bond, the bond's value is its maturity value ($100) plus its final coupon payment ($4.2). Thus, it is $104.2.

Exhibit 7: The 1-Year Rates for Year 1
Using the 2-Year 4.2% On-the-Run Issue: First Trial

					•	100.000
		98.486 ↗	N_{HH}		4.2
	•	4.2				
	↗ N_H	5.8017% ↘				
• 99.691				•	100.000
N 3.5000% ↘		99.475 ↗	N_{HL}		4.2
	•	4.2				
	N_L	4.7500% ↘		•	100.000
			N_{LL}		4.2

3b. Calculate the present value of the bond's value found in 3a for the higher rate in the second year. The appropriate discount rate is the higher 1-year rate, 5.8017% in our example. The present value is $98.486 (= $104.2/1.058017). This is the value of V_H that we referred to earlier.

3c. Calculate the present value of the bond's value found in 3a for the lower rate. The discount rate assumed for the lower 1-year rate is 4.75%. The present value is $99.475 (= $104.2/1.0475) and is the value of V_L.

3d. Add the coupon to both V_H and V_L to get the cash flow at N_H and N_L, respectively. In our example we have $102.686 for the higher rate and $103.675 for the lower rate.

3e. Calculate the present value of the two values using the 1-year rate r_*. At this point in the valuation, r_* is the root rate, 3.50%. Therefore,

$$\frac{V_H + C}{1 + r_*} = \frac{\$102.686}{1.035} = \$99.213$$

and

$$\frac{V_L + C}{1 + r_*} = \frac{\$103.675}{1.035} = \$100.169$$

Step 4: Calculate the average present value of the two cash flows in Step 3. This is the value we referred to earlier as:

$$\text{Value at a node} = \frac{1}{2}\left[\frac{V_H + C}{(1 + r_*)} + \frac{V_L + C}{(1 + r_*)}\right]$$

In our example, we have

$$\text{Value at a node} = \frac{1}{2}[\$99.213 + \$100.169] = \$99.691$$

Exhibit 8: The 1-Year Rates for Year 1
Using the 2-Year 4.2% On-the-Run Issue

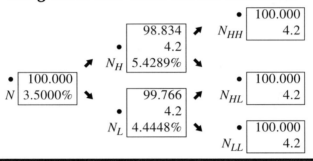

Step 5: Compare the value in Step 4 to the bond's market value. If the two values are the same, then the r_1 used in this trial is the one we seek. This is the 1-year rate that would then be used in the binomial interest rate tree for the lower rate and to obtain the corresponding higher rate. If, instead, the value found in step 4 is not equal to the market value of the bond, this means that the value r_1 in this trial is not the 1-year rate that is consistent with (1) the volatility assumption, (2) the process assumed to generate the 1-year rate, and (3) the observed market value of the bond. In this case, the five steps are repeated with a different value for r_1.

When r_1 is 4.75%, a value of $99.691 results in Step 4 which is less than the observed market price of $100. Therefore, 4.75% is too large and the five steps must be repeated trying a lower rate for r_1.

Let's jump right to the correct rate for r_1 in this example and rework steps 1 through 5. This occurs when r_1 is 4.4448%. The corresponding binomial interest rate tree is shown in Exhibit 8.

Step 1: In this trial we select a value of 4.4448% for r_1, the lower 1-year rate.

Step 2: The corresponding value for the higher 1-year rate is 5.4289% $(=4.4448\%e^{2 \times 0.10})$.

Step 3: The bond's value one year from now is determined as follows:
3a. The bond's value two years from now is $104.2, just as in the first trial.

    3b. The present value of the bond's value found in 3a for the higher 1-year rate, V_H, is $98.834 (= $104.2/1.054289).

    3c. The present value of the bond's value found in 3a for the lower 1-year rate, V_L, is $99.766 (= $104.2/1.044448).

    3d. Adding the coupon to V_H and V_L, we get $103.034 as the cash flow for the higher rate and $103.966 as the cash flow for the lower rate.

3e. The present value of the two cash flows using the 1-year rate at the node to the left, 3.5%, gives

$$\frac{V_H + C}{1 + r_*} = \frac{\$103.034}{1.035} = \$99.550$$

and,

$$\frac{V_L + C}{1 + r_*} = \frac{\$103.966}{1.035} = \$100.450$$

Step 4: The average present value is $100, which is the value at the node.

Step 5: Since the average present value is equal to the observed market price of $100, r_1 or $r_{1,L}$ is 4.4448% and $r_{1,H}$ is 5.4289%.

We can "grow" this tree for one more year by determining r_2. We would use the 3-year on-the-run issue, the 4.7% coupon bond, to get r_2. The same five steps are used in an iterative process to find the 1-year rates in the tree two years from now. Our objective is to find the value of r_2 that will produce a bond value of $100 (since the 3-year on-the-run issue has a market price of $100) and is consistent with (1) a volatility assumption of 10%, (2) a current 1-year rate of 3.5%, and (3) the two rates one year from now of 4.4448% (the lower rate) and 5.4289% (the higher rate). We will not describe how to complete the tree using the 3-year and 4-year on-the-run issues. Exhibit 9 shows the binomial interest rate tree for the on-the-run issues in Exhibit 3.

Valuing an Option-Free Bond with the Tree Now consider an option-free bond of this issuer with three years remaining to maturity and a coupon rate of 6.5%. The value of this bond can be calculated by discounting the cash flow at the spot rates in Exhibit 3 as shown below:

$$\frac{\$6.5}{(1.035)^1} + \frac{\$6.5}{(1.042147)^2} + \frac{\$6.5}{(1.047345)^3} + \frac{\$100 + \$6.5}{(1.052707)^4} = \$104.643$$

An option-free bond that is valued using the binomial interest rate tree should have the same value as discounting by the spot rates.

Exhibit 9 is the binomial interest rate tree that can then be used to value any bond for this issuer with a maturity up to four years. To illustrate how to use the binomial interest rate tree, consider once again the 6.5% option-free bond with three years remaining to maturity. Also assume that the issuer's on-the-run yield curve is the one in Exhibit 3, hence the appropriate binomial interest rate tree is the one in Exhibit 9. Exhibit 10 shows the various values in the discounting process, and produces a bond value of $104.643.

Exhibit 9: Binomial Interest Rate Tree for Valuing Up to a 4-Year Bond for Issuer (10% Volatility Assumed)

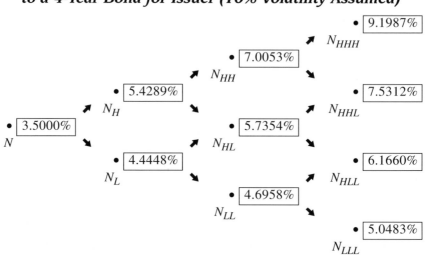

This value is identical to the bond value found when we discounted at the spot rates. This clearly demonstrates that the valuation model is consistent with the standard valuation model for an option-free bond.

Valuing a Callable Corporate Bond Now we will demonstrate how the binomial interest rate tree can be applied to value a callable bond. The valuation process proceeds in the same fashion as in the case of an option-free bond, but with one exception: when the call option may be exercised by the issuer, the bond value at a node must be changed to reflect the lesser of its values if it is not called (i.e., the value obtained by applying the recursive valuation formula described above) and the call price.

For example, consider a 6.5% bond with four years remaining to maturity that is callable in one year at $100. Exhibit 11 shows two values at each node of the binomial interest rate tree. The discounting process explained above is used to calculate the first of the two values at each node. The second value is the value based on whether the issue will be called. For simplicity, let's assume that this issuer calls the issue if it exceeds the call price of $100. Then, in Exhibit 11 at nodes N_L, N_H, N_{LL}, N_{HL}, N_{LLL}, and N_{HLL}, the values from the recursive valuation formula are $101.968, $100.032, $101.723, $100.270, $101.382, and $100.315. These values exceed the assumed call price ($100) and therefore the second value is $100 rather than the calculated value. It is the second value that is used in subsequent calculations. The root of the tree indicates that the value for this callable bond is $102.899.

Exhibit 10: Valuing an Option-Free Bond with Four Years to Maturity and a Coupon Rate of 6.5% (10% Volatility Assumed)

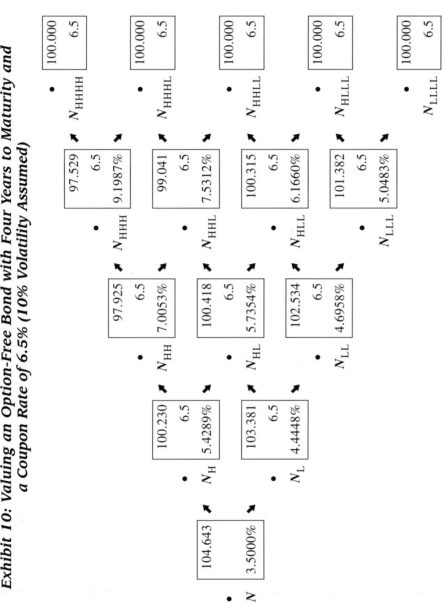

Exhibit 11: Valuing a Callable Bond with Four Years to Maturity, a Coupon Rate of 6.5%, and Callable in One Year at 100 (10% Volatility Assumed)

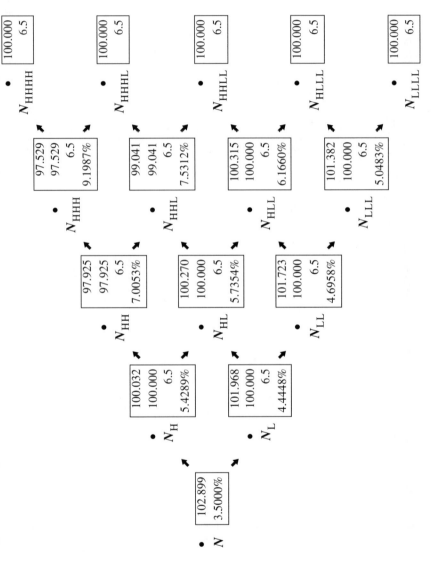

The question that we have not addressed in our illustration, which is nonetheless important, is the circumstances under which the issuer will call the bond. A detailed explanation of the call rule is beyond the scope of this chapter. Basically, it involves determining when it would be economic for the issuer on an after-tax basis to call the issue.

The bond valuation framework presented here can be used to analyze other embedded options such as put options, caps and floors on floating-rate notes, and interest sensitive structured notes.

Volatility and the Theoretical Value In our illustration, interest rate volatility was assumed to be 10%. The volatility assumption has an important impact on the theoretical value. More specifically, the higher the expected volatility, the higher the value of an option. The same is true for an option embedded in a bond. Correspondingly, this affects the value of the bond with an embedded option.

For example, for a callable bond, a higher interest rate volatility assumption means that the value of the call option increases, and, since the value of the option-free bond is not affected, the value of the callable bond must be lower. For a putable bond, higher interest rate volatility means that its value will be higher.

To illustrate this, suppose that a 20% volatility is assumed rather than 10%. The value of the hypothetical callable bond is $102.108 if volatility is assumed to be 20% compared to $102.899 if volatility is assumed to be 10%. The hypothetical putable bond at 20% volatility has a value of $106.010 compared to $105.327 at 10% volatility.

In the construction of the binomial interest rate, it was assumed that volatility is the same for each year. The methodology can be extended to incorporate a term structure of volatility.

Option-Adjusted Spread Suppose the market price of the 3-year 6.5% callable bond is $102.218 and the theoretical value assuming 10% volatility is $102.899. This means that this bond is cheap by $0.681 according to the valuation model. Bond market participants prefer to think not in terms of a bond's price being cheap or expensive in dollar terms but rather in terms of a yield spread — a cheap bond trades at a higher yield spread and an expensive bond at a lower yield spread.

The OAS is the constant spread that when added to all the short-term rates on the binomial interest rate tree will make the theoretical value equal to the market price. In our illustration, if the market price is $102.218, the OAS would be the constant spread added to every rate in Exhibit 9 that will make the theoretical value equal to $102.218. The solution in this case would be 35 basis points.

As with the value of a bond with an embedded option, the OAS will depend on the volatility assumption. For a given bond price, the higher the interest rate volatility assumed, the lower the OAS for a callable bond and the higher the OAS for a putable bond. For example, if volatility is 20% rather than 10%, it can be demonstrated that the OAS would be –11 basis points.

This illustration clearly demonstrates the importance of the volatility assumption. Assuming volatility of 10%, the OAS is 35 basis points. At 20% volatility, the OAS declines and, in this case, is negative and therefore overvalued.

MONTE CARLO METHOD

The second method for valuing bonds with embedded options is the Monte Carlo simulation, or simply Monte Carlo, method. The method involves simulating a sufficiently large number of potential interest rate paths in order to assess the value of a security along these different paths. This method is the most flexible of the two valuation methodologies for valuing interest rate sensitive instruments where the history of interest rates is important. Mortgage-backed securities are commonly valued using this method. Some dealers use Monte Carlo simulation to value callable and putable bonds.

Interest Rate History and Path-Dependent Cash Flows For some fixed-income securities and derivative instruments the periodic cash flows are *path-dependent*. This means that the cash flow received in one period is determined not only by the current interest rate level, but also by the path that interest rates took to get to the current level.

In the case of mortgage passthrough securities (or simply, passthroughs), prepayments are path-dependent because this month's prepayment rate depends on whether there have been prior opportunities to refinance since the underlying mortgages were originated. Unlike passthroughs, the decision as to whether a corporate issuer will elect to refund an issue when the current rate is below the issue's coupon rate is not dependent on how rates evolved over time to the current level.

Moreover, in the case of adjustable-rate mortgages (ARMs), prepayments are not only path-dependent but the periodic coupon rate depends on the history of the reference rate upon which the coupon rate is determined. This is because ARMs have periodic caps and floors as well as a lifetime cap and floor. For example, an ARM whose coupon rate resets annually could have the following restriction on the coupon rate: (1) the rate cannot change by more than 200 basis points each year and (2) the rate cannot be more than 500 basis points from the initial coupon rate.

Pools of passthroughs are used as collateral for the creation of collateralized mortgage obligations (CMOs). Consequently, for CMOs there are typically two sources of path dependency in a CMO tranche's cash flows. First, the collateral prepayments are path-dependent as discussed above. Second, the cash flow to be received in the current month by a CMO tranche depends on the outstanding balances of the other tranches in the deal. Thus, we need the history of prepayments to calculate these balances.

Valuing Mortgage-Backed Securities[5] Conceptually, the valuation of passthroughs using the Monte Carlo method is simple. In practice, however, it is very complex. The simulation involves generating a set of cash flows based on simulated future mortgage refinancing rates, which in turn imply simulated prepayment rates.

Valuation modeling for CMOs is similar to valuation modeling for passthroughs, although the difficulties are amplified because the issuer has sliced and diced both the prepayment and interest rate risk into smaller pieces called tranches. The sensitivity of the passthroughs comprising the collateral to these two risks is not transmitted equally to every tranche. Some of the tranches wind up more sensitive to prepayment and interest rate risk than the collateral, while some of them are much less sensitive.

The typical model used to generate random interest rate paths takes as input today's term structure of interest rates and a volatility assumption. The term structure of interest rates is the theoretical spot rate (or zero coupon) curve implied by today's Treasury securities. The volatility assumption determines the dispersion of future interest rates in the simulation. The simulations are normalized so that the average simulated price of a zero-coupon Treasury bond equals today's actual price.

Each model has its own model of the evolution of future interest rates and its own volatility assumptions. Typically, there are no significant differences in the interest rate models of dealer firms and vendors, although their volatility assumptions can be significantly different.

The random paths of interest rates should be generated from an arbitrage-free model of the future term structure of interest rates. By arbitrage-free it is meant that the model replicates today's term structure of interest rates, an input of the model, and that for all future dates there is no possible arbitrage within the model. We will explain how this is done later.

The simulation works by generating many scenarios of future interest rate paths. In each month of the scenario, a monthly interest rate and a mortgage refinancing rate are generated. The monthly interest rates are used to discount the projected cash flows in the scenario. The mortgage refinancing rate is needed to determine the cash flow because it represents the opportunity cost the mortgagor is facing at that time.

If the refinancing rates are high relative to the mortgagor's original coupon rate (i.e., the rate on the mortgagor's loan), the mortgagor will have less incentive to refinance, or even a positive disincentive (i.e., the homeowner will avoid moving in order to avoid refinancing). If the refinancing rate is low relative to the mortgagor's original coupon rate, the mortgagor has an incentive to refinance.

---

[5] Portions of the material in this section are adapted from Frank J. Fabozzi and Scott F. Richard, "Valuation of CMOs," Chapter 6 in Frank J. Fabozzi (ed.), *CMO Portfolio Management* (Summit, N.J.: Frank J. Fabozzi Associates, 1994).

Exhibit 12: Simulated Paths
of 1-Month Future Interest Rates

Month	Interest Rate Path Number						
	1	2	3	...	n	...	N
1	$f_1(1)$	$f_1(2)$	$f_1(3)$	...	$f_1(n)$	...	$f_1(N)$
2	$f_2(1)$	$f_2(2)$	$f_2(3)$	...	$f_2(n)$	...	$f_2(N)$
3	$f_3(1)$	$f_3(2)$	$f_3(3)$	...	$f_3(n)$	...	$f_3(N)$
t	$f_t(1)$	$f_t(2)$	$f_t(3)$	...	$f_t(n)$	...	$f_t(N)$
358	$f_{358}(1)$	$f_{358}(2)$	$f_{358}(3)$	...	$f_{358}(n)$	...	$f_{358}(N)$
359	$f_{359}(1)$	$f_{359}(2)$	$f_{359}(3)$	...	$f_{359}(n)$	...	$f_{359}(N)$
360	$f_{360}(1)$	$f_{360}(2)$	$f_{360}(3)$	...	$f_{360}(n)$	...	$f_{360}(N)$

Notation:

$f_t(n)$ = 1-month future interest rate for month t on path n

N = number of interest rate paths

Prepayments are projected by feeding the refinancing rate and loan characteristics, such as age, into a prepayment model. Given the projected prepayments the cash flow along an interest rate path can be determined.

To make this more concrete, consider a newly issued mortgage passthrough security with a maturity of 360 months. Exhibit 12 shows N simulated interest rate path scenarios. Each scenario consists of a path of 360 simulated 1-month future interest rates. Just how many paths should be generated is explained later. Exhibit 13 shows the paths of simulated mortgage refinancing rates corresponding to the scenarios shown in Exhibit 12. Assuming these mortgage refinancing rates, the cash flow for each scenario path is shown in Exhibit 14.

Given the cash flow on an interest rate path, its present value can be calculated. The discount rate for determining the present value is the simulated spot rate for each month on the interest rate path plus an appropriate spread. The spot rate on a path can be determined from the simulated future monthly rates. The relationship that holds between the simulated spot rate for month T on path n and the simulated future 1-month rates is:

$$z_T(n) = \{[1 + f_1(n)][1 + f_2(n)]...[1 + f_T(n)]\}^{1/T} - 1$$

where

$z_T(n)$ = simulated spot rate for month T on path n

$f_j(n)$ = simulated future 1-month rate for month j on path n

Consequently, the interest rate path for the simulated future 1-month rates can be converted to the interest rate path for the simulated monthly spot rates as shown in Exhibit 15.

Exhibit 13: Simulated Paths of Mortgage Refinancing Rates

Month	\multicolumn{7}{c}{Interest Rate Path Number}
	1	2	3	...	n	...	N
1	$r_1(1)$	$r_1(2)$	$r_1(3)$	...	$r_1(n)$	...	$r_1(N)$
2	$r_2(1)$	$r_2(2)$	$r_2(3)$	...	$r_2(n)$	...	$r_2(N)$
3	$r_3(1)$	$r_3(2)$	$r_3(3)$	...	$r_3(n)$	...	$r_3(N)$
t	$r_t(1)$	$r_t(2)$	$r_t(3)$	...	$r_t(n)$	...	$r_t(N)$
358	$r_{358}(1)$	$r_{358}(2)$	$r_{358}(3)$	...	$r_{358}(n)$	...	$r_{358}(N)$
359	$r_{359}(1)$	$r_{359}(2)$	$r_{359}(3)$	...	$r_{359}(n)$	...	$r_{359}(N)$
360	$r_{360}(1)$	$r_{360}(2)$	$r_{360}(3)$	...	$r_{360}(n)$	...	$r_{360}(N)$

Notation:
$r_t(n)$ = mortgage refinancing rate for month t on path n
N = number of interest rate paths

Exhibit 14: Simulated Cash Flow
on Each of the Interest Rate Paths

Month	\multicolumn{7}{c}{Interest Rate Path Number}
	1	2	3	...	n	...	N
1	$C_1(1)$	$C_1(2)$	$C_1(3)$	...	$C_1(n)$	...	$C_1(N)$
2	$C_2(1)$	$C_2(2)$	$C_2(3)$	...	$C_2(n)$	...	$C_2(N)$
3	$C_3(1)$	$C_3(2)$	$C_3(3)$	...	$C_3(n)$	...	$C_3(N)$
t	$C_t(1)$	$C_t(2)$	$C_t(3)$	...	$C_t(n)$	...	$C_t(N)$
358	$C_{358}(1)$	$C_{358}(2)$	$C_{358}(3)$	...	$C_{358}(n)$	...	$C_{358}(N)$
359	$C_{359}(1)$	$C_{359}(2)$	$C_{359}(3)$	...	$C_{359}(n)$	...	$C_{359}(N)$
360	$C_{360}(1)$	$C_{360}(2)$	$C_{360}(3)$	...	$C_{360}(n)$	...	$C_{360}(N)$

Notation:
$C_t(n)$ = cash flow for month t on path n
N = number of interest rate paths

Exhibit 15: Simulated Paths of Monthly Spot Rates

Month	\multicolumn{7}{c}{Interest Rate Path Number}
	1	2	3	...	n	...	N
1	$z_1(1)$	$z_1(2)$	$z_1(3)$	...	$z_1(n)$	...	$z_1(N)$
2	$z_2(1)$	$z_2(2)$	$z_2(3)$	...	$z_2(n)$	...	$z_2(N)$
3	$z_3(1)$	$z_3(2)$	$z_3(3)$	...	$z_3(n)$	...	$z_3(N)$
t	$z_t(1)$	$z_t(2)$	$z_t(3)$	...	$z_t(n)$	...	$z_t(N)$
358	$z_{358}(1)$	$z_{358}(2)$	$z_{358}(3)$	...	$z_{358}(n)$	...	$z_{358}(N)$
359	$z_{359}(1)$	$z_{359}(2)$	$z_{359}(3)$	...	$z_{359}(n)$	...	$z_{359}(N)$
360	$z_{360}(1)$	$z_{360}(2)$	$z_{360}(3)$	...	$z_{360}(n)$	...	$z_{360}(N)$

Notation:
$z_t(n)$ = spot rate for month t on path n
N = number of interest rate paths

Therefore, the present value of the cash flow for month T on interest rate path n discounted at the simulated spot rate for month T plus some spread is:

$$PV[C_T(n)] = \frac{C_T(n)}{[1 + z_T(n) + K]^T}$$

where

$PV[C_T(n)]$ = present value of cash flow for month T on path n
$C_T(n)$ = cash flow for month T on path n
$z_T(n)$ = spot rate for month T on path n
K = spread

The present value for path n is the sum of the present value of the cash flow for each month on path n. That is,

$$PV[Path(n)] = PV[C_1(n)] + PV[C_2(n)] +... + PV[C_{360}(n)]$$

where $PV[Path(n)]$ is the present value of interest rate path n.

Determining the Theoretical Value The present value of a given interest rate path can be thought of as the theoretical value of a passthrough if that path was actually realized. The theoretical value of the passthrough can be determined by calculating the average of the theoretical value of all the interest rate paths. That is,

$$\text{Theoretical value} = \frac{PV[Path(1)] + PV[Path(2)] + ... + PV[Path(N)]}{N}$$

where N is the number of interest rate paths.

This procedure for valuing a passthrough is also followed for a CMO tranche. The cash flow for each month on each interest rate path is found according to the principal repayment and interest distribution rules of the deal. In order to do this, a CMO structuring model is needed. In any analysis of CMOs, one of the major stumbling blocks is getting a good CMO structuring model.

Option-Adjusted Spread As explained earlier, the option-adjusted spread is a measure of the yield spread that can be used to convert dollar differences between theoretical value and market price. It represents a spread over the issuer's spot rate curve or benchmark.

In the Monte Carlo model, the OAS is the spread that when added to all the spot rates on all interest rate paths will make the average present value of the paths equal to the observed market price (plus accrued interest). Mathematically, OAS is the spread that will satisfy the following condition:

$$\text{Market Price} = \frac{PV[Path(1)] + PV[Path(2)] + ... + PV[Path(N)]}{N}$$

where N is the number of interest rate paths.

Some Technical Issues In the binomial method for valuing bonds, the interest rate tree is constructed so that it is arbitrage free. That is, if any on-the-run issue is valued, the value produced by the model is equal to the market price. This means that the tree is calibrated to the market. In contrast, in our discussion of the Monte Carlo method, there is no mechanism that we have described above that will assure the valuation model will produce a value for an on-the-run Treasury security (the benchmark in the case of agency mortgage-backed securities) equal to the market price. In practice, this is accomplished by adding a *drift term* to the short-term return generating process (Exhibit 12) so that the value produced by the Monte Carlo method for all on-the-run Treasury securities is their market price.[6] A technical explanation of this process is beyond the scope of this chapter.[7]

There is also another adjustment made to the interest rate paths. Restrictions on interest rate movements must be built into the model to prevent interest rates from reaching levels that are believed to be unreasonable (e.g., an interest rate of zero or an interest rate of 30%). This is done by incorporating *mean reversion* into the model. By this it is meant that at some point, the interest rate is forced toward some estimated average (mean) value.

The specification of the relationship between short-term rates and refinancing rates is necessary. Empirical evidence on the relationship is also necessary. More specifically, the correlation between the short-term and long-term rates must be estimated.

The number of interest rate paths determines how "good" the estimate is, not relative to the truth but relative to the valuation model used. The more paths, the more the theoretical value tends to settle down. It is a statistical sampling problem. Most Monte Carlo models employ some form of *variance reduction* to cut down on the number of sample paths necessary to get a good statistical sample. Variance reduction techniques allow us to obtain value estimates within a tick. By this we mean that if the model is used to generate more scenarios, value estimates from the model will not change by more than a tick. So, for example, if 1,024 paths are used to obtain the estimate value for a CMO tranche, there is little more information to be had from the OAS model by generating more than that number of paths. (For some very sensitive CMO tranches, more paths may be needed to estimate value within one tick.)

Distribution of Path Present Values The Monte Carlo simulation method is a commonly used management science tool in business. It is employed when the outcome of a business decision depends on the outcome of several random variables. The product of the simulation is the average value and the probability distribution of the possible outcomes.

---

[6] This is equivalent to saying that the OAS produced by the model is zero.

[7] For an explanation of how this is done, see Lakhbir S. Hayre and Kenneth Lauterbach, "Stochastic Valuation of Debt Securities," in Frank J. Fabozzi (ed.), *Managing Institutional Assets* (New York: Harper & Row, 1990), pp. 321-364.

Unfortunately, the use of Monte Carlo simulation to value fixed-income securities has been limited to just the reporting of the average value, which is referred to as the theoretical value of the security. This means that all of the information about the distribution of the path present values is ignored. Yet, this information is quite valuable.

For example, consider a well protected PAC bond. The distribution of the present value for the paths should be concentrated around the theoretical value. That is, the standard deviation should be small. In contrast, for a support tranche, the distribution of the present value for the paths could be wide, or equivalently, the standard deviation could be large.

Therefore, before using the theoretical value for a mortgage-backed security generated from the Monte Carlo method, a manager should ask for information about the distribution of the path's present values.

Key Points

1. *Valuation is the process of determining the fair value of a financial asset.*

2. *The fundamental principle of valuation is that the value of any financial asset is the present value of the expected cash flow, where the cash flow is the cash that is expected to be received each period from an investment.*

3. *For any bond in which neither the issuer nor the investor can alter the repayment of the principal before its contractual due date, the cash flow can easily be determined assuming that the issuer does not default.*

4. *The difficulty in determining the cash flow arises for bonds where either the issuer or the investor can alter the cash flow.*

5. *The base interest rate in valuing bonds is the rate on default-free securities and U.S. Treasury securities are viewed as default-free securities.*

6. *The traditional valuation methodology is to discount every cash flow of a bond by the same interest rate (discount rate), thereby incorrectly viewing each security as the same package of cash flows.*

7. *The proper approach values a bond as a package of cash flows, with each cash flow viewed as a zero-coupon instrument and each cash flow discounted at its own unique discount rate.*

8. *To properly value bonds, the rate on zero-coupon Treasury securities must be determined.*

9. *The Treasury yield curve indicates the relationship between the yield on Treasury securities and maturity; however, the securities included are a combination of zero-coupon instruments (that is, Treasury bills) and Treasury coupon securities.*

10. *Since the U.S. Treasury does not issue zero-coupon securities with a maturity greater than one year, a theoretical spot rate (i.e. zero-coupon rate) curve must be constructed from the yield curve.*

11. *One approach to constructing the spot rate curve is bootstrapping, the basic principle of which is that the value of the cash flow from an on-the-run Treasury issue when discounted at the spot rates should be equal to the observed market price.*

12. From a Treasury spot rate curve, the value of any default-free security can be determined.

13. The economic force that assures that Treasury securities will be priced based on spot rates is the opportunity for government dealers to profitably strip Treasury securities or for investors to risklessly enhance portfolio returns.

14. To value a security with credit risk, it is necessary to determine a term structure of credit risk or equivalently a zero-coupon credit spread.

15. Evidence suggests that the credit spread increases with maturity and the lower the credit rating, the steeper the curve.

16. Adding the zero-coupon credit spread for a particular credit quality within a sector to the Treasury spot rate curve gives the benchmark spot rate curve that should be used to value a security.

17. There are two valuation methodologies that are being used to value bonds with embedded options: the binomial method and the Monte Carlo simulation method.

18. The methodologies seek to determine the fair or theoretical value of the bond.

19. The option-adjusted spread (OAS) converts the cheapness or richness of a bond into a spread over the future possible spot rate curves.

20. The spread is option adjusted because it allows for future interest rate volatility to affect the cash flows.

21. The user of a valuation model is exposed to modeling risk and should test the sensitivity of the model to alternative assumptions.

22. The binomial method involves generating a binomial interest rate tree based on (1) an issuer's on-the-run yield curve, (2) an assumed interest rate generation process, and (3) an assumed interest rate volatility.

23. The uncertainty of interest rates is introduced into the model by introducing the volatility of interest rates.

24. In valuing a bond using the binomial interest rate tree, the cash flows at a node are modified to take into account any embedded options.

25. *The option-adjusted spread is the constant spread that when added to the short rates in the binomial interest rate tree will produce a valuation for the bond equal to the market price of the bond.*

26. *The cash flow of mortgage-backed securities is path dependent and consequently the Monte Carlo method is commonly used to value these securities.*

27. *The Monte Carlo method involves randomly generating many scenarios of future interest rate paths based on some volatility assumption for interest rates.*

28. *The random paths of interest rates should be generated from an arbitrage-free model of the future term structure of interest rates.*

29. *The Monte Carlo method applied to mortgage-backed securities involves randomly generating a set of cash flows based on simulated future mortgage refinancing rates.*

30. *The theoretical value of a security on any interest rate path is the present value of the cash flow on that path where the spot rates are those on the corresponding interest rate path.*

31. *The theoretical value of a security is the average of the theoretical values over all the interest rate paths.*

32. *In the Monte Carlo method, the option-adjusted spread is the spread that when added to all the spot rates on all interest rate paths will make the average present value of the paths equal to the observed market price (plus accrued interest).*

33. *Information about the distribution of the present value for the interest rate paths provides guidance as to the degree of uncertainty associated with the theoretical value derived from the Monte Carlo method.*

Chapter 3
Measuring Level Risk:
Duration and Convexity

To effectively control a portfolio's exposure to interest rate risk, it is necessary to quantify the sensitivity of a portfolio to a change in rates. In this chapter we explain how this is done. The most popular measure of interest rate risk is duration, a concept we introduced in Chapter 1. We will explain this measure and demonstrate its limitations. We will then look at another measures that can be used to supplement duration.

The objectives of this chapter are to:

1. illustrate the price volatility properties of an option-free bond;

2. provide a general formula that can be used to calculate the duration of any security;

3. explain why the traditional duration measure, modified duration, is of limited value in determining the duration of a security with an embedded option;

4. distinguish between modified duration, effective duration, and dollar duration;

5. explain what is meant by negative convexity for a callable bond and a mortgage passthrough security;

6. explain what the convexity measure of a bond is and the distinction between modified convexity and effective convexity;

7. describe the relationship between Macaulay duration and modified duration;

8. explain how the duration of a floater and inverse floater are determined;

9. market-based approaches for estimating duration of a mortgage-backed security; and,

10. explain how to control interest rate risk in active bond portfolio strategies.

Exhibit 1: Price/Yield Relationship
for Four Hypothetical Bonds

Yield (%)	Price ($)			
	6%/5 year	6%/20 year	9%/5 year	9%/20 year
4.00	108.9826	127.3555	122.4565	168.3887
5.00	104.3760	112.5514	117.5041	150.2056
5.50	102.1600	106.0195	115.1201	142.1367
5.90	100.4276	101.1651	113.2556	136.1193
5.99	100.0427	100.1157	112.8412	134.8159
6.00	100.0000	100.0000	112.7953	134.6722
6.01	99.9574	99.8845	112.7494	134.5287
6.10	99.5746	98.8535	112.3373	133.2472
6.50	97.8944	94.4479	110.5280	127.7605
7.00	95.8417	89.3225	108.3166	121.3551
8.00	91.8891	80.2072	104.0554	109.8964

PRICE VOLATILITY CHARACTERISTICS
OF OPTION-FREE BONDS

A fundamental principle of an option-free bond (that is, a bond that does not have any embedded options) is that the price of the bond changes in the opposite direction from a change in the bond's yield. Exhibit 1 illustrates this property for four hypothetical bonds, where the bond prices are shown assuming a par value of $100.

When the price/yield relationship for any option-free bond is graphed, it exhibits the shape shown in Exhibit 2. Notice that as the yield rises, the price of the option-free bond declines. However, this relationship is not linear (that is, it is not a straight line). The shape of the price/yield relationship for any option-free bond is referred to as *convex*. The price/yield relationship that we have discussed refers to an instantaneous change in yield.

Properties of Option-Free Bonds
Exhibit 3 uses the four hypothetical bonds in Exhibit 1 to show the percentage change in each bond's price for various changes in the yield, assuming that the initial yield for all four bonds is 6%. An examination of Exhibit 3 reveals several properties concerning the price volatility of an option-free bond.

Property 1: Although the prices of all option-free bonds move in the opposite direction from the change in yield, the percentage price change is not the same for all bonds.

Property 2: For small changes in yield, the percentage price change for a given bond is roughly the same whether the yield increases or decreases.

Exhibit 2: Price/Yield Relationship for an Option-Free Bond

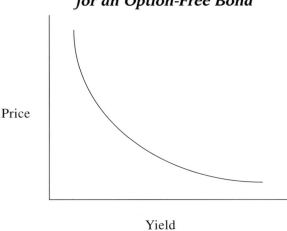

Price

Yield

Property 3: For large changes in yield, the percentage price change is not the same for an increase in yield as it is for a decrease in yield.

Property 4: For a given large change in basis points, the percentage price increase is greater than the percentage price decrease.

The implication of Property 4 is that if an investor is long a bond, the price appreciation that will be realized if the yield decreases is greater than the capital loss that will be realized if the yield rises by the same number of basis points. For an investor who is short a bond, the reverse is true: the potential capital loss is greater than the potential capital gain if the yield changes by a given number of basis points.

An explanation for these four properties of bond price volatility lies in the convex shape of the price/yield relationship.

Characteristics of a Bond that Affect its Price Volatility

There are two characteristics of an option-free bond that determine its price volatility: coupon and term to maturity.

Characteristic 1: For a given term to maturity and initial yield, the lower the coupon rate the greater the price volatility of a bond.

Characteristic 2: For a given coupon rate and initial yield, the longer the term to maturity, the greater the price volatility.

These properties can be verified by examining Exhibit 3.

Exhibit 3: Instantaneous Percentage Price Change for Four Hypothetical Bonds
(Initial yield for all four bonds is 6%)

New Yield (%)	Percent Price Change			
	6%/5 year	6%/20 year	9%/5 year	9%/20 year
4.00	8.98	27.36	8.57	25.04
5.00	4.38	12.55	4.17	11.53
5.50	2.16	6.02	2.06	5.54
5.90	0.43	1.17	0.41	1.07
5.99	0.04	0.12	0.04	0.11
6.01	−0.04	−0.12	−0.04	−0.11
6.10	−0.43	−1.15	−0.41	−1.06
6.50	−2.11	−5.55	−2.01	−5.13
7.00	−4.16	−10.68	−3.97	−9.89
8.00	−8.11	−19.79	−7.75	−18.40

An implication of the second characteristic is that investors who want to increase a portfolio's price volatility because they expect interest rates to fall, all other factors being constant, should hold bonds with long maturities in the portfolio. To reduce a portfolio's price volatility in anticipation of a rise in interest rates, bonds with shorter-term maturities should be held in the portfolio.

The Effects of Yield to Maturity

We cannot ignore the fact that credit considerations cause different bonds to trade at different yields, even if they have the same coupon and maturity. How, then, holding other factors constant, does the yield to maturity affect a bond's price volatility? As it turns out, the higher the yield to maturity that a bond trades at, the lower the price volatility.

To see this, we can compare a 6% 20-year bond initially selling at a yield of 6%, and a 6% 20-year bond initially selling at a yield of 10%. The former is initially at a price of 100, and the latter carries a price of 65.68. Now, if the yield on both bonds increase by 100 basis points, the first bond trades down by 10.68 points (10.68%). After the assumed increase in yield, the second bond will trade at a price of 59.88, for a price decline of only 5.80 points (or 8.83%). Thus, we see that the bond that trades at a lower yield is more volatile in both percentage price change and absolute price change, as long as the other bond characteristics are the same.

An implication of this is that, for a given change in yields, price volatility is lower when the yield level in the market is high, and price volatility is higher when the yield level is low.

PRICE VALUE OF A BASIS POINT AS A MEASURE OF INTEREST RATE RISK

One measure of the dollar price sensitivity of a bond to interest rate changes is the *price value of a basis point* (PVBP). This measure, also referred to as the *dollar value of an 01* (D01), is the change in the price of a bond if the yield changes by 1 basis point. Typically, the price value of a basis point is expressed as the absolute value of the change in price; consequently, the greater the price value of a basis point, the greater the dollar price volatility. As we noted earlier, price changes are almost symmetric for small changes in yield. Thus, it does not make a great deal of difference whether we increase or decrease yields to calculate the price value of a basis point. In practice, an average of the change resulting from both an up and a down movement in yield is used.

We will illustrate the calculation of the price value of a basis point using the 9% 20-year bond assuming this bond is selling to yield 6%. As can be seen in Exhibit 1:

$$\text{yield at } 6.00\% \;=\; 134.6722$$
$$\text{yield at } 5.99\% \;=\; 134.8159$$
$$\text{yield at } 6.01\% \;=\; 134.5287$$

The PVBP per $100 of par value if the yield decreases by one basis point is:

$$134.8159 - 134.6722 = 0.1437$$

This value is almost identical to the PVBP if the yield increases by one point:

$$134.6722 - 134.5287 = 0.1435$$

Some investors calculate the price value of more than one basis point.[1] The principle of calculating the price value of any number of basis points is the same. For example, the price value of 10 basis points is found by computing the difference between the initial price and the price if the yield changed by 10 basis points. Consider once again the 9% 20-year bond trading to yield 9%, then:

$$\text{yield at } 6.00\% \;=\; 134.6722$$
$$\text{yield at } 5.90\% \;=\; 136.1193$$
$$\text{yield at } 6.10\% \;=\; 133.2472$$

The price value of 10 basis points per $100 of par value if the yield decreases by 10 basis points is:

$$136.1193 - 134.6722 = 1.4471$$

The price value of 10 basis points per $100 of par value if the yield decreases by 10 basis points is:

$$134.6722 - 133.2472 = 1.4250$$

---

[1] For example, in the municipal bond market it is common to calculate the price value of 5 basis points.

The price value of 10 basis is then the average of the two changes:

$(1.4471 + 1.4250)/2 = 1.4361$

Since the relationship is still nearly symmetric for a 10 basis point change in yield up or down, the price value of 10 basis points is approximately equal to 10 times the price value of one basis point. However, for larger changes in yield, there will be a difference between the price value of a basis point if the yield is increased or decreased, and the price change for a large number of basis points can no longer be approximated by multiplying the price value of one basis point by the number of basis points. Most investors who derive the price values of a basis point by calculating price changes for large movements in yields (such as 100 basis points), will average the PVBPs for an up move and a down move to get the PVBP of interest.

DURATION AS A MEASURE OF INTEREST RATE RISK

The most obvious way to measure a bond's price sensitivity as a percentage of its current price to changes in interest rates is to change rates by a small number of basis points and calculate how its price will change.

To do this, we introduce the following notation. Let

Δy = change in the yield of the bond (in decimal)
V_+ = the estimated value of the bond if the yield is increased by Δy
V_- = the estimated value of the bond if the yield is decreased by Δy
V_0 = initial price of the bond (per \$100 of par value)

There are two key points to keep in mind in the foregoing discussion. First, the change in yield referred to above is the same change in yield for all maturities. This assumption is commonly referred to as a *parallel yield curve shift assumption*. Thus, the foregoing discussion about the price sensitivity of a security to interest rate changes is limited to parallel shifts in the yield curve. Later in this chapter we will address the case where the yield curve shifts in a nonparallel manner.

Second, the notation refers to the estimated value of the bond. This value is obtained from a valuation model. Consequently, *the resulting measure of the price sensitivity of a security to interest rates changes is only as good as the valuation model employed to obtain the estimated value of the bond.*

Now let's focus on the measure of interest. We are interested in the percentage change in the price of a security when interest rates change. The percentage change in price per basis point change is found by dividing the percentage price change by the number of basis points (Δy times 100). That is:

$$\frac{V_- - V_0}{V_0(\Delta y)100}$$

Similarly, the percentage change in price per basis point change for an increase in yield (Δy times 100) is:

$$\frac{V_0 - V_+}{V_0(\Delta y)100}$$

As explained earlier, the percentage price change for an increase and decrease in interest rates may not be the same. Consequently, the average percentage price change per basis point change in yield can be calculated. This is done as follows:

$$\frac{1}{2}\left[\frac{V_- - V_0}{V_0(\Delta y)100} + \frac{V_0 - V_+}{V_0(\Delta y)100}\right]$$

or equivalently,

$$\frac{V_- - V_+}{2V_0(\Delta y)100}$$

The approximate percentage price change for a 100 basis point change in yield is found by multiplying the previous formula by 100. The name popularly used to refer to the approximate percentage price change is *duration*. Thus,

$$\text{Duration} = \frac{V_- - V_+}{2V_0(\Delta y)} \qquad (1)$$

To illustrate this formula, consider the following option-free bond: a 9% 20-year bond trading to yield 6%. The initial price or value (V_0) is 134.6722. Suppose the yield is changed by 20 basis points. If the yield is decreased to 5.8%, the value of this bond (V_-) would be 137.5888. If the yield is increased to 6.2%, the value of this bond (V_+) would be 131.8439. Thus,

$$\Delta y = 0.0020$$
$$V_+ = 131.8439$$
$$V_- = 137.5888$$
$$V_0 = 134.6722$$

Substituting these values into the duration formula,

$$\text{Duration} = \frac{137.5888 - 131.8439}{2(134.6722)(0.002)} = 10.66$$

Interpreting Duration

The duration of a security can be interpreted as the approximate percentage change in the price for a 100 basis point parallel shift in the yield curve. Thus a bond with a duration of 4.8 will change by approximately 4.8% for a 100 basis point parallel shift in the yield curve. For a 50 basis point parallel shift in the yield curve, the bond's price will change by approximately 2.4%; for a 25 basis point parallel shift in the yield curve, 1.2%, etc.

A manager who anticipates a decline in interest rates will extend (i.e., increase) the portfolio's duration. Suppose that the manager increases the present portfolio duration of 4 to 6. This means that for a 100 basis point change in interest rates, the portfolio will change by about 2% more than if the portfolio duration was left unchanged.

Dollar Duration

Duration is related to percentage price change. However, for two bonds with the same duration, the dollar price change will not be the same. For example, consider two bonds, W and X. Suppose that both bonds have a duration of 5, but that W is trading at par while X is trading at 90. A 100 basis point change for both bonds will change the price by approximately 5%. This means a price change of $5 (5% times $100) for W and a price change of $4.5 (5% times $90) for X.

The dollar price volatility of a bond can be measured by multiplying modified duration by the full dollar price and the number of basis points (in decimal form). That is:

$$\text{Dollar price change} = \text{Modified duration} \times \text{Dollar price} \times \text{Yield change (in decimal)}$$

The dollar price volatility for a 100 basis point change in yield is:

$$\text{Dollar price change} = \text{Modified duration} \times \text{Dollar price} \times 0.01$$

or equivalently,

$$\text{Dollar price change} = \text{Modified duration} \times \text{Dollar price}/100$$

The dollar price change calculated using the above formula is called *dollar duration*. In some contexts, dollar duration refers to the price change for a 100 basis point change in yield. The dollar duration for any number of basis points can be computed by scaling the dollar price change accordingly. For example, for a 50 basis point change in yields, the dollar price change or dollar duration is:

$$\text{Dollar price change} = \text{Modified duration} \times \text{Dollar price}/200$$

For a one basis point change in yield, the dollar price change will give the same result as the price value of a basis point.

The dollar duration for a 100 basis point change in yield for bonds W and X is:

For bond W: Dollar duration $= 5 \times 100/100$ $= 5.0$
For bond X: Dollar duration $= 5 \times 90/100$ $= 4.5$

Exhibit 4: Price/Yield Relationship for a Noncallable Bond and a Callable Bond

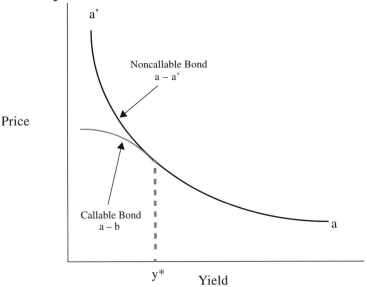

Modified Duration Versus Effective Duration

A popular form of duration that is used by practitioners is modified duration. Modified duration is the approximate percentage change in a bond's price for a 100 basis point parallel shift in the yield curve *assuming that the bond's cash flow does not change when the yield curve shifts*. What this means is that in calculating the values of V_- and V_+ in equation (1), the same cash flow used to calculate V_0 is used. Therefore, the change in the bond's price when the yield curve is shifted by a small number of basis points is due solely to discounting at the new yield level.

The assumption that the cash flow will not change when the yield curve shifts in a parallel fashion makes sense for option-free bonds such as noncallable Treasury securities. This is because the payments made by the U.S. Department of the Treasury to holders of its obligations does not change when the yield curve changes. However, the same cannot be said for callable and putable bonds and mortgage-backed securities. For these securities, a change in yield will alter the expected cash flow.

The price/yield relationship for callable bonds and mortgage passthrough securities is shown in Exhibit 4. As yields in the market decline, the likelihood that yields will decline further so that the issuer or homeowner will benefit from calling the bond increases. The exact yield level at which investors begin to view the issue likely to be called may not be known, but we do know that there is some level. In Exhibit 4, at yield levels below y*, the price/yield relationship for the callable bond departs from the price/yield relationship for the noncallable bond. If, for example, the market yield is such that a noncallable bond would be selling for 109, but since it is callable would be called at 104, investors would not pay 109. If they did and the bond is called, investors would receive 104 (the call price) for a bond they purchased for 109. Notice that for a range of yields below y*, there is price compression — that is, there is limited price appreciation as yields decline. The portion of the callable bond price/yield relationship below y* is said to be *negatively convex.*

Negative convexity means that the price appreciation will be less than the price depreciation for a large change in yield of a given number of basis points. An option-free bond is said to exhibit *positive convexity*; that is, the price appreciation will be greater than the price depreciation for a large change in yield. The price changes resulting from bonds exhibiting positive convexity and negative convexity are summarized below:

Change in interest rates	Absolute value of percentage price change for:	
	Positive convexity	Negative convexity
−100 basis points	X%	less than Y%
+100 basis points	less than X%	Y%

The valuation models that we described in Chapter 2 take into account how shifts in the yield curve will affect cash flow. Thus, when V_- and V_+ are the values produced from these valuation models, the resulting duration takes into account both the discounting at different interest rates and how the cash flow can change. When duration is calculated in this manner, it is referred to as *effective duration* or *option-adjusted duration*. Exhibit 5 summarizes the distinction between modified duration and effective duration.

The difference between modified duration and effective duration for bonds with an embedded option can be quite dramatic. For example, a callable bond could have a modified duration of 5 but an effective duration of only 4. For certain collateralized mortgage obligations, the modified duration could be 7 and the effective duration 20! Thus, using modified duration as a measure of the price sensitivity of a security to a parallel shift in the yield curve would be misleading. The more appropriate measure for any bond with an embedded option is effective duration.

The values used in the duration formula are those obtained from a valuation model. For the binomial model, this is done by shifting the on-the-run yield curve down a small number of basis points and then reconstructing the binomial interest rate tree. The bond is then revalued using the new binomial interest rate tree to obtain V_-.[2] To obtain V_+, the on-the-run yield curve is shifted up by a small number of basis points and the reconstructed binomial interest rate tree is used to value the bond. In the Monte Carlo simulation model for valuation, the short-term rates are shifted up and down on each interest rate path and the bond revalued.[3]

---

[2] More specifically, the initial OAS is added to the rate at each node of the new binomial interest rate tree.

[3] For a description of this process, see Chapter 11 in Frank J. Fabozzi, *Bond Portfolio Management* (New Hope, PA: Frank J. Fabozzi Associates, 1996).

Exhibit 5: Modified Duration Versus Effective Duration

Duration
Interpretation: Generic description of the sensitivity of a bond's price (as a percentage of initial price) to a parallel shift in the yield curve

Modified Duration	Effective Duration
Duration measure in which it is assumed that yield changes do not change the expected cash flow	Duration in which recognition is given to the fact that yield changes may change the expected cash flow

Macaulay Duration

It is worth comparing the modified duration formula presented above to that commonly found in the literature. It is common in the literature to find the following formula for modified duration:[4]

$$\frac{1}{(1 + \text{yield}/k)}\left[\frac{1\text{PVCF}_1 + 2\text{PVCF}_2 + 3\text{PVCF}_3 + ... + n\text{PVCF}_n}{k \times \text{Price}}\right] \qquad (2)$$

where

k	=	number of periods, or payments, per year (e.g., k = 2 for semiannual pay bonds and k = 12 for monthly pay bonds)
n	=	number of periods until maturity (i.e., number of years to maturity times k)
yield	=	yield to maturity of the bond
PVCF$_t$	=	present value of the cash flow in period t discounted at the yield to maturity

The expression in the brackets of the modified duration formula given by equation (2) is a measure formulated in 1938 by Frederick Macaulay.[5] This measure is popularly referred to as *Macaulay duration*. Thus, modified duration is commonly expressed as:

$$\text{Modified duration} = \frac{\text{Macaulay duration}}{(1 + \text{yield}/k)}$$

The general formulation for duration as given by equation (1) provides a short-cut procedure for determining a bond's modified duration. Because it is easier to calculate the modified duration using the short-cut procedure, many vendors of analytical software will use equation (1) rather than equation (2) to reduce

---

[4] More specifically, this is the formula for modified duration for a bond on a coupon anniversary date.

[5] Frederick Macaulay, *Some Theoretical Problems Suggested by the Movement of Interest Rates, Bond Yields, and Stock Prices in the U.S. Since 1856* (New York: National Bureau of Economic Research, 1938).

computation time. But, once again, it must be emphasized that modified duration is a flawed measure of a bond's price sensitivity to interest rate changes for a bond with an embedded option.

Portfolio Duration

A portfolio's (effective) duration can be obtained by calculating the weighted average of the duration of the bonds in the portfolio. The weight is the proportion of the portfolio that a security comprises. Mathematically, a portfolio's duration can be calculated as follows:

$$W_1D_1 + W_2D_2 + W_3D_3 + \ldots + W_KD_K$$

where

W_i = market value of bond i/market value of the portfolio
D_i = effective duration of bond i
K = number of bonds in the portfolio

To illustrate this calculation, consider the following three-bond portfolio in which all three bonds are option free:

Bond	Par amount owned	Market Value
10% 5-year	$4 million	$4,000,000
8% 15-year	5 million	4,231,375
14% 30-year	1 million	1,378,586

In this illustration, it is assumed that the next coupon payment for each bond is six months from now. The market value for the portfolio is $9,609,961. Since each bond is option free, the modified duration can be used. The market price per $100 value of each bond, its yield to maturity, and its duration are given below:

Bond	Price ($)	Yield to Maturity (%)	Duration
10% 5-year	100.0000	10	3.861
8% 15-year	84.6275	10	8.047
14% 30-year	137.8590	10	9.168

In this illustration, K is equal to 3 and:

$$W_1 = 4,000,000/9,609,961 = 0.416 \quad D_1 = 3.861$$
$$W_2 = 4,231,375/9,609,961 = 0.440 \quad D_2 = 8.047$$
$$W_3 = 1,378,586/9,609,961 = 0.144 \quad D_3 = 9.168$$

The portfolio's duration is:

$$0.416 (3.861) + 0.440 (8.047) + 0.144 (9.168) = 6.47$$

A portfolio duration of 6.47 means that for a 100 basis change in the yield for *all* three bonds, the market value of the portfolio will change by approximately 6.47%. But keep in mind, the yield on all three bonds must change by 100 basis points for the duration measure to be useful. This is a critical assumption and its importance cannot be overemphasized. We shall return to this point in the next chapter.

Similarly, the dollar duration of a portfolio can be obtained by calculating the weighted average of the dollar duration of the bonds in the portfolio.

Duration for Noncallable Corporate Bonds

In recent years, the issuance of noncallable corporate bonds has increased. The yield on a noncallable corporate bond is composed of the Treasury base rate plus a credit spread. Duration measures the sensitivity of the price of a security to the general level of interest rates. Thus the duration of a noncallable corporate bond depends on the change in the level of Treasury rates and the change in credit spreads. If the change in Treasury rates and credit spreads is highly correlated, a duration measure for a noncallable corporate bond will do an effective job of estimating its price sensitivity to rate changes. However, if the correlation is low, duration will not be an effective measure of price sensitivity.

Ilmanen, McGuire, and Warga empirically examined this issue.[6] For the period covering 1985 to December 1991, they analyzed the relative monthly performance of investment grade noncallable corporate bonds due to general market-wide parallel yield shifts (duration and convexity) and a change in credit spreads. They found that for a portfolio of Aaa-rated bonds, duration is able to explain almost 90% of a portfolio's returns. For portfolios comprising Aaa- and Aa-rated bonds, duration explains about 80% of a portfolio's returns. However, for portfolios comprised of all investment grade noncallable corporate bonds, only 35% of a portfolio's returns are explained by duration. By incorporating credit spread as a variable to explain portfolio returns, no major improvement is made in the explanatory power. The conclusion of Ilmanen, McGuire, and Warga is that while duration does a good job of explaining returns for portfolios of Aaa- and Aa-rated noncallable, it does not do so for portfolios that include A- and Baa-rated issues.

Duration of a Floater

For a floating-rate security, the greater the reset frequency, the smaller the duration. When the coupon reset date is close, the duration is close to zero. All of this assumes that the spread over the reference rate that the market requires does not change.

Duration of an Inverse Floater

An inverse floater is a security whose coupon rate changes inversely with the change in the reference rate. It is common to create an inverse floater by splitting a fixed-rate security into a floater and an inverse floater. There are inverse floaters in the corporate, municipal, and CMO markets, the largest issuance being in the

---

[6] Annti Ilmanen, Donald McGuire, and Arthur Warga, "The Value of Duration as a Risk Measure for Corporate Debt," *Journal of Fixed Income* (June 1994), pp. 70-79.

latter market. The fixed-rate security from which the floater and inverse floater are created is called the collateral.

The duration of an inverse floater will be a multiple of the duration of the collateral from which it is created. To see this, suppose that a 30-year fixed-rate bond with a market value of $100 million is split into a floater and an inverse floater with a market value of $80 and $20 million, respectively. Assume also that the duration for the collateral (i.e., the 30-year fixed-rate bond) is 8. For a 100 basis point change in interest rates, the collateral's value will change by approximately 8% or $8 million (8% times $100 million). This means that by splitting the collateral's value, the combined change in value for a 100 basis change in interest rates for the floater and inverse floater must be $8 million. If the duration of the floater is small as just explained, this means that the entire $8 million change in value must come from the inverse floater. For this to occur, the duration of the inverse floater must be 40. That is, a duration of 40 will mean a 40% change in the value of the inverse floater for a 100 basis point change in interest rates and a change in value of $8 million (40% times $20 million).

Notice from our illustration that the duration of the inverse floater is greater than the number of years to maturity of the collateral. Managers who interpret duration in terms of years (i.e., Macaulay duration) are confused that a security can have a duration greater than the collateral from which it is created.

In general, assuming that the duration of the floater is close to zero, it can be shown that the duration of an inverse floater is:[7]

Duration of inverse floater

$$= (1 + L)(\text{Duration of collateral}) \times \frac{\text{Collateral price}}{\text{Inverse price}}$$

where L = leverage of inverse floater.

Controlling Interest Rate Risk in Active Bond Portfolio Strategies

Bond portfolio strategies can be classified as either active portfolio strategies or structured portfolio strategies. Essential to all active strategies is specification of expectations about the factors that influence the performance of bonds. Structured portfolio strategies involve minimal expectational input. The goal is to design a portfolio so as to replicate the performance of a bond index or to satisfy predetermined liabilities.

There are four types of active strategies: rate expectations strategies, yield curve strategies, yield spread strategies, and individual bond selection strategies. Here we will explain how to control the interest rate risk for all but yield curve strategies. Measuring and controlling risk in yield curve strategies is the subject of later chapters.

---

[7] William Leach, "A Portfolio Manager's Perspective of Inverses and Inverse IOs," in Frank J. Fabozzi, (ed.), *CMO Portfolio Management* (Summit, NJ: Frank J. Fabozzi Associates, 1994), p. 159.

Rate expectations strategies seek to capitalize on expectations about interest rate movements. A manager who believes that he or she can accurately forecast the future level of interest rates will alter the portfolio's sensitivity to interest rate changes. As duration is a measure of interest rate sensitivity, this involves increasing a portfolio's duration if interest rates are expected to fall and reducing duration if interest rates are expected to rise. For those managers whose benchmark is a bond index, this means increasing the portfolio duration relative to the index if interest rates are expected to fall and reducing it if interest rates are expected to rise. The degree to which the duration of the managed portfolio is permitted to diverge from that of the bond index may be limited by the client.

A portfolio's duration may be altered by swapping (or exchanging) bonds in the portfolio for new bonds that will achieve the target portfolio duration. Such swaps are commonly referred to as rate anticipation swaps. Alternatively, a more efficient means for altering the duration of a bond portfolio is to use interest rate futures contracts. As we explain in Chapter 8, buying futures increases a portfolio's duration, while selling futures decreases it.

Yield spread strategies involve positioning a portfolio to capitalize on expected changes in yield spreads between sectors of the bond market. Swapping (or exchanging) one bond for another when the manager believes that the prevailing yield spread between two bonds in the market is out of line with their historical yield spread, and that the yield spread will realign by the end of the investment horizon, are called intermarket spread swaps.

Individual security selection strategies involve identifying mispriced securities and taking a position in those securities so as to benefit when the market realigns. The most common strategy identifies an issue as undervalued because either (1) its yield is higher than that of comparably rated issues, or (2) its yield is expected to decline (and price therefore rise) because credit analysis indicates that its rating will improve.

A swap in which a manager exchanges one bond for another bond that is similar in terms of coupon, maturity, and credit quality, but offers a higher yield, is called a substitution swap. This swap depends on a capital market imperfection. Such situations sometimes exist in the bond market owing to temporary market imbalances and the fragmented nature of the non-Treasury bond market. The risk the manager faces in undertaking a substitution swap is that the bond purchased may not be truly identical to the bond for which it is exchanged.

What is critical in assessing yield spread and individual security selection strategies when an intermarket swap or substitution swap are being contemplated is to compare positions that have the same dollar duration. To understand why, consider two bonds, X and Y. Suppose that the price of bond X is 80 and has a modified duration of 5 while bond Y has a price of 90 and has a modified duration of 4. Since modified duration is the approximate percentage change per 100 basis point change in yield, a 100 basis points change in yield for bond X would change its price by about 5%. Based on a price of 80, its price will change by about $4 per $80 of market value. Thus, its dollar duration for a 100 basis point change in yield is $4 per $80 of market value. Similarly, for bond Y, its dollar duration for a 100 basis point change in yield per $90 of market value can be determined. In this case it is $3.6. So, if bonds X and Y are being considered as alternative investments in some strategy other than one based on anticipating interest rate movements, the amount of each bond in the strategy should be such that they will both have the same dollar duration.

To illustrate this, suppose that a manager owns $10 million of par value of bond X which has a market value of $8 million. The dollar duration of bond X per 100 basis point change in yield for the $8 million market value is $400,000. Suppose further that this manager is considering exchanging bond X that she owns in her portfolio for bond Y. If the manager wants to have the same interest rate exposure (i.e., dollar duration) for bond Y that she currently has for bond X, she will buy a market value amount of bond Y with the same dollar duration. If the manager purchased $10 million of *par value* of bond Y and therefore $9 million of *market value* of bond Y, the dollar value change per 100 basis change in yield would be only $360,000. If, instead, the manager purchased $10 million of *market value* of bond Y, the dollar duration per 100 basis point change in yield would be $400,000. Since bond Y is trading at 90, $11.11 million of par value of bond Y must be purchased to keep the dollar duration of the position from bond Y the same as for bond X.

Mathematically, this problem can be expressed as follows. Let:

$\$D_X$ = dollar duration per 100 basis point change in yield for bond X for the market value of bond X held

MD_Y = modified duration for bond Y

MV_Y = market value of bond Y needed to obtain the same dollar duration as bond X

Then, the following equation sets the dollar duration for bond X equal to the dollar duration for bond Y:

$$\$D_X = (MD_Y/100)\, MV_Y$$

Solving for MV_Y,

$$MV_Y = \$D_X\, /\, (MD_Y/100)$$

Dividing by the price per $1 of par value of bond Y gives the par value of Y that has an approximately equivalent dollar duration as bond X.

In our illustration, $\$D_X$ is $400,000 and MD_Y is 4, then

$$MV_Y = \$400,000/(4/100) = \$10,000,000$$

Since the market value of bond Y is 90 per $100 of par value, the price per $1 of par value is 0.9. Dividing $10 million by 0.9 indicates that the par value of bond Y that should be purchased is $11.11 million.

Failure to adjust a portfolio repositioning based on some expected change in yield spread so as to hold the dollar duration the same means that the outcome of the portfolio will be affected by not only the expected change in the yield spread but also a change in the yield level. Thus, a manager would be making a conscious yield spread bet and possibly an undesired bet on the level of interest rates.

Price Sensitivity to Nonparallel Yield Curve Shifts

Both modified duration and effective duration assume that any change in interest rates is the result of a parallel shift in the yield curve. For some fixed-income securities, the price sensitivity to most nonparallel shifts will be very close to the estimated price sensitivity for a parallel shift in the yield curve. This is generally true for option-free bonds with a bullet maturity. However, for sinking-fund bonds and bonds with embedded options, particularly mortgage-backed securities, the price sensitivity to a nonparallel shift in the yield curve can be quite different from that estimated for a parallel shift.

We will illustrate the significance of the parallel yield curve assumption in the next chapter.

MARKET-BASED APPROACHES TO DURATION ESTIMATION FOR AN MBS

For mortgage-backed securities, two completely different approaches than modified and effective duration are used by some managers — empirical duration and coupon curve duration. The two approaches are based on observed market prices.

Empirical Duration

Empirical duration, sometimes referred to as *implied duration*, is the sensitivity of a mortgage-backed security (MBS) as estimated empirically from historical prices and yields.[8] Regression analysis, a statistical technique described in Chapter 7, is used to estimate the relationship. More specifically, the relationship estimated is the percentage change in the price of the MBS of interest to the change in the general level of Treasury yields.

To obtain the empirical duration, Paul DeRossa, Laurie Goodman, and Mike Zazzarino suggest the following relationship be estimated using multiple regression analysis:[9]

---

[8] The first attempt to calculate empirical duration was by Scott M. Pinkus and Marie A. Chandoha, "The Relative Price Volatility of Mortgage Securities," *Journal of Portfolio Management* (Summer 1986), pp. 9-22.

[9] Paul DeRossa, Laurie Goodman, and Mike Zazzarino, "Duration Estimates on Mortgage-Backed Securities," *Journal of Portfolio Management* (Winter 1993), pp. 32-37.

$$\text{Percentage change in price} = c + b_1(\Delta y) + b_2(P - 100)(\Delta y)$$
$$+ b_3[(P - 100)^2(\Delta y) \text{ if P} > 100, \text{ otherwise } 0] + \text{error term}$$

where

P = price (with par equal to 100)
Δy = change in yield

and c, b_1, b_2, and b_3 are the parameters to be estimated.

The inclusion of the second and third terms in the relationship is to allow for the price sensitivity to vary depending on the price level of the mortgages. The reason for the inclusion of the error term is explained in Chapter 7.

The expectation is that the parameter c would be equal to zero when the relationship is estimated. The expected sign of b_2 is negative. That is, there is an inverse relationship between yield changes and price changes. Finally, the terms b_2 and b_3 are expected to have a positive sign.

DeRossa, Goodman, and Zazzarino estimated the relationship using daily data for the 5-year period (11/19/86 to 11/18/91) for Ginnie Mae and Fannie Mae 8s, 9s, 10s, and 11s. The yield used was the 10-year Treasury, although they indicate that nearly identical results were realized if they used the 7-year Treasury. In all of their estimated regressions, all of the parameters had the expected sign.

Given the estimated relationship, the empirical duration for different coupons at different price levels can be found by dividing the estimated relationship by the change in yield. That is:

$$\text{Duration} = \frac{\text{Percentage change in price}}{\Delta y} = c + b_1 + b_2(P - 100)$$
$$+ b_3[(P - 100)^2(\Delta y) \text{ if P} > 100, \text{ otherwise } 0]$$

For an MBS trading at par, P is 100, and the empirical duration is therefore b_1.

There are three advantages to the empirical duration approach.[10] First, the duration estimate does not rely on any theoretical formulas or analytical assumptions. Second, the estimation of the required parameters are easy to compute using regression analysis. Finally, the only inputs that are needed are a reliable price series and Treasury yield series.

There are disadvantages.[11] First, a reliable price series for the data may not be available. For example, there may be no price series available for a thinly traded mortgage derivative security or the prices may be matrix priced or model priced rather than actual transaction prices. Second, an empirical relationship

---

[10] See Bennett W. Golub, "Towards a New Approach to Measuring Mortgage Duration," Chapter 32 in Frank J. Fabozzi (ed.), *The Handbook of Mortgage-Backed Securities* (Chicago: Probus Publishing, 1995), p. 672.

[11] Ibid.

does not impose a structure for the options embedded in an MBS and this can distort the empirical duration. Third, the price history may lag current market conditions. This may occur after a sharp and sustained shock to interest rates has been realized. Finally, the volatility of the spread to Treasury yields can distort how the price of an MBS reacts to yield changes.

Coupon Curve Duration

The *coupon curve duration* is a second approach that uses market prices to estimate the duration of an MBS. It is an easier approach to duration estimation than empirical duration. The approach, first suggested by Douglas Breeden,[12] starts with the coupon curve of prices for similar MBS. By rolling up and down the coupon curve of prices, the duration can be obtained. Because of the way it is estimated, this approach to duration estimation was referred to by Breeden as the "roll-up, roll-down approach." The prices obtained from rolling up and rolling down the coupon curve of prices are substituted into the approximation formula for duration given by equation (1).

To illustrate this approach, let's use the coupon curve of prices for Ginnie Maes in June 1994. A portion of the coupon curve of prices for that month was as follows:

Coupon	Price
6%	85.19
7%	92.06
8%	98.38
9%	103.34
10%	107.28
11%	111.19

Suppose that the coupon curve duration for the 8s is sought. If the yield declines by 100 basis points, the assumption is that the price of the 8s will increase to the price of the 9s. Thus, the price will increase from 98.38 to 103.34. Similarly, if the yield increases by 100 basis points, the assumption is that the price of the 8s will decline to the price of the 7s (92.06). Using the duration formula given by equation (1), the corresponding values are:

$$V_0 = 98.38$$
$$V_- = 103.34$$
$$V_+ = 92.06$$
$$\Delta y = 0.01$$

The estimated duration based on the coupon curve is then:

$$\text{Duration} = \frac{103.34 - 92.06}{2(98.38)(0.01)} = 5.73$$

---

[12] Douglas Breeden, "Risk, Return, and Hedging of Fixed-Rate Mortgages," *Journal of Fixed Income* (September 1991), pp. 85-107.

Breeden of Smith Breeden Associates tested the coupon curve durations and found them to be relatively accurate.[13] Bennett Golub of BlackRock Financial Management reports a similar finding.[14]

While the advantages of the coupon curve duration are the simplicity of its calculation and the fact that current prices embody market expectations, there are disadvantages. The approach is limited to generic MBS and difficult to use for mortgage derivatives.

CONVEXITY MEASURE AS A SECOND ORDER APPROXIMATION OF PRICE CHANGE

Notice that the duration measure indicates that regardless of whether the yield curve is shifted up or down, the approximate percentage price change is the same. However, this does not agree with the properties of a bond's price volatility described earlier in this chapter. Specifically, Property 2 states that for small changes in yield the percentage price change will be the same for an increase or decrease in yield. Property 3 states that for large changes in yield this is not true. This suggests that duration is only a good approximation of the percentage price change for a small change in yield.

To see this, consider once again the 9% 20-year bond selling to yield 6% with a duration of 10.66. If yields increase instantaneously by 10 basis points (from 6% to 6.1%), then using duration the approximate percentage price change would be −1.066% (−10.66% divided by 10, remembering that duration is the percentage price change for a 100 basis point change in yield). Notice from Exhibit 3 that the actual percentage price change is −1.07%. Similarly, if the yield decreases instantaneously by 10 basis points (from 6.00% to 5.90%), then the percentage change in price would be +1.066%. From Exhibit 3, the actual percentage price change would be +1.07%. This example illustrates that for small changes in yield, duration does an excellent job of approximating the percentage price change.

Instead of a small change in yield, let's assume that yields increase by 200 basis points, from 6% to 8%. The approximate percentage price change is −21.32% (−10.66% times 2). As can be seen from Exhibit 3, the actual percentage change in price is only −18.40%. Moreover, if the yield decreases by 200 basis points from 6% to 4%, the approximate percentage price change based on duration would be +21.32%, compared to an actual percentage price change of +25.04%. Thus, the approximation is not as good for a 200 basis point change in yield.

Duration is in fact a first approximation for a small parallel shift in the yield curve. The approximation can be improved by using a second approxima-

[13] Breeden, "Risk, Return, and Hedging of Fixed-Rate Mortgages."
[14] Golub, "Towards a New Approach to Measuring Mortgage Duration," p. 673.

tion. This approximation is referred to as a *bond's convexity.*[15] The use of this term in the industry is unfortunate since the term convexity is also used to describe the shape or curvature of the price/yield relationship, as explained earlier in this chapter. The convexity measure of a bond can be used to approximate the change in price that is not explained by duration.

Convexity Measure

The convexity measure of any bond can be approximated using the following formula:

$$\text{Convexity measure} = \frac{V_+ + V_- - 2V_0}{2V_0(\Delta y)^2} \tag{3}$$

where the notation is the same as used earlier for duration [equation (1)].

For our hypothetical 9% 20-year bond selling to yield 6%, we know that for a 20-basis-point-change in yield

$$\Delta y = 0.0020$$
$$V_+ = 131.8439$$
$$V_- = 137.5888$$
$$V_0 = 134.6722$$

Substituting these values into the convexity measure formula,

$$\text{Convexity measure} = \frac{137.5888 + 131.8439 - 2(134.6722)}{2(134.6722)(0.002)^2} = 81.96$$

Percentage Price Change Adjustment for Convexity

Given the convexity measure, the approximate percentage price change adjustment due to the bond's convexity (i.e., the percentage price change not explained by duration) is:

$$\text{Convexity measure} \times (\Delta y)^2$$

For example, for the 9% coupon bond maturing in 20 years, the convexity adjustment to the percentage price change if the yield increases from 6% to 8% is

---

[15] Mathematically, any function can be estimated by a series of approximations referred to as a Taylor series. Each approximation or term of the Taylor series is based on the corresponding derivative. For a bond, duration is the first approximation to price change and is related to the first derivative of the bond's price. The convexity measure is the second approximation and related to the second derivative of the bond's price. It turns out that in general the first two approximations do a good job of estimating the bond's price so no additional derivatives are needed. The derivation is provided in Chapter 4 of Frank J. Fabozzi, *Bond Markets, Analysis, and Strategies* (Englewood Cliffs, N.J.: Prentice Hall, 1996).

$$81.96 \times (0.02)^2 = 0.0328 = 3.28\%$$

If the yield decreases from 6% to 4%, the convexity adjustment to the approximate percentage price change would also be 3.28%.

The approximate percentage price change based on duration and the convexity adjustment is found by simply adding the two estimates. So, for example, if yields change from 6% to 8%, the estimated percentage price change would be:

Estimated change approximated by duration	$= -21.32\%$
Estimated adjustment for convexity	$= +3.28\%$
Total estimated percentage price change	$= -18.04\%$

The actual percentage price change is −18.40%.

For a decrease of 200 basis points, from 6% to 4%, the approximate percentage price change would be as follows:

Estimated change approximated by duration	$= +21.32\%$
Estimated adjustment for convexity	$= +3.28\%$
Total estimated percentage price change	$= +24.60\%$

The actual percentage price change is +25.04%. Thus, duration, with the convexity adjustment, does a good job of estimating the sensitivity of a bond's price change to large changes in yield.

Modified Convexity and Effective Convexity

The prices used in equation (3) to calculate convexity can be obtained by either assuming that when the yield curve shifts in a parallel way the expected cash flow does not change or it does change. In the former case, the resulting convexity is referred to as *modified convexity*.[16] Actually, in the industry, convexity is not qualified by the adjective modified. Thus, in practice the term convexity typically means the cash flow is assumed not to change when yields change. Effective convexity, in contrast, assumes that the cash flow does change when yields change. This is the same distinction made for duration.

As with duration, for bonds with embedded options there could be quite a difference between the calculated modified convexity and effective convexity. In fact, for all option-free bonds, either convexity measure will have a positive

---

[16] The formula for modified convexity is

$$\frac{1(2)PVCF_1 + 2(3)PVCF_2 + 3(4)PVCF_3 + \ldots + n(n+1)PVCF_n}{(1 + yield/k)^2 \ k^2 \ Price}$$

Using this formula, the modified convexity for the 9% 20-year bond selling to yield 6% is 82.04. While this number is slightly different from that obtained using equation (3), when we use this measure to obtain the approximate percentage price change due to convexity, the result will be the same.

value.[17] For callable bonds and mortgage-backed securities, the calculated effective convexity can be negative when the calculated modified convexity gives a positive value.

---

[17] Hence, dealer firms such as Goldman Sachs refer to the convexity adjustment as the "convexity gain."

KEY POINTS

1. *The price/yield relationship for an option-free bond is convex.*

2. *A property of an option-free bond is that for a small change in yield, the percentage price change is roughly the same whether the yield increases or decreases.*

3. *A property of an option-free bond is that for a large change in yield, the percentage price change is not the same for an increase in yield as it is for a decrease in yield.*

4. *A property of an option-free bond is that for a given change in basis points, the percentage price increase is greater than the percentage price decrease.*

5. *The coupon and maturity of an option-free bond affect its price volatility.*

6. *For a given term to maturity and initial yield, the lower the coupon rate the greater the price volatility of a bond.*

7. *For a given coupon rate and initial yield, the longer the term to maturity, the greater the price volatility.*

8. *For a given change in yield, price volatility is less when yield levels in the market are high than when yield levels are low.*

9. *The percentage price change of a bond can be estimated by changing the yield by a small number of basis points and observing how the price changes.*

10. *Modified duration is the approximate percentage change in a bond's price for a 100 basis point parallel shift in the yield curve assuming that the bond's cash flow does not change when the yield curve shifts.*

11. *Callable bonds and mortgage passthrough securities exhibit negative convexity which means that the percentage price change for a rise in rates is greater than for a decline in rates by the same number of basis points.*

12. *Modified duration is not a useful measure of the price sensitivity for bonds with embedded options.*

13. *Effective duration or option-adjusted duration is the approximate percentage price change of a bond for a 100 basis point parallel shift in the yield curve allowing for the cash flow to change as a result of the change in yield.*

14. *The difference between modified duration and effective duration for bonds with an embedded option can be quite dramatic.*

15. *The duration measure is only as good as the valuation model from which it is derived.*

16. *The dollar duration of a bond measures the dollar price change when interest rates change.*

17. *A rate expectations strategy involves positioning the duration of a portfolio based on whether rates are expected to increase or decrease.*

18. *For a manager pursuing a rate expectation strategy, the portfolio duration relative to the bond index will be increased if interest rates are expected to fall and the duration will be reduced relative to the bond index if interest rates are expected to rise.*

19. *When contemplating an intermarket spread swap or a substitution swap, it is important to keep the dollar duration of the portfolio constant.*

20. *Two market-based approaches have been used to estimate the duration of a mortgage-backed security — empirical duration and coupon curve duration.*

21. *Empirical duration, or implied duration, uses historical price series for a mortgage-backed securities and data on Treasury yields to statistically estimate duration.*

22. *The coupon curve duration is calculated from observed prices for similar mortgage-backed securities at given point in time by rolling up and rolling down the coupon curve of prices.*

23. *The estimate of the price sensitivity of a bond based on duration can be improved by using a bond's convexity measure.*

24. *As with duration, the convexity of a bond can be measured assuming that the cash flow does not change when yield changes (modified convexity) or assuming that it does change when yield changes (effective convexity).*

25. *Both modified duration and effective duration assume that any change in interest rates is the result of a parallel shift in the yield curve.*

Chapter 4
Measuring Yield Curve Risk

The Treasury yield curve shows the relationship between yield and maturity for Treasury securities. When using a portfolio's duration to measure the exposure to interest rates, it is assumed that any change in interest rates is the result of a parallel shift in the yield curve. A parallel shift means that the yield for all maturities changes by the same number of basis points.

In this chapter, we will see that duration is an inadequate measure of interest rate risk when the yield curve does not change in a parallel manner. As a result, it is necessary to approximate the exposure of a portfolio or a position to shifts in the yield curve. Several basic approaches for measuring this exposure are described in this chapter.

The objectives of this chapter are to:

1. describe the types of shifts that have been observed for the yield curve;

2. demonstrate why duration and convexity do not provide information about the risk of a portfolio if the yield curve does not shift in a parallel fashion;

3. discuss the two general approaches to measuring yield curve risk;

4. explain the reshaping duration measure of yield curve risk;

5. explain the slope elasticity measure of yield curve risk; and,

6. explain the risk point method for assessing yield curve risk.

TYPES OF YIELD CURVE SHIFTS

Historically, the yield curve has taken on various shapes. These shapes are shown in Exhibit 1. An *upward sloping yield curve* (also called a *positive* or *normal yield curve*) is one in which yield increases with maturity. A *downward sloping yield curve* (also called an *inverted yield curve*) is one in which the yield declines with maturity. For a flat yield curve, the yield is approximately the same at each maturity. Finally, for a *humped yield curve*, the yield increases with maturity initially, and then subsequently declines with maturity.

Exhibit 1: Historically Observed Yield Curve Shapes

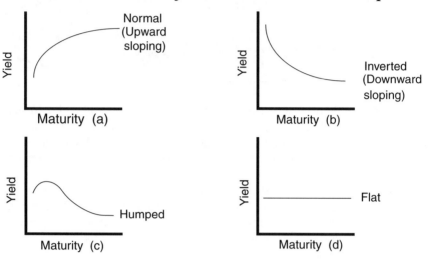

Historically, the following yield curve shifts have been observed, each of which is shown in Exhibit 2:[1]

- a parallel shift
- a twist in the slope of the yield curve (i.e., a flattening or steepening of the yield curve)
- a change in the humpedness of the yield curve (such a change is referred to as a *butterfly shift*)

DURATION, CONVEXITY, AND NONPARALLEL YIELD CURVE SHIFTS

Let's first look at how two portfolios with the same duration may perform quite differently if the yield curve does not shift in a parallel fashion. To illustrate this, consider the three bonds shown in Exhibit 3. Bond A is the short-term bond, bond B is the long-term bond, and bond C is the intermediate-term bond. Each bond is selling at par, and it is assumed the next coupon payment is six months from now. The duration and convexity for each bond are calculated in the exhibit. Since the bonds are trading at par value, the duration and convexities are then the dollar duration and dollar convexity per $100 of par value.

---

[1] For evidence on how shifts in the yield curve affected returns on Treasuries, see Frank J. Jones, "Yield Curve Strategies," *Journal of Fixed Income* (September 1991), pp. 43-41, and Robert Litterman and José Scheinkman, "Common Factors Affecting Bond Returns," *Journal of Fixed Income* (June 1991), pp. 54-61.

Exhibit 2: Types of Yield Curve Shifts

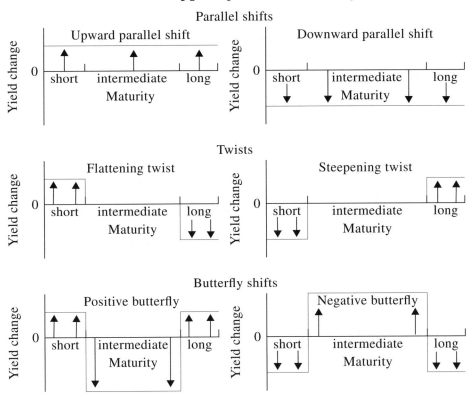

Exhibit 3: Three Hypothetical Bonds to Illustrate the Limitations of Duration and Convexity

Bond	Coupon rate (%)	Price ($)	Yield to maturity (%)	Maturity (years)
A	6.500	100	6.500	5
B	8.000	100	8.000	20
C	7.500	100	7.500	10

Calculation of duration: Change yield up and down by 10 basis points

Bond	V_+ ($)	V_- ($)	Duration	Convexity
A	99.5799	100.4222	4.21122	10.67912
B	99.0177	100.9970	9.89681	73.63737
C	99.3083	100.6979	6.94821	31.09724

Suppose that the following two portfolios are constructed. The first portfolio consists of only bond C, the 10-year bond, and shall be referred to as the "bullet portfolio." The second portfolio consists of 51.86% of bond A and 48.14% of bond B and this portfolio shall be referred to as the "barbell portfolio."

The dollar duration of the bullet portfolio is 6.49821. Recall that dollar duration is a measure of the dollar price sensitivity of a bond or portfolio. The dollar duration of the barbell is the weighted average of the dollar duration of the two bonds and is computed below:

$$0.5186 (4.21122) + 0.4814 (9.89681) = 6.49821$$

The dollar duration of the barbell is equal to the dollar duration of the bullet. In fact, the barbell portfolio was designed to produce this result.

Duration is just a first approximation of the change in price resulting from a change in interest rates. The convexity measure provides a second approximation. The dollar convexity measure of the two portfolios is not equal. The dollar convexity measure of the bullet portfolio is 31.09724. The dollar convexity measure of the barbell is a weighted average of the dollar convexity measure of the two bonds. That is,

$$0.5186 (10.67912) + 0.4814 (73.63737) = 40.98658$$

Thus, the bullet has a dollar convexity measure that is less than that of the barbell portfolio. Below is a summary of the dollar duration and dollar convexity of the two portfolios:

	Portfolio	
Parameter	Bullet	Barbell
Dollar duration	6.49821	6.49821
Dollar convexity	31.09724	40.98658

Let's use scenario analysis to look at the interest rate risk exposure of these two portfolios assuming a 6-month investment horizon. The second, third, and fourth columns of Exhibit 4 show the new price plus coupon of each bond assuming yields change by the number of basis points shown in the first column. Since Exhibit 4 assumed all yields change by the same number of basis points, the results are based on a parallel yield curve assumption. The fifth and sixth columns show what happens to the two portfolios.

We have shown only shifts of yields of +60 basis points and greater since for smaller changes there is a positive return for both portfolios. The last column of Exhibit 4 shows the difference in the loss over a 6-month investment horizon for the two portfolios assuming a parallel shift in the yield curve.[2]

---

[2] Note that no assumption is needed for the reinvestment rate since the three bonds shown in Exhibit 1 are assumed to be trading right after a coupon payment has been made and therefore there is no accrued interest.

Exhibit 4: Risk Exposure of Bullet and Barbell Portfolios with Same Duration Over a 6-Month Horizon Assuming a Parallel Yield Curve Shift

Yield change	Price plus coupon($)			Loss(%)		
(in b.p.)	A	B	C	Bullet	Barbell	Difference*
60	100.9729	98.3740	99.8265	−0.35	−0.56	0.21
80	100.2279	96.6046	98.5627	−2.87	−3.03	0.16
100	99.4896	94.8852	97.3203	−5.36	−5.45	0.09
120	98.7582	93.2142	96.0988	−7.80	−7.82	0.02
140	98.0334	91.5900	94.8979	−10.20	−10.14	−0.07
160	97.3153	90.0110	93.7171	−12.57	−12.40	−0.16
180	96.6037	88.4758	92.5562	−14.89	−14.62	−0.27
200	95.8987	86.9830	91.4146	−17.17	−16.79	−0.38
220	95.2000	85.5311	90.2921	−19.42	−18.91	−0.51
240	94.5078	84.1188	89.1883	−21.62	−20.99	−0.64
260	93.8218	82.7448	88.1029	−23.79	−23.02	−0.77
280	93.1421	81.4080	87.0355	−25.93	−25.01	−0.92
300	92.4686	80.1070	85.9857	−28.03	−26.96	−1.06

* Bullet loss minus barbell loss.

Notice that despite the same dollar duration, the losses are not the same. For a parallel shift in the yield curve, the loss is less for the bullet portfolio as long as the yield curve does not shift by more than 120 basis points.

Now let's look at what happens if the yield curve does not shift in a parallel fashion. Obviously, there are an infinite number of possible yield curve shifts. To demonstrate the limitations of duration, we will use just two possible yield curve shifts.

In Exhibit 5 it is assumed that if the yield on bond C (the intermediate-term bond) changes by the amount shown in the first column, bond A (the short-term bond) will change by the same amount minus 30 basis points, whereas bond B (the long-term bond) will change by the same amount shown in the first column plus 30 basis points. That is, the nonparallel shift assumed is a steepening of the yield curve by 60 basis points. For this yield curve shift, the barbell has less yield curve exposure as long as bond C does not increase more than 260 basis points.

In Exhibit 6, the nonparallel shift assumes that for a change in bond C's yield, the yield on bond A will change by the same amount plus 30 basis points, whereas that on bond B will change by the same amount minus 30 points. That is, it assumes that the yield curve will flatten by 60 basis points. In this case, the yield curve risk for the barbell is greater than that for the bullet for any rise in yield for bond C of 60 basis points or more.

Exhibit 5: Risk Exposure of Bullet and Barbell Portfolios with Same Duration Over a 6-Month Horizon Assuming a 60 Basis Point Steepening of the Yield Curve

Yield change	Price plus coupon($)			Loss(%)		
for C (in b.p.)	A	B	C	Bullet	Barbell	Difference[*]
60	102.1036	95.7387	99.8265	−0.35	−1.92	1.57
80	101.3481	94.0437	98.5627	−2.87	−4.34	1.46
100	100.5995	92.3963	97.3203	−5.36	−6.70	1.34
120	99.8579	90.7949	96.0988	−7.80	− 9.01	1.21
140	99.1230	89.2380	94.8979	−10.20	−11.27	1.07
160	98.3949	87.7242	93.7171	−12.57	−13.48	0.92
180	97.6735	86.2520	92.5562	−14.89	−15.65	0.76
200	96.9587	84.8200	91.4146	−17.17	−17.77	0.60
220	96.2504	83.4271	90.2921	−19.42	−19.85	0.43
240	95.5485	82.0718	89.1883	−21.62	−21.88	0.25
260	94.8531	80.7531	88.1029	−23.79	−23.87	0.07
280	94.1640	79.4696	87.0355	−25.93	−25.82	−0.11
300	93.4812	78.2204	85.9857	−28.03	−27.73	−0.30

* Bullet loss minus barbell loss.
Yield curve assumption: Change in yield of bond C (column 1) results in a change in the yield of bond A minus 30 basis point. Change in yield of bond C (column 1) results in a change in the yield of bond B plus 30 basis point.

Exhibit 6: Risk Exposure of Bullet and Barbell Portfolios with Same Duration Over a 6-Month Horizon Assuming a 60 Basis Point Flattening of the Yield Curve

Yield change	Price plus coupon($)			Loss(%)		
for C (in b.p.)	A	B	C	Bullet	Barbell	Difference[*]
60	99.8579	101.1257	99.8265	−0.35	0.94	−1.28
80	99.1230	99.2780	98.5627	−2.87	−1.60	−1.27
100	98.3949	97.4829	97.3203	−5.36	−4.09	−1.27
120	97.6735	95.7387	96.0988	−7.80	−6.52	−1.29
140	96.9587	94.0437	94.8979	−10.20	−8.89	−1.32
160	96.2504	92.3963	93.7171	−12.57	−11.21	−1.36
180	95.5485	90.7949	92.5562	−14.89	−13.48	−1.41
200	94.8531	89.2380	91.4146	−17.17	−15.70	−1.47
220	94.1640	87.7242	90.2921	−19.42	−17.87	−1.54
240	93.4812	86.2520	89.1883	−21.62	−20.00	−1.63
260	92.8046	84.8200	88.1029	−23.79	−22.08	−1.72
280	92.1341	83.4271	87.0355	−25.93	−24.11	−1.81
300	91.4697	82.0718	85.9857	−28.03	−26.11	−1.92

* Bullet loss minus barbell loss.
Yield curve assumption: Change in yield of bond C (column 1) results in a change in the yield of bond A plus 30 basis point. Change in yield of bond C (column 1) results in a change in the yield of bond B minus 30 basis point.

YIELD CURVE RISK MEASURES

It should be clear from our illustrations that neither the duration nor the convexity of a portfolio or position measures the exposure to yield curve risk. The sensitivity of a portfolio to changes in the shape of the yield curve can be approximated. There have been several approaches suggested in the literature to accomplish this. There are two fundamental approaches.

The first approach is to look at the sensitivity of a portfolio to a change in the slope of the yield curve. The slope is defined as the spread between points on the yield curve. We will describe two examples of this approach below — yield curve reshaping duration and slope elasticity. The second approach is to change yields on the yield curve and determine the sensitivity of a portfolio or position to a change in each yield. Thus the sensitivity of a portfolio or position is defined for points on the yield curve. We will describe one approach below — the risk point method.

The second approach is superior to the first approach for assessing yield curve risk. However, the first approach can be used to quickly estimate the exposure of a portfolio or position to yield curve risk.

MANAGING LEVEL AND YIELD CURVE RISK INDEPENDENTLY

Shortly we will define various measures of yield curve risk. Given the exposure of a portfolio or position to shifts in the level of interest rates (as measured by duration) and to shifts in the yield curve, a manager should be able to make an informed decision about what kind of hedge to put on or how to manage that risk.

Yield curve slope risk and level risk can, for the most part, be managed independently. The reason for this is that the correlation between changes in the level of rates and yield curve slope is low. What if it were the case that whenever rates rose the yield curve got steeper, or when rates fell the yield curve flattened? In that case, changes in yield curve slope and changes in the level of rates would be highly correlated and a manager would have to consider the effect or exposure of a portfolio to changes both in the level of rates and in slope simultaneously. A manager could not effectively separate the two effects.

The relationship of changes in the level of rates to changes in yield curve slope is an empirical question. Schumacher, Dektar, and Fabozzi investigated this question by calculating the historical correlation between changes in the slope of the yield curve and changes in the level of rates.[3] In their analysis the level of rates is defined as the average of the 6-month, 5-year, and 30-year Treasury yields. Based on monthly data for the period 12/82 to 12/92, they find that the correlation is 0.12

---

[3] Michael P. Schumacher, Daniel C. Dektar, and Frank J. Fabozzi, "Yield Curve Risk of CMO Bonds," in Frank J. Fabozzi (ed.), *CMO Portfolio Management* (Summit, NJ: Frank J. Fabozzi Associates, 1994). An adaptation of this chapter appears as Chapter 13 in this book.

between changes in the level of rates and changes in the slope of the yield curve.[4] While it is not zero, it is low enough to give a manager comfort that yield curve slope exposure can be calculated and managed independently of parallel interest rate shifts. This is an important property since if this were not the case, a manager would have to establish an elaborate Monte Carlo model to assess the joint effect of level and slope exposures based on a correlation between the two factors.

YIELD CURVE RESHAPING DURATION

The first approach to estimating yield curve risk in terms of changes in the slope of the yield curve requires a definition of what is meant by the slope of the yield curve. There are several definitions that have been used to describe the slope of the yield curve. Some market participants define yield curve slope as the difference in the Treasury yield curve at two maturity levels. For instance, the yield curve slope can be defined as the difference between the yield on the 10-year on-the-run Treasury and the 2-year on-the-run Treasury.

Rather than looking at just two points, some market participants break down the yield curve to the spread between various maturity sectors. For example, yield curve slope can be defined as the difference between the 10-year and 2-year on-the-run Treasuries and the 30-year and 10-year on-the-run Treasuries. With this definition, an investor is looking at the slope at the short end of the yield curve (the 10-year/2-year spread) and the long end of the yield curve (the 30-year/10-year spread).

The *yield curve reshaping duration* introduced by Klaffky, Ma, and Nozari focuses on three points on the yield curve: 2-year, 10-year and 30-year, and the spread between the 10-year and 2-year issue and the spread between the 30-year and 10-year issue.[5] The former spread is referred to as the short-end of the yield curve, and the latter spread the long-end of the yield curve. Klaffky, Ma and Nozari refer to the sensitivity of a portfolio to changes in the short end of the yield curve as *short-end duration* (SEDUR) and to changes in the long-end of the yield curve as *long-end duration* (LEDUR). These concepts, however, are applicable to other points on the yield curve.

To calculate the SEDUR of each bond in the portfolio, the percentage change in the bond's price is calculated for (1) a steepening of the yield curve at the short end by 50 basis points, and (2) a flattening of the yield curve at the short end of the yield curve by 50 basis points. Then the bond's SEDUR is computed as follows:

$$\text{SEDUR} = \frac{V_s - V_f}{2V_0 \Delta y}$$

---

[4] The correlation would probably be somewhat higher if a longer differencing interval were used.

[5] Thomas E. Klaffky, Y.Y. Ma, and Ardavan Nozari, "Managing Yield Curve Exposure: Introducing Reshaping Durations," *Journal of Fixed Income* (December 1992), pp. 5-15

where

V_s = bond's price if the short-end of the yield curve steepens by 50 basis points

V_f = bond's price if the short-end of the yield curve flattens by 50 basis points

V_0 = bond's current market price

To calculate the LEDUR, the same procedure is used for each bond in the portfolio: calculate the price for (1) a flattening of the yield curve at the long end by 50 basis points, and (2) a steepening of the yield curve at the long end of the yield curve by 50 basis points. Then the bond's LEDUR is computed in the following manner:

$$\text{LEDUR} = \frac{V_f - V_s}{2V_0\Delta y}$$

The SEDUR and LEDUR are equivalent to the formula for approximating duration given in the previous chapter.

We will use the three bonds in Exhibit 7, bonds U, V, and W, to demonstrate how to calculate SEDUR and LEDUR. From these three bonds two portfolios are constructed as shown in the second panel of the exhibit. Portfolio 1 is concentrated in the 10-year maturity sector, while Portfolio 2 is more heavily distributed in the 2-year and 30-year maturity sectors. Both portfolios, however, have the same dollar duration of 6.877182.

The SEDUR for the 2-year issue, bond U, is found by steepening the yield curve by 50 basis points and flattening it by 50 basis points. These values can be found by decreasing the yield on the 2-year by 50 basis points and increasing it by 50 basis points. The resulting values are V_s = 99.0763 and V_f = 100.9349. Using the formula for SEDUR:

$$\frac{100.9349 - 99.0763}{2(100)(0.005)} = 1.85860$$

The SEDUR for the 30-year bond is zero. Since the analysis proceeds from the shifting of the yield curve holding the 10-year yield constant, the SEDUR for the 10-year issue is zero.

Similarly, for the 2-year bond and the 10-year bond the LEDUR is zero. For the 30-year bond, the LEDUR is found by steepening the yield curve by 50 basis points and flattening it by 50 basis points. This means increasing and decreasing the yield on the 30-year by 50 basis points. The resulting values are V_s = 96.5259 and V_f = 103.6348. Using the formula for LEDUR:

$$\frac{103.6348 - 96.5259}{2(100)(0.005)} = 7.10899$$

Exhibit 7: Bonds and Portfolios Used to Illustrate the Calculation of SEDUR and LEDUR

Bond	Coupon rate (%)	Price ($)	Yield to maturity (%)	Maturity (years)
U	6.0	100	6.0	2
V	8.0	100	8.0	30
W	7.0	100	7.0	10

Portfolios

	Percentage of bond in portfolio	
Bond	Portfolio 1	Portfolio 2
U	42.5	22.0
V	47.5	22.0
W	10.0	56.0

Dollar Duration and Convexity

	Dollar duration	Dollar convexity
Bond U	1.85855	2.22220
Bond V	11.31258	107.12569
Bond W	7.10631	32.15018
Portfolio 1	6.87718	51.86454
Portfolio 2	6.87718	42.06064

The SEDUR and LEDUR for each bond are summarized in Exhibit 7. The portfolio SEDUR and LEDUR are the weighted averages of the corresponding durations for each bond in the portfolio. The SEDUR for the two portfolios is calculated as follows:

Portfolio 1: 0.425 (1.85860) + 0.475 (0) + 0.10 (0) = 0.789
Portfolio 2: 0.22 (1.85860) + 0.22 (0) + 0.56 (0) = 0.409

The LEDUR for the two portfolios is calculated as follows:

Portfolio 1: 0.425 (0) + 0.475 (0) + 0.10 (7.10889) = 0.711
Portfolio 2: 0.22 (0) + 0.22 (0) + 0.56 (7.10889) = 3.981

The various duration measures for the two portfolios are summarized below:

	Duration	SEDUR	LEDUR
Portfolio 1	6.88	0.789	0.711
Portfolio 2	6.88	0.409	3.981

These measures indicate that while both portfolios are exposed to the same risk for a small parallel shift in the level of interest rates, for a nonparallel shift, portfolio 1's exposure at the short end of the yield curve is about twice that of portfolio 2's. That is, if the short end of the yield curve shifted by 50 basis points, portfolio 1's value will change by 0.39% while portfolio 2's would change by about 0.20%. Portfolio 2's exposure to a shift in the long end of the yield curve, however, is considerably greater than portfolio 1's. A shift of 50 basis points at the long end will change portfolio 2's value by approximately 2% but portfolio 1's by about 0.36%. As emphasized earlier in the chapter, just focusing on duration would have masked the yield curve exposure.

So far, we have looked at only bonds with maturities at the three points on the yield curve that are used to define the short end and long end. The methodology can be generalized to other maturities as follows:

(1) the shift in yields begins with the 10-year Treasury
(2) at the short end, the steepening or flattening of the yield curve for any maturity other than two years is proportionate to the 10-year to 2-year spread. For example, suppose that the 10- to 2-year spread is 200 basis points and that the 10- to 7-year spread is 120 basis points. Assume that the yield spread widens by 50 basis points, a 25% increase in the spread. The yield spread for the 10- to 7-year spread is then assumed to widen by 20 basis points (50 basis points − 0.25 × 120). The SEDUR for the 7-year is then calculated assuming a 20 basis point change in the spread, not 50 basis points.
(3) at the long end, the steepening or widening for any bond with a maturity greater than ten years is assumed to be proportionate to the change in the 30-year to 10-year spread.

SLOPE ELASTICITY MEASURE

The *slope elasticity measure*, introduced by Schumacher, Dektar, and Fabozzi for managing the yield curve risk of portfolios of collateralized mortgage obligation bonds, also looks at the sensitivity of a position or portfolio to changes in the slope of the yield curve.[6] However, it does not decompose the yield curve into two segments. Instead, Schumacher, Dektar, and Fabozzi define the yield curve slope as the spread between the 30-year on-the-run Treasury yield and the 3-month Treasury bill yield (i.e., basically the longest and the shortest points on the Treasury yield curve). They find that while this is not a perfect definition, it captures most of the effect of changes in yield curve slope.

They then define changes in the yield curve as follows: Half of any basis point change in the yield curve slope results from a change in the 3-month yield and half from a change in the 30-year yield. For example, with a 200 basis point steepening of the yield curve, the assumption is that 100 basis points of that steepening come from a rise in the 30-year yield, and another 100 basis points come from a fall in the 3-month yield.

[6] Schumacher, Dektar, and Fabozzi, "Yield Curve Risk of CMO Bonds."

The sensitivity of a bond's price to changes in the yield curve is simply its *slope elasticity*. They define slope elasticity as the approximate negative percentage change in a bond's price resulting from a 100 basis point change in the slope of the curve. Slope elasticity is calculated as follows: increase and decrease the yield curve slope, calculate the price change for these two scenarios after adjusting for the price effect of a change in the level of yields, and compare the prices to the initial price. More specifically, the slope elasticity for each scenario is calculated as follows:

$$\frac{\text{Price effect of a change in slope/Base price}}{\text{Change in yield curve slope}}$$

The slope elasticity is then the average of the slope elasticity for the two scenarios.

A bond or portfolio that benefits when the yield curve flattens is said to have *positive slope elasticity*; a bond or a portfolio that benefits when the yield curve steepens is said to have *negative slope elasticity*. The definition of yield curve risk follows from that of slope elasticity. It is defined as the exposure of the bond to changes in the slope of the yield curve.

In Chapter 13, we show to use the slope elasticity methodology for controlling the yield curve risk of a mortgage-backed securities portfolio.

RISK POINT METHOD

The second approach is to look at how changes in Treasury yields for different maturities individually and then collectively affect the value of a bond and the value of a portfolio. This is the approach used by Ho ("key rate duration"),[7] Reitano ("partial duration"),[8] Fong ("functional duration"),[9] and Dattatreya and Fabozzi ("risk point method").[10] We will illustrate the risk point method here.

Dattatreya and Fabozzi define the *risk point* of a bond or portfolio with reference to a specific hedge instrument. For this reason, it can also be called *relative dollar duration*. It represents the change in the value of the bond or portfolio due to a 1-basis point change in the yield of the hedge. Dividing the risk point by the dollar duration of the hedge, we get the dollar amount of the hedge instrument to be used as a hedge. This hedge amount will protect the portfolio against risk from small changes in the market sector represented by the hedge instrument.

---

[7] Thomas Y. Ho, "Key Rate Durations: Measures of Interest Rate Risks," *Journal of Fixed Income* (September 1992), pp. 29-44.

[8] Robert R. Reitano, "Non-Parallel Yield Curve Shifts and Immunization," *Journal of Portfolio Management* (Spring 1992), pp. 36-43.

[9] This measure was developed by Gifford Fong Associates and is described in Chapter 3 of Frank J. Fabozzi and H. Gifford Fong, *Advanced Fixed Income Portfolio Management* (Chicago: Probus Publishing, 1994).

[10] Ravi E. Dattatreya and Frank J. Fabozzi, "The Risk Point Method for Measuring and Controlling Yield Curve Risk," *Financial Analysts Journal* (July-August 1995), pp. 45-54. The explanation of the risk point method in this section is adapted from this article.

This approach to risk measurement focuses more on hedge instruments than on specific yield curve sectors (such as defined by the slope of the yield curve or a short and long yield curve slope of the yield curve) or specific maturity sectors. The reason for this is that it may be of little use to look at risk for which there is no tool for hedging or management.

Unlike dollar duration, which measures the *total* interest rate risk, the risk point measures only one component of the total risk. This component represents the risk due to a change in yields in a given maturity sector. Thus, to determine a complete risk or hedge, a full set of risk points, relative to a set of hedge instruments, is needed. From this set of risk points the portfolio of hedge instruments that will hedge a given portfolio can be determined.

The risk point method consists of three main steps:

Step 1. Specification of the acceptable hedge instruments.

Step 2. Application of a valuation model that values the assets and liabilities *relative* to the prices of the hedge instruments.

Step 3. Change the yield of one of the hedge instruments by a small amount, keeping all other yields the same. With the new yield, revalue the portfolio. The change in its value (expressed as dollars per 1-basis point change) is the risk point of the portfolio. This gives the amount of the hedge instrument needed for hedging by simply equating the dollar duration of a 1-basis point change of the hedge to the risk point of the portfolio.

In our illustration below, Step 1 includes all the on-the-run Treasury issues in the set of hedge instruments that we consider. Treasury bills are included to handle cash flows occurring in the short term. Derivative instruments that can be used to control interest rate risk should be included in an actual situation.

Step 2 begins with the Treasury par yield curve. For securities with credit risk, an appropriate spread is added.[11] A spot rate curve is then generated. This procedure is described in Chapter 2. From the spot rate curve, the discount function can be generated and the value of a bond can be calculated.

To implement Step 3, the risk point corresponding to a given hedge is determined. This is done as follows. First, the yield on the hedge instrument is changed by 1 basis point. Then the spot rates are recomputed using this new yield for the particular hedge instrument, keeping the yield for all other hedges the same as before. The value of the bond (or portfolio) is now recomputed. The change in the value of the bond due to the change in the yield of the hedge gives us the risk point of the bond relative to that hedge instrument. This procedure is repeated for all hedge instruments in the set of hedges chosen. The risk point relative to a hedge can be used to determine the amount of the hedge to be bought (or sold) to hedge it against changes in the price of that hedge.

---

[11] The spread is the swap spread as quoted in the swap market.

Exhibit 8: The Hedging Instruments with Yields

Maturity (years)	Treasury yield (%)	Spread (bp)	Total
0.5	4.932	28	5.212
1	5.520	29	5.810
2	6.234	31	6.544
3	6.563	35	6.913
5	7.074	32	7.394
10	7.466	41	7.876

To illustrate this procedure, suppose that the yield for the Treasury securities and the corresponding spread shown in Exhibit 8 are those prevailing at the time of the analysis. Exhibit 9 shows the spot rate curve and discount function. (The spot rates for maturities between the maturities for the on-the-run issues are simple linear interpolations.)

Suppose that a 10-year bond with a 10% coupon is owned. The value of that bond per $100 par value using the spot rate curve in Exhibit 9 is $114.740102. We can use Step 3 to find the risk point for this bond. This is done by increasing the yield on the 10-year on-the-run Treasury issue in Exhibit 8 by 1 basis point, from 7.466% to 7.476%. The new yield (after considering the spread) changes from 7.876% to 7.886%. Exhibit 10 shows the new discount functions and spot rates. Compare the values in Exhibits 9 and 10. Notice that the change in the 10-year rate impacts the discount function and the spot rates only beyond year 5 in our example.

Using the spot rate curve in Exhibit 10 to value the 10-year 10% bond, we would find that the value declines to $114.667571. Thus, the value of the bond has fallen by $0.072531 ($114.740102 − 114.667571). This number is the change in dollars for every $100 par holding of the bond. This is the risk point for the 10-year 10% bond relative to the 10-year Treasury.

The risk point is usually computed for a given par holding of a security. The risk points for this bond per $10,000 par holding relative to all the other hedges are shown in the fifth column of Exhibit 11. Also shown here are a few other results that should be of interest to managers. The sixth column shows the fraction (as a percentage) of the total risk represented by any given sector. For example, approximately 95.4% of the risk in this bond is in the 10-year sector. The last column expresses the risk point as a percentage of the total value of the bond. The numbers in this column are similar to duration. These two columns, along with the risk points themselves, form a more complete picture of the yield curve risk in the 10% bond under consideration.[12]

---

[12] The idea of duration-like risk point can be extended to convexity. This is explained in Dattatreya and Fabozzi, "The Risk Point Method for Measuring and Controlling Yield Curve Risk."

Exhibit 9: Bootstrapping: Getting the Spot Rate Curve from the Par Curve

Maturity (years)	Par yields (%)	Interpolated par yields (%)	Discount function	Cumulative factor	Spot rates
0.5	5.212	5.212000	0.974602	0.974602	5.212000
1.0	5.810	5.810000	0.944257	1.918859	5.818712
1.5		6.177000	0.912552	2.831411	6.194689
2.0	6.544	6.544000	0.878608	3.710019	6.576629
2.5		6.728500	0.846701	4.556720	6.768333
3.0	6.913	6.913000	0.814349	5.371069	6.964043
3.5		7.033250	0.783565	6.154633	7.091448
4.0		7.153500	0.752934	6.907567	7.221785
4.5		7.273750	0.722504	7.630071	7.354956
5.0	7.394	7.394000	0.692321	8.322392	7.490986
5.5		7.442200	0.665550	8.987942	7.541282
6.0		7.490400	0.639435	9.627377	7.593429
6.5		7.538600	0.613973	10.241350	7.647266
7.0		7.586800	0.589156	10.830505	7.702698
7.5		7.635000	0.564977	11.395483	7.759674
8.0		7.683200	0.541431	11.936914	7.818175
8.5		7.731400	0.518511	12.455425	7.878204
9.0		7.779600	0.496207	12.951632	7.939786
9.5		7.827800	0.474514	13.426147	8.002961
10.0	7.876	7.876000	0.453423	13.879569	8.067783

Exhibit 10: Recomputed Spot Rate Zero Curve after Incrementing 10-Year Yield by 1 Basis Point

Maturity (years)	Par yields (%)	Interpolated par yields (%)	Discount function	Cumulative factor	Spot rates
0.5	5.212	5.212000	0.974602	0.974602	5.212000
1.0	5.810	5.810000	0.944257	1.918859	5.818712
1.5		6.177000	0.912552	2.831411	6.194689
2.0	6.544	6.544000	0.878608	3.710019	6.576629
2.5		6.728500	0.846701	4.556720	6.768333
3.0	6.913	6.913000	0.814349	5.371069	6.964043
3.5		7.033250	0.783565	6.154633	7.091448
4.0		7.153500	0.752934	6.907567	7.221785
4.5		7.273750	0.722504	7.630071	7.354956
5.0	7.394	7.394000	0.692321	8.322392	7.490986
5.5		7.443200	0.665506	8.987898	7.542511
6.0		7.492400	0.639344	9.627243	7.595897
6.5		7.541600	0.613830	10.241072	7.650990
7.0		7.590800	0.588957	10.830029	7.707698
7.5		7.640000	0.564721	11.394750	7.765973
8.0		7.689200	0.541114	11.935864	7.825799
8.5		7.738400	0.518130	12.453994	7.887182
9.0		7.787600	0.495762	12.949756	7.950151
9.5		7.836800	0.474003	13.423759	8.014749
10.0	7.886	7.886000	0.452845	13.876605	8.081033

Exhibit 11: Risk Points for the 10-Year 10% Bond
(Per $10,000 Par Holding)

Maturity (years)	Treasury yield	Spread (bp)	Total	Risk point	Percent of total risk	Percent of total PV
0.5	4.932	28	5.212	−0.002566	0.033757	−0.002236
1.0	5.520	29	5.810	−0.009118	0.119968	−0.007947
2.0	6.234	31	6.544	−0.021308	0.280349	−0.018571
3.0	6.563	35	6.913	−0.055563	0.731037	−0.048425
5.0	7.074	32	7.394	−0.258960	3.407101	−0.225693
10.0	7.466	41	7.876	−7.253094	95.427787	−6.321324
			Totals:	−7.600610	100.000000	−6.624196

KEY POINTS

1. Four shapes have been observed for the Treasury yield curve — upward sloping, inverted, flat, and humped.

2. Historically, the types of yield curve shifts that been observed are a parallel shift, a twist in the slope of the yield curve (i.e., a flattening or steepening of the yield curve), and a change in the humpedness of the yield curve.

3. A parallel shift in the yield curve means that the yield for all maturities changes by the same number of basis points.

4. When using a portfolio's duration and convexity to measure the exposure to interest rates, it is assumed that the yield curve shifts in a parallel fashion.

5. For a nonparallel shift in the yield curve, duration and convexity do not provide adequate information about the risk exposure.

6. Exposure of a portfolio or position to a shift in the yield curve is called yield curve risk.

8. There are two fundamental approaches to measuring yield curve risk — exposure due to a change in the slope of the yield curve and exposure to the change in yield for particular points on the yield curve.

9. Yield curve slope risk and level risk can, for the most part, be managed independently.

10. In estimating yield curve slope risk, it is necessary to define what is meant by the slope of the yield curve.

11. The yield curve reshaping duration measure decomposes the yield curve into a short end and a long end.

12. The sensitivity of a portfolio to changes in the short end of the yield curve is called short-end duration (SEDUR) and to changes in the long-end of the yield curve is called long-end duration (LEDUR).

13. Slope elasticity looks at the sensitivity of a position or portfolio to changes in the slope of the yield curve.

14. Slope elasticity does not decompose the yield curve into two segments but defines the yield curve slope as the spread between the 30-year on-the-run Treasury yield and the 3-month Treasury bill yield.

15. *Slope elasticity is defined as the approximate negative percentage change in a bond's price resulting from a 100 basis point change in the slope of the curve.*

16. *With slope elasticity, changes in the yield curve are defined as follows: half of any basis point change in the yield curve slope results from a change in the 3-month yield and half from a change in the 30-year yield.*

17. *The risk point of a bond or a portfolio is defined with reference to a specific hedge instrument.*

18. *The risk point represents the change in the value of the bond or portfolio due to a 1-basis point change in the yield of the hedge.*

19. *The risk point method focuses more on hedge instruments than on specific yield curve sectors or specific maturity sectors.*

Chapter 5

Probability Distributions and their Properties

In this chapter and the two that follow we look at several concepts from probability theory and statistical theory that are needed for measuring interest rate risk. In this chapter we introduce the concept of a probability distribution and look at two key parameters of a probability distribution — expected value and standard deviation. Our focus then turns to one particular probability distribution known as the normal distribution. We then look at the value at risk framework and how it relies on probability theory.

The objectives of this chapter are to:

1. explain what is meant by a random variable;

2. describe what a probability distribution is;

3. explain how to calculate the variance and standard deviation;

3. describe the fundamental properties of the normal probability distribution;

4. demonstrate several applications of the normal probability distribution;

5. describe what a skewed distribution is;

6. explain the value at risk framework and its limitations; and,

7. describe how a probability distribution can be obtained using Monte Carlo simulation.

RANDOM VARIABLE AND PROBABILITY DISTRIBUTION

A *random variable* is a variable for which a probability can be assigned to each possible value that can be taken by the variable. A random variable is sometimes referred to as a *stochastic variable*. A *probability distribution* or *probability func-*

tion describes all the values that the random variable can take on and the probability associated with each.

Let's use some notation. If we let X denote a random variable, then we use a subscript to denote specific values of the random variable. For example, X_i refers to the ith value for the random variable X. The probability of a specific value for the random variable X is typically denoted by stating the specific value [i.e., $P(X =$ specific value)] or by using the subscript notation [i.e., $P(X_i)$].

To illustrate the above concepts, consider a position established today in a 20-year zero-coupon bond. Suppose that the par value of this position is $50 million. The bond is purchased at a yield of 8%. The price is $20.8289 per $100 par, so the purchase price of $50 million par of this bond is $10,414,452. The manager is concerned with the potential loss that would be realized from this position two weeks from now. The loss will depend on the yield on zero-coupon bonds with 19 years and 50 weeks remaining to maturity.

Exhibit 1 shows the nine possible yields that the manager believes can occur two weeks from now. The exhibit shows the probability of each possible yield two weeks from now. Notice that the sum of the probabilities is one. The random variable in this illustration is the yield two weeks from now and it can take on nine possible outcomes. This is the probability distribution for the yield.

Rather than defining the random variable as the yield, the random variable can be the profit/loss of the position two weeks from now. There is a profit/loss corresponding to each yield. This is shown in Exhibit 1. The probability distribution for the profit/loss is the same as the probability distribution for the yield. The probability that the loss will be $182,702 is 15%. If X denotes the profit/loss, then $P(X = \$182,702)$ or $P(X_7)$ is 15%. The probability that there will be a loss on the position is the probability of a yield higher than 8%. In our illustration it is 50%.

STATISTICAL MEASURES OF A PROBABILITY DISTRIBUTION

Various measures are used to summarize the probability distribution of a random variable. The two most often used measures are the expected value and the variance (or standard deviation).

Expected Value

The *expected value* of a probability distribution is the weighted average of the distribution. The weights in this case are the probabilities associated with the random variable X. The expected value of a random variable is denoted by $E(X)$ and is computed as follows:

$$E(X) = P_1 X_1 + P_2 X_2 + ... + P_n X_n$$

where P_i is the probability associated with the outcome X_i.

Exhibit 1: Probability for Yield Distribution and Profit/Loss Distribution in Two Weeks for a Position in 20-Year Zero-Coupon Bonds

Purchase price: $20.8289
Par position: $50,000,000
Dollar position: $10,414,452

	Yield (%)	Probability (%)	Two weeks from now		
			Bond Price ($)	Market Value ($)	Profit/loss ($)
1	7.6	1.5	22.52833	11,264,164	849,712
2	7.7	10.0	22.09892	11,049,462	635,010
3	7.8	12.5	21.67790	10,838,952	424,500
4	7.9	15.0	21.26510	10,632,552	218,099
5	8.0	22.0	20.86036	10,430,178	15,725
6	8.1	15.0	20.46350	10,231,750	−182,702
7	8.2	12.5	20.07438	10,037,190	−377,262
8	8.3	10.0	19.69284	9,846,421	−568,032
9	8.4	1.5	19.31873	9,659,366	−755,086
	Total	100.0			

Exhibit 2 shows how to calculate the expected value for the profit/loss position for the $50 million par value 20-year zero-coupon bond whose probability distribution is shown in Exhibit 1. The expected value is $22,791.

Variance

A manager is interested not only in the expected value of a probability distribution but also in the dispersion of the random variable around the expected value. A measure of dispersion of the probability distribution is the *variance* of the distribution. The variance of a random variable X, denoted by var(X), is computed from the following formula:

$$\text{var}(X) = [X_1 - E(X)]^2 P_1 + [X_2 - E(X)]^2 P_2 + ... + [X_n - E(X)]^2 P_n$$

Notice that the variance is simply a weighted average of the deviations of each possible outcome from the expected value, where the weight is the probability of an outcome occurring. The greater the variance, the greater the distribution of the possible outcomes for the random variable. The reason that the deviations from the expected value are squared is to avoid outcomes above and below the expected value from cancelling each other out.

The problem with using the variance as a measure of dispersion is that it is in terms of squared units of the random variable. Consequently, the square root of the variance, called the *standard deviation,* is used as a better measure of the degree of dispersion. Mathematically this can be expressed as follows:

$$\text{std}(X) = \sqrt{\text{var}(X)}$$

where std(X) denotes the standard deviation of the random variable X.

Exhibit 2: Calculation of Expected Value

	Yield (%)	Probability (%)	Profit/loss ($)	Probability × Profit/loss ($)
1	7.6	1.5	849,712	12,746
2	7.7	10.0	635,010	63,501
3	7.8	12.5	424,500	53,062
4	7.9	15.0	218,099	32,715
5	8.0	22.0	15,725	3,460
6	8.1	15.0	−182,702	−27,405
7	8.2	12.5	−377,262	−47,158
8	8.3	10.0	−568,032	−56,803
9	8.4	1.5	−755,086	−11,326
			Expected value	$22,791

Exhibit 3 shows how to calculate the variance for the profit/loss of the position whose probability distribution is shown in Exhibit 1.

Discrete versus Continuous Probability Distributions

A probability distribution can be classified according to the values that a random variable can realize. When the value of the random variable can only take on specific values, then the probability distribution is referred to as a *discrete probability distribution*. For example, in our illustration, we assumed only nine specific values for the random variable. Hence, to this point we have been working with a discrete probability distribution. If, instead, the random variable can take on any possible value within the range of outcomes, then the probability distribution is said to a *continuous probability distribution*.

When a random variable is either the price, yield, or return on a financial asset, the distribution can be assumed to be a continuous probability distribution. This means that it is possible to obtain, for example, a price of 95.43231 or 109.34872 and any value in between. In practice, we know that financial assets are not quoted in such a way. Nevertheless, there is no loss in describing the distribution as continuous. However, what is important in using a continuous distribution is that in moving from one price to the next, there is no major jump. For example, if the price declines from 95.14 to 70.50, it is assumed that there are trades that are executed at prices at small increments below 95.14 before getting to 70.50. In contrast, if the price can just "jump" from 95.14 to 70.50, then the distribution is referred to as a *jump process*.

NORMAL PROBABILITY DISTRIBUTION

In many applications involving probability distributions, it is assumed that the underlying probability distribution is a *normal distribution*. An example of a normal distribution is shown in Exhibit 4. A normal distribution is an example of a continuous probability distribution.

Exhibit 3: Calculation of Variance and Standard Deviation

	Yield (%)	Probability (%)	Profit/loss ($)	Expected value ($)	(Profit/loss − EV)^2 × Probability
1	7.6	1.5	849,712	22,791	10,256,973,964
2	7.7	10.0	635,010	22,791	37,481,153,671
3	7.8	12.5	424,500	22,791	20,171,254,459
4	7.9	15.0	218,099	22,791	5,721,793,349
5	8.0	22.0	15,725	22,791	10,983,298
6	8.1	15.0	−182,702	22,791	6,334,118,886
7	8.2	12.5	−377,262	22,791	20,005,314,706
8	8.3	10.0	−568,032	22,791	34,907,144,650
9	8.4	1.5	−755,086	22,791	9,076,399,869
				Variance	143,965,136,853

Standard deviation $= \sqrt{143,965,136,853} = \$379,427$

The area under the normal distribution or normal curve between any two points on the horizontal axis is the probability of obtaining a value between those two values. For example, the probability of realizing a value for the random variable X that is between X_1 and X_2 in Exhibit 4 is shown by the shaded area. Mathematically, the probability of realizing a value for X between these two variables can be written as follows:

$$P(X_1 < X < X_2)$$

The entire area under the normal curve is equal to 1 which means the sum of the probabilities is 1.

Properties of the Normal Distribution
The normal distribution has the following properties:

1. The point in the middle of the normal curve is the expected value for the distribution.

2. The distribution is symmetric around the expected value. That is, half of the distribution is to the left of the expected value and the other half is to the right. Thus, the probability of obtaining a value less than the expected value is 50%. The probability of obtaining a value greater than the expected value is also 50%.

3. The probability that the actual outcome will be within a range of one standard deviation above the expected value and one standard deviation below the expected value is 68.3%.

Exhibit 4: Normal Distribution

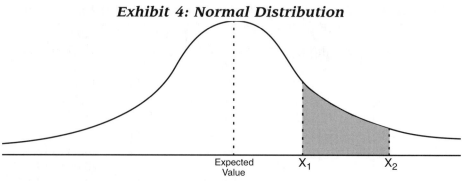

Probability of realizing a value between X_1 and X_2 is shaded area.

4. The probability that the actual outcome will be within a range of two standard deviations above the expected value and two standard deviations below the expected value is 95.5%.

5. The probability that the actual outcome will be within a range of three standard deviations above the expected value and three standard deviations below the expected value is 99.7%.

Exhibit 5 graphically presents these properties.

Suppose that a manager estimates a position one week from now has an expected profit of $40,000 with a standard deviation of $100,000, and that the probability distribution can be approximated well by a normal distribution. The probability is 68.3% that one week from now the profit will be between −$60,000 (the expected value of $40,000 minus one standard deviation of $100,000) and $140,000 (the expected value of $40,000 plus one standard deviation of $100,000). The probability is 95.5% that the profit will be between −$160,000 (the expected value minus two standard deviations) and $240,000 (the expected value plus two standard deviations).

Suppose that the standard deviation is believed to be $70,000 rather than $100,000. Then the probability is 68.3% that the profit will be between −$30,000 and $110,000; the probability is 95.5% that the profit will be between −$100,000 and $180,000. *Notice that the smaller the standard deviation, the narrower the range for the possible outcome for a given probability.*

Using Normal Distribution Tables

Tables are available that give the probability of obtaining a value between any two values of a normal probability distribution. All that must be known in order to determine the probability is the expected value and the standard deviation.

The normal distribution table is constructed for a normal distribution that has an expected value of 0 and a standard deviation of 1. In order to use the table it is necessary to convert the normal distribution under consideration into a distribution that has an expected value of 0 and a standard deviation of 1. This is done by standardizing the values of the distribution under consideration.

Exhibit 5: Properties of a Normal Distribution

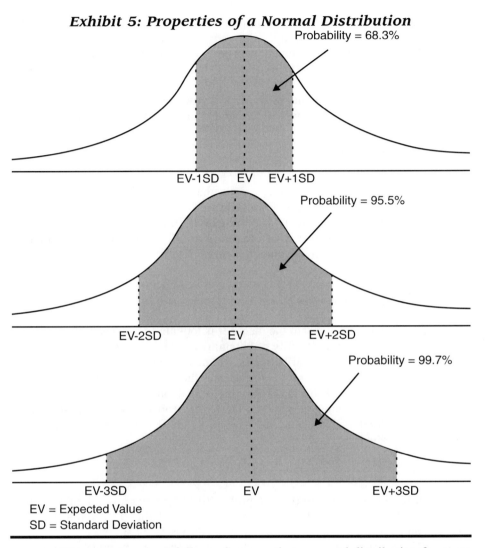

EV = Expected Value
SD = Standard Deviation

The procedure is as follows. Suppose that a normal distribution for some random variable X has an expected value $E(X)$ and a standard deviation denoted by $\text{std}(X)$. To standardize any particular value, say X_1, the following is computed:

$$z_1 = \frac{X_1 - E(X)}{\text{std}(X)}$$

where z_1 is the *standardized value* for X_1. The standardized value is also called the *normal deviate*.

Exhibit 6 is an abridged table that shows the area under the normal curve, which, as stated before, represents probability. This particular table shows the probability of obtaining a value greater than some specified value in standardized form in the right-hand tail of the distribution. This is the shaded area shown in the normal curve at the top of Exhibit 6.

The illustrations to follow demonstrate how to use the table. We will use the same example as earlier: the expected value of the profit of the position is $40,000 and the standard deviation is $100,000.

Suppose that the manager wants to know the probability of realizing a value greater than $90,000. The standardized value (z) corresponding to $90,000 is 0.5, as shown below:

$$\frac{\$90,000 - \$40,000}{\$100,000} = 0.5$$

The probability of obtaining a value greater than $90,000 is the same as a standardized value greater than 0.5. From Exhibit 6, the probability of obtaining a standardized value greater than 0.5 is 0.4801 or 48.01%.

Suppose the probability of obtaining a loss is sought by the manager. This is equivalent to realizing a value of X that is less than zero. The standardized value is −0.4, as shown below:

$$\frac{\$0 - \$40,000}{\$100,000} = -0.4$$

The negative value indicates that the manager is looking for values in the left-hand tail. From Exhibit 6, the probability of obtaining a value greater than 0.4 is 0.4840 or 48.4%. Since the normal distribution is symmetric, the probability of realizing a standardized value greater than 0.4 is the same as the probability of realizing a standardized value less −0.4. Thus, the probability of realizing a loss is 48.4%.

Suppose the manager wants to know the probability of realizing a loss greater than $150,000. The value of X is then −$150,000 and the corresponding standardized value is:

$$\frac{-\$150,000 - \$40,000}{\$100,000} = -1.1$$

From Exhibit 6 it can be seen that the probability of getting a standardized value greater than 1.1 is 13.57%. Thus, the probability of realizing a standardized value of less than −1.1 or equivalently a loss of $150,000 is 13.57%.

The standardized value is nothing more than the number of standard deviations above the expected value since the expected value of z is zero. From an examination of Exhibit 6, we can see the properties of a normal distribution that we discussed earlier. For example, look at the value in the table for a standardized value equal to 2. The probability is 2.28%. This is the probability of realizing a value in each of the tails of the normal distribution. Doubling this probability gives 4.56%, which is the probability of realizing a value in either of the two tails. This means that the probability of getting a value between the two tails is 95.44%. This agrees with the third property of the normal probability distribution that we stated above — there is a 95.5% probability of getting a value between two standard deviations below and above the expected value.

Exhibit 6: Normal Distribution Table

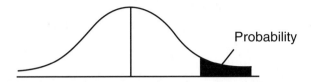

Probability

z	0.00	0.01	0.02	0.03	0.04	0.05	0.06	0.07	0.08	0.09
0.0	0.5000	0.4960	0.4920	0.4880	0.4840	0.4801	0.4761	0.4721	0.4681	0.4641
0.1	0.4602	0.4562	0.4522	0.4483	0.4443	0.4404	0.4364	0.4325	0.4286	0.4247
0.2	0.4207	0.4168	0.4129	0.4090	0.4052	0.4013	0.3974	0.3936	0.3897	0.3859
0.3	0.3821	0.3783	0.3745	0.3707	0.3669	0.3632	0.3594	0.3557	0.3520	0.3483
0.4	0.3446	0.3409	0.3372	0.3336	0.3300	0.3264	0.3228	0.3192	0.3156	0.3121
0.5	0.3085	0.3050	0.3015	0.2981	0.2946	0.2912	0.2877	0.2843	0.2810	0.2776
0.6	0.2743	0.2709	0.2676	0.2643	0.2611	0.2578	0.2546	0.2514	0.2483	0.2451
0.7	0.2420	0.2389	0.2358	0.2327	0.2296	0.2266	0.2236	0.2206	0.2177	0.2148
0.8	0.2110	0.2090	0.2061	0.2033	0.2005	0.1977	0.1949	0.1922	0.1894	0.1867
0.9	0.1841	0.1814	0.1788	0.1762	0.1736	0.1711	0.1685	0.1660	0.1635	0.1611
1.0	0.1587	0.1562	0.1539	0.1515	0.1492	0.1469	0.1449	0.1423	0.1401	0.1379
1.1	0.1357	0.1335	0.1314	0.1292	0.1271	0.1251	0.1230	0.1210	0.1190	0.1170
1.2	0.1151	0.1131	0.1112	0.1093	0.1075	0.1056	0.1038	0.1020	0.1003	0.0985
1.3	0.0968	0.0951	0.0934	0.0918	0.0901	0.0885	0.0869	0.0853	0.0838	0.0823
1.4	0.0808	0.0793	0.0778	0.0764	0.0749	0.0735	0.0721	0.0708	0.0694	0.0681
1.5	.0668	0.0655	0.0643	0.0630	0.0618	0.0606	0.0594	0.0582	0.0571	0.0559
1.6	.0548	0.0537	0.0526	0.0516	0.0505	0.0495	0.0485	0.0475	0.0465	0.0455
1.7	.0446	0.0436	0.0427	0.0418	0.0409	0.0401	0.0392	0.0384	0.0375	0.0367
1.8	.0359	0.0351	0.0344	0.0336	0.0329	0.0322	0.0314	0.0307	0.0301	0.0294
1.9	.0287	0.0281	0.0274	0.0268	0.0262	0.0256	0.0250	0.0244	0.0239	0.0233
2.0	0.0228	0.0222	0.0217	0.0212	0.0207	0.0202	0.0197	0.0192	0.0188	0.0183
2.1	0.0179	0.0174	0.0170	0.0166	0.0162	0.0158	0.0154	0.0150	0.0146	0.0143
2.2	0.0139	0.0136	0.0132	0.0129	0.0125	0.0122	0.0119	0.0116	0.0113	0.0110
2.3	0.0107	0.0104	0.0102	0.0099	0.0096	0.0094	0.0091	0.0089	0.0087	0.0084
2.4	0.0082	0.0080	0.0078	0.0075	0.0073	0.0071	0.0069	0.0068	0.0066	0.0064
2.5	0.0062	0.0060	0.0059	0.0057	0.0055	0.0054	0.0052	0.0051	0.0049	0.0048
2.6	0.0047	0.0045	0.0044	0.0043	0.0041	0.0040	0.0039	0.0038	0.0037	0.0036
2.7	0.0035	0.0034	0.0033	0.0032	0.0031	0.0030	0.0029	0.0028	0.0027	0.0026
2.8	0.0026	0.0025	0.0024	0.0023	0.0023	0.0022	0.0021	0.0021	0.0020	0.0019
2.9	0.0019	0.0018	0.0018	0.0017	0.0016	0.0016	0.0015	0.0015	0.0014	0.0014
3.0	0.0013	0.0013	0.0013	0.0012	0.0012	0.0011	0.0011	0.0011	0.0010	0.0010

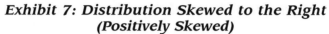

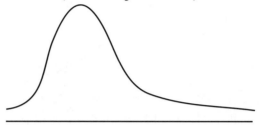

Exhibit 7: Distribution Skewed to the Right (Positively Skewed)

The Appropriateness of Using a Normal Distribution

In a normal distribution, the expected value (mean) and the standard deviation are all the information needed to make statements about the probabilities of outcomes. In order to apply the normal distribution to make statements about probabilities, it is necessary to assess whether a historical distribution (i.e., a distribution created from observed data) is normally distributed.

For example, a property of the normal probability distribution is that the distribution is symmetric around the expected value. However, a probability distribution might be best characterized like those shown in Exhibits 7 and 8. Such distributions are referred to as *skewed distributions*. The skewed distribution shown in Exhibit 7 is one which has a long tail on the right hand side of the distribution. Such a distribution is referred to as a *positively skewed distribution*. Exhibit 8 shows a skewed distribution that has a long tail on the left hand side of the distribution and is called a *negatively skewed distribution*.[1]

In addition to skewness, a historical distribution may have more outliers (i.e., observations in the tails) than the normal distribution predicts. Distributions with this characteristic are said to have "fat tails." Or, a historical distribution may have a higher peak around the expected value than is predicted by the normal distribution.[2]

The following two questions must be addressed to determine whether a historical distribution can be characterized as a normal distribution:

1. Does the data fit the values predicted by the normal distribution?
2. Are the returns today independent of the returns of the prior periods?

Goodness of Fit Most introductory courses in statistics explain how to test if the historical data for some random variable can be characterized by a normal distribution. Basically the test involves breaking the historical observations into intervals. For each interval, the number of expected or predicted observations based on the normal probability distribution are determined. Then the number predicted for the interval and the number actually observed are compared. This is done for all intervals. Statistical tests can then be used to determine if the historically observed distribution differs significantly from a normal distribution.

---

[1] A normal distribution is said to have zero skewedness.
[2] *Kurtosis* is a measure of the peakedness of a probability distribution.

Exhibit 8: Distribution Skewed to the Left (Negatively Skewed)

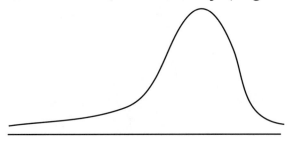

Let's look at the evidence on bond returns. For bonds, there is a lower limit on the loss. For Treasury securities, the limit depends on how high rates can rise. Since Treasury rates have never exceeded 15% this places a lower bound on a negative return from holding a bond. However, there is maximum return. Assuming that negative interest rates are not possible, the maximum price for a bond is the undiscounted value of the cash flow (i.e., the sum of the interest payments and maturity value). In turn, this determines the maximum return. On balance, government bond return distributions are negatively skewed. JP Morgan reports that this occurs for government bonds and swaps.[3] Moreover, government bond returns exhibit fat tails and a peakedness greater than predicted by the normal distribution.

One way to overcome the problem of negative skewedness of bond returns is to convert returns into the logarithm of returns. The transformation to logarithm of returns tends to pull in the outlier negative returns resulting in a distribution that is approximately normal. The resulting probability distribution of logarithm returns is said to be *lognormally distributed.*

For options and derivatives with option-like features such as caps and floors, one would expect a skewed distribution. The reason is that a long position in an option has a maximum loss equal to the option price but an extremely high upside potential. It is difficult to measure the riskiness of such positions with a standard deviation.

Independence of Returns For any probability distribution, it is important to assess whether the value of a random variable in one period is affected by the value that the random variable took on in a prior period. Casting this in terms of returns, it is important to know whether the return that can be realized today is affected by the return in a prior period. The terms *serial correlation* and *autocorrelation* are used to describe the correlation between the return in different periods. JP Morgan's analysis suggests that there is only a small positive serial correlation for government bond returns.[4]

---

[3] *RiskMetrics™ — Technical Document*, JP Morgan, May 26, 1995, New York, p. 48.

[4] *RiskMetrics™ — Technical Document*, p. 48.

Exhibit 9: Graphical Depiction of VaR

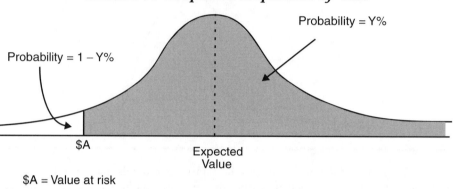

VALUE AT RISK

Suppose that a risk manager wants to make the following statement: "There is a Y% probability that the loss in value from a position will be less than $A in the next T days." The $A in this statement is popularly referred to as the *value at risk* (VaR). The VaR can be determined from probability theory assuming a normal distribution, the expected value and standard deviation of the distribution, the specified probability (Y%), and the number of days (T).

The VaR can be exhibited graphically. Exhibit 9 shows a normal probability distribution for the change in the value of a position over the next T days. The VaR is the loss of $A where the probability to the right of that value is Y%. Or equivalently, the VaR is where the probability to the left of that value (i.e., the probability in the tail) is equal to 1−Y%.

Let's see how we obtain the VaR using a numerical example. Suppose that the probability distribution for the change in value of a position over the next four days is normally distribution with an expected value of zero and a standard deviation of $20,000. Assume also that the probability specified by the manager is 95%. From the normal distribution table (Exhibit 6), the standardized value that will give a probability in the tail of 5% can be found. This is done by searching the table for where the probability is 5%. From Exhibit 6, this is where the standardized value is about 1.65.

The standardized value indicates the number of standard deviations above or below the expected value. The VaR is the value which is 1.65 standard deviations *below* the expected value. Since the expected value of the change in value of a position over the next four days is zero and the standard deviation is $20,000, then the VaR is $33,000. Therefore, there is a 95% probability that the loss in value from a position will be less than $33,000 in the next four days.

Alternatively, the VaR can be expressed as follows: "There is a 1−Y% probability that the loss in value over the next T days will be greater than $A." In our example, there is a 5% probability that the loss in value over the next four days will be greater than $33,000.

Daily Earnings at Risk

VaR begins with measuring the *daily earnings at risk* (DEaR). This is simply the value at risk for a day. For a single position in a bond, DEaR is measured as follows using the duration approach to risk management described in Chapter 1:

DEaR = market value of position
     × sensitivity of the value of position to a 1 basis point adverse change in yield
     × adverse yield movement per day (in basis points)

Since the duration of a position is the approximate percentage change for a 100 basis point change in yield, dividing the duration by 100 gives the percentage change in value for a 100 basis point change in yield. That is,

percentage change in value for a 100 basis point change in yield
     = duration/100

Dividing by 100 gives the percentage change in value for a 1 basis point change in yield. That is,

percentage change in value for a 1 basis point change in yield
     = duration/10,000

DEaR can then be restated as follows:

DEaR = market value of position × duration/10,000
     × adverse yield movement per day (in basis points)

The adverse yield movement per day is a based on the daily yield volatility and the probability specified. In the next chapter we will see how daily yield volatility can be estimated. It is the forecasted daily standard deviation of yield changes. The adverse yield movement per day is 100 times the product of the forecasted daily standard deviation of yield changes and the standardized value from the normal distribution. That is,

adverse yield movement per day (in basis points)
     = forecasted daily standard deviation
     × standardized value from normal distribution × 100

For example, suppose that the forecasted daily standard deviation for the yield change of the Treasury 30-year zero-coupon bond is 0.63%. Assuming a normal probability distribution, then the standardized value is 1.65 if a probability of 95% is sought for the VaR. Therefore, the adverse yield movement per day is:

$$\text{adverse yield movement per day} = 0.0063 \times 1.65 \times 100$$
$$= 10.395 \text{ basis points}$$

If the market value of a position of Treasury 30-year zero-coupon bonds is $5,000,000 and its duration is 4, then the DEaR is:

$$\text{DEaR} = \$5,000,000 \times 4/10,000 \times 10.395$$
$$= \$20,790$$

In JP Morgan's RiskMetrics^{TM}, a 95% probability is used. The Basel Committee proposed a probability of 99%. This translates into a standardized value assuming a normal distribution of 2.32.

Relationship Between DEaR and VaR

Given the DEaR, the VaR is calculated as follows:

$$\text{VaR} = \text{DEaR} \sqrt{\text{Days expected until position can be neutralized}}$$

where days expected until position can be neutralized is the number of days that it is expected it will take to neutralize the risk of the position.

The Basel Committee proposed 10 business days for the days expected until a position can be neutralized. RiskMetrics^{TM} assumes 1 business day for trading positions and 25 business days for investment positions. Thus, for trading positions, the DEaR and the VaR are equal.

Limitations of VaR

There are several criticisms that have been levied against the VaR framework. First, VaR depends on good estimates for the sensitivity of a position to rate changes and for daily volatility of yield changes as measured by the daily standard deviation. As explained in Chapter 3, for a complex security, estimating the effective duration is not simple. Even if the full valuation approach is employed, a good valuation model is needed. Moreover, as demonstrated in the next chapter, there could be substantial variations in the forecasted daily standard deviation. In a recent study, Tanya Beder found that there is a wide variation in the VaR for a given position based on different assumptions about the required inputs.[5]

A second limitation of the VaR framework is that it assumes the distribution of yield changes is normally distributed. Finally, multiplying the DEaR by the square root of the number of days expected until the position can be neutralized assumes that the distribution for the daily percentage change in yield is not serially correlated.

---

[5] See Tanya Styblo Beder, "VAR: Seductive but Dangerous," *Financial Analysts Journal* (September-October 1995), pp. 12-24.

CONFIDENCE INTERVALS

When a range for the possible values of a random variable and a probability associated with that range are calculated, the range is referred is as a *confidence interval*. In general, for a normal distribution, the confidence interval is calculated as follows:

(expected value − standardized value × standard deviation) to
(expected value + standardized value × standard deviation)

The standardized value indicates the number of standard deviations way from the expected value and corresponds to a particular probability. For example, suppose a manager wants a confidence interval of 95%. This means that there will be 2.5% in each tail. From Exhibit 6, we see that a standardized value with a 2.5% probability is 1.96. Thus, a 95% confidence interval is:

(expected value − 1.96 × standard deviation) to
(expected value + 1.96 × standard deviation)

For example, suppose that a manager wants to construct a confidence interval for the change in the value of a position over the next four days. Assuming that the change in value is normally distribution with an expected value of zero and a standard deviation of $20,000, then a 95% confidence interval would be:

($0 − 1.96 × $20,000) to ($0 + 1.96 × $20,000) or −$39,200 to $39,200

MONTE CARLO SIMULATION

The probability distribution for the change in the value of a bond or derivative instrument such as an option may depend on the outcome of a number of random variables. For example, the change in the value of a bond will depend on the sensitivity of the bond's value to rate changes, changes in the shape of the yield curve, and its yield volatility. In the case of mortgage-backed securities, it will also depend on the change in prepayment speeds. Each random variable will have its own probability distribution and there may be some random variables that may not be normally distributed. Moreover, each of the random variables that affects the change in value of a bond may not be independent. That is, there may be a significant correlation between the random variables. (We'll discuss correlation in Chapter 7.)

One way to evaluate the risk of a bond position is to evaluate all possible combinations of potential outcomes for the random variables and develop a probability distribution based on the change in the bond's value from all combinations. However, since each random variable may have a substantial number of possible outcomes, evaluation of all possible combinations of outcomes is usually impractical. Rather than evaluate all possible combinations of potential outcomes, a large number of combinations of outcomes can be evaluated. This approach is called scenario analysis. Scenario analysis, however, has a major drawback: the assessment of risk will depend on the scenarios analyzed.

An alternative to complete enumeration of the outcomes and scenario analysis for developing a probability distribution is *Monte Carlo simulation*. We described this methodology in Chapter 2 where we explained how it is used for valuing mortgage-backed securities.

There are 10 steps in a Monte Carlo simulation. Each step is described below.

Step 1. The performance measure must be specified. For risk measurement, the appropriate performance measure is the change in the value of a bond.

Step 2. The problem under investigation must be expressed mathematically. The mathematical description of the problem must include all important variables and their interactions. The variables in the mathematical model will be either *deterministic* or *random*. A deterministic variable can take only one value; a random variable can take on more than one value.

Step 3. For those variables that are random variables, a probability distribution for each must be specified.

Step 4. For each random variable, representative numbers must be assigned to each possible outcome based on the probability distribution.

Step 5. A random number must be attained for each random variable.[6]

Step 6. For each random number, the corresponding value of the random variable must be determined.

Step 7. The corresponding value of each random variable found in the previous step must be used to determine the value of the performance measure.

Step 8. The value of the performance measure found in step 7 is recorded.

Step 9. Steps 5 through 8 must be repeated many times.[7] The repetition of steps 5 through 8 is known as a *trial*.

Step 10. On the basis of the value for the performance measure for each trial recorded in step 8, a probability distribution is constructed.

The probability distribution developed in step 10 can be used to determine a bond's VaR.

In practice, some of the deterministic variables are actually unknown but are assigned some assumed value in the Monte Carlo simulation. The simulation is repeated with different assumed values for the deterministic variables that are unknown in order to assess the impact of these variables on the probability distribution.

When there is more than one asset in a position, Monte Carlo simulation can consider the interaction (or correlation) amongst the prices and rates for all assets. The correlations are estimated using historical data. The probability distribution generated for a position will then depend on the correlation between the price or rates of each asset. The sensitivity of the probability distribution can be examined by repeating the Monte Carlo simulation using a different set of correlations.

---

[6] Most computers have a built-in random number generator.

[7] The number of trials is determined by a technique called variance reduction.

KEY POINTS

1. *A random variable is a variable for which a probability can be assigned to each possible value that can be taken by the variable.*

2. *A probability distribution describes all the values that the random variable can take on and the probability associated with each.*

3. *The expected value of a probability distribution is the weighted average of the distribution.*

4. *Variance is a measure of the dispersion of the random variable around its expected value.*

5. *The standard deviation is the square root of the variance.*

6. *The greater the standard deviation, the greater the variability of the random variable around the expected value.*

7. *A discrete probability distribution is one in which the random variable can only take on specific values, while a random variable can take on any possible value within the range of outcomes for a continuous probability distribution.*

8. *In jump process, a random variable can realize large movements without taking on interim values.*

9. *A normal distribution is a symmetric probability distribution that is used in many business applications.*

10. *The area under the normal distribution or normal curve between any two points on the horizontal axis is the probability of obtaining a value between those two values.*

11. *If a random variable follows a normal distribution then the expected value and the standard deviation are the only two parameters that are needed to make statements about the probability of outcomes for that random variable.*

12. *In order to apply the normal distribution to make statements about probabilities, it is necessary to assess whether a historical distribution is properly characterized as normally distributed.*

13. *There are statistical tests that can be used to determine whether a historical distribution can be characterized as a normal distribution.*

14. *A skewed distribution is a probability distribution which is not symmetric around the expected value.*

15. *A positively skewed distribution is one in which there is a long tail to the right; a negatively skewed distribution is one in which there is a long tail to the left.*

16. *Serial correlation or autocorrelation is the correlation between returns over time.*

17. *There is only a small positive serial correlation for government bond returns.*

18. *The value at risk is the amount that a loss is not expected to exceed over some time period with a specified probability.*

19. *The value at risk is determined from probability theory assuming a normal distribution, the expected value and standard deviation of the distribution, a specified probability, and the number of days.*

20. *Value at risk begins with measuring the daily earnings at risk.*

21. *Value at risk is the product of the daily earnings at risk and the square root of the number of days expected until a position can be neutralized.*

22. *Value at risk depends on good estimates for the sensitivity of a position to rate changes and the daily volatility of yield changes.*

23. *A confidence interval gives a range for possible values of a random variable and a probability associated with that range.*

24. *For complex bonds and bond positions, Monte Carlo simulation can be used to obtain a probability distribution.*

Chapter 6
Measuring and Forecasting Yield Volatility from Historical Data

The standard deviation is a measure of the variation of a random variable around its mean or expected value. Consequently, the standard deviation is commonly used as a measure of the volatility of prices or yields. Because volatility plays such a key role in interest rate risk control, we shall discuss how the standard deviation is calculated from historical data, as well as approaches to forecasting the standard deviation. At the end of this chapter, we tie in yield volatility to the value at risk framework.

The objectives of this chapter are to:

1. explain how the standard deviation is estimated from historical yield data;

2. show how the daily standard deviation is affected by the number of observations and the time period used;

3. explain the different ways in which the daily standard deviation can be annualized;

4. describe the different approaches for forecasting volatility; and,

5. explain what implied volatility is.

CALCULATING STANDARD DEVIATION FROM HISTORICAL DATA

In the previous chapter, we showed how to calculate the standard deviation and variance of a random variable given a discrete probability distribution. The variance of a random variable using historical data is calculated using the following formula:

$$\text{Variance} = \sum_{t=1}^{T} \frac{(X_t - \bar{X})^2}{T - 1} \tag{1}$$

and then

$$\text{Standard deviation} = \sqrt{\text{Variance}}$$

where

X_t = observation t on variable X
X = the sample mean for variable X
T = the number of observations in the sample

Our focus in this book will be on yield volatility. More specifically, we are interested in the percentage change in daily yields. So, X_t will denote the percentage change in yield from day t and the prior day, t-1. If we let y_t denote the yield on day t and y_{t-1} denote the yield on day t-1, then X_t which is the natural logarithm of percentage change in yield between two days, can be expressed as:

$$X_t = 100[\text{Ln}(y_t/y_{t-1})]$$

For example, on 10/18/95 the Treasury 30-year zero rate was 6.555% and on 10/19/95 it was 6.593%. Therefore, the natural logarithm of X for 10/19/95 is:

$$X = 100[\text{Ln}(6.593/6.555)] = 0.57804$$

To illustrate how to calculate a daily standard deviation from historical data, consider the data in Exhibit 1 which shows the yield on Treasury 30-year zeros from 10/8/95 to 11/12/95 in the second column. From the 26 observations, 25 days of daily percentage yield changes are calculated in the third column. The fourth column shows the square of the deviations of the observations from the mean. The bottom of Exhibit 1 shows the calculation of the daily mean for the 25 observations, the variance, and the standard deviation. The daily standard deviation is 0.6360493%.

The daily standard deviation will vary depending on the 25 days selected. For example, the daily yields from 8/20/95 to 9/24/95 were used to generate 25 daily percentage yield changes. The computed daily standard deviation was 0.8452714%.

Determining the Number of Observations

In our illustration, we used 25 observations for the daily percentage change in yield. The appropriate number depends on the situation at hand. For example, traders concerned with overnight positions might use the 10 most recent days (i.e., two weeks). A bond portfolio manager who is concerned with longer term volatility might use 25 days (about one month).

The selection of the number of observations can have a significant effect on the calculated daily standard deviation. This can be seen in Exhibit 2 which shows the daily standard deviation for the Treasury 30-year zero, Treasury 10-year zero, Treasury 5-year zero, and 3-month LIBOR for 60 days, 25 days, 10 days, and 683 days ending 11/12/95.

Exhibit 1: Calculation of Daily Standard Deviation Based on 25 Daily Observations for 30-Year Treasury Zero (October 9, 1995 to November 12, 1995)

t	Date	y_t	$X_t = 100[Ln(y_t/y_{t-1})]$	$(X_t - \overline{X})^2$
0	08-Oct-95	6.694		
1	09-Oct-95	6.699	0.06720	0.02599
2	10-Oct-95	6.710	0.16407	0.06660
3	11-Oct-95	6.675	−0.52297	0.18401
4	12-Oct-95	6.555	−1.81311	2.95875
5	15-Oct-95	6.583	0.42625	0.27066
6	16-Oct-95	6.569	−0.21290	0.01413
7	17-Oct-95	6.583	0.21290	0.09419
8	18-Oct-95	6.555	−0.42625	0.11038
9	19-Oct-95	6.593	0.57804	0.45164
10	22-Oct-95	6.620	0.40869	0.25270
11	23-Oct-95	6.568	−0.78860	0.48246
12	24-Oct-95	6.575	0.10652	0.04021
13	25-Oct-95	6.646	1.07406	1.36438
14	26-Oct-95	6.607	−0.58855	0.24457
15	29-Oct-95	6.612	0.07565	0.02878
16	30-Oct-95	6.575	−0.56116	0.21823
17	31-Oct-95	6.552	−0.35042	0.06575
18	01-Nov-95	6.515	−0.56631	0.22307
19	02-Nov-95	6.533	0.27590	0.13684
20	05-Nov-95	6.543	0.15295	0.06099
21	06-Nov-95	6.559	0.24424	0.11441
22	07-Nov-95	6.500	−0.90360	0.65543
23	08-Nov-95	6.546	0.70520	0.63873
24	09-Nov-95	6.589	0.65474	0.56063
25	12-Nov-95	6.539	−0.76173	0.44586
		Total	−2.35025	9.7094094

Sample mean $= \overline{X} = \dfrac{-2.35025}{25} = -0.09401\%$

Variance $= \dfrac{9.7094094}{25-1} = 0.4045587$

Std $= \sqrt{0.4045587} = 0.6360493\%$

Annualizing the Standard Deviation

If serial correlation is not significant, the daily standard deviation can be annualized by multiplying it by the square root of the number of days in a year. That is,

$$\text{Daily standard deviation} \times \sqrt{\text{Number of days in a year}}$$

Market practice varies with respect to the number of days in the year that should be used in the annualizing formula above. Typically, either 250 days, 260 days, or 365 days are used.

Thus, in calculating an annual standard deviation, the manager must decide on:

1. the number of daily observations to use
2. the number of days in the year to use to annualize the daily standard deviation.

Exhibit 2 shows the difference in the annual standard deviation for the daily standard deviation based on the different number of observations and using 250 days, 260 days, and 365 days to annualize. Exhibit 3 compares the 25-day annual standard deviation for two different time periods for the 30-year zero, 10-year zero, 5-year zero, and 3-month LIBOR.

Constructing Confidence Intervals

What does it mean if the annual standard deviation or annual yield volatility for a 30-year zero is 12%? It means that if the prevailing yield on the 30-year zero is 6.5%, the annual standard is 78 basis points (6.5% times 12%).

Assuming that the yield volatility is approximately normally distributed, the annual standard deviation can be used to construct a confidence interval for a yield one year from now. This is done by using the following generalization of the formula for the confidence interval given in the previous chapter:

(current yield − standardized z value × standard deviation) to
(current yield + standardized z value × standard deviation)

For a 90% confidence, recall that the standardized value is 1.65. To illustrate the calculation of the confidence interval, assume the current yield for the Treasury 30-year zero is 6.5% and the annual standard deviation is 12%. Therefore the annual standard deviation is 78 basis points or 0.78%. A 90% confidence interval would then be:

$(6.5\% - 1.65 \times 0.78\%)$ to $(6.5\% + 1.65 \times 0.78\%)$
$= 4.94\%$ to 7.787%

Exhibit 2: Comparison of Daily and Annual Volatility for a Different Number of Observations (ending date November 12, 1995) for Various Instruments

Number. of observations	Daily standard deviation (%)	Annualized standard deviation (%)		
		250 days	260 days	365 days
Treasury 30-Year Zero				
683	0.4901505	7.75	7.90	9.36
60	0.6282858	9.93	10.13	12.00
25	0.6360493	10.06	10.26	12.15
10	0.6242041	9.87	10.06	11.93
Treasury 10-Year Zero				
683	0.7497844	11.86	12.09	14.32
60	0.7408469	11.71	11.95	14.15
25	0.7091771	11.21	11.44	13.55
10	0.7458877	11.79	12.03	14.25
Treasury 5-Year Zero				
683	1.0413025	16.46	16.79	19.89
60	0.8267317	13.07	13.33	15.79
25	0.7224093	11.42	11.65	13.80
10	0.8345784	13.20	13.46	15.94
3-Month LIBOR				
683	0.7495924	11.85	12.09	14.32
60	0.2993957	4.73	4.83	5.72
25	0.1465032	2.32	2.36	2.80
10	0.2366242	3.74	3.82	4.52

Exhibit 3: Comparison of Daily Standard Deviation Calculated for Two 25 Day Periods for Various Instruments

Dates		Daily standard deviation(%)	Annualized standard deviation(%)		
From	To		250 days	260 days	365 days
Treasury 30-Year Zero					
10/8/95	11/12/95	0.6360493	10.06	10.26	12.15
8/20/95	9/24/95	0.8452714	13.36	13.63	16.15
Treasury 10-Year Zero					
10/8/95	11/12/95	0.7091771	11.21	11.44	13.55
8/20/95	9/24/95	0.9044855	14.30	14.58	17.28
Treasury 5-Year Zero					
10/8/95	11/12/95	0.7224093	11.42	11.65	13.80
8/20/95	9/24/95	0.8145416	12.88	13.13	15.56
3-Month LIBOR					
10/8/95	11/12/95	0.1465032	2.32	2.36	2.80
8/20/95	9/24/95	0.2523040	3.99	4.07	4.82

FORECASTING YIELD VOLATILITY

As can be seen, the yield volatility as measured by the standard deviation can vary based on the time period selected and the number of observations. Now we turn to the issue of forecasting yield volatility. There are several methods. Before describing these methods, let's address the question of what mean should be used in the calculation of the forecasted standard deviation.

Suppose at the end of 10/24/95 a trader is interested in a forecast for volatility using the 10 most recent days of trading and updating that forecast at the end of each trading day. What mean value should be used?

The trader can calculate a 10-day moving average of the daily percentage yield change. Exhibit 1 shows the daily percentage change in yield for the Treasury 30-year zero from 10/9/95 to 11/12/95. To calculate a moving average of the daily percentage yield change on 10/24/95, the trader would use the 10 trading days from 10/11/95 to 10/24/95. At the end of 10/25/95, the trader will calculate the 10-day average by using the percentage yield change on 11/25/95 and would exclude the percentage yield change on 10/11/95. That is, the trader will use the 10 trading days from 10/12/95 to 10/25/95.

Exhibit 4 shows the 10-day moving average calculated from 10/24/95 to 11/12/95. Notice the considerable variation over this period. The 10-day moving average ranges from −0.20324% to 0.07902%. For the period from 4/15/93 to 11/12/95, the 10-day moving average ranged from −0.61705% to 0.60298%.

Rather than using a moving average, it is more appropriate to use an expectation of the average. Longerstacey and Zangari argue that it would be more appropriate to use a mean value of zero.[1] In that case, the variance as given by equation (1) simplifies to:

$$\text{Variance} = \sum_{t=1}^{T} \frac{X_t^2}{T-1} \tag{2}$$

Now let's look at the various methods for forecasting daily volatility.

Equally-Weighted Average Method

The daily standard deviation given by equation (2) assigns an equal weight to all observations. So, if a trader is calculating volatility based on the most recent 10 days of trading, each day is given a weight of 10%.

For example, suppose that a trader is interested in the daily volatility of the Treasury 30-year zero yield and decides to use the 10 most recent trading days. Exhibit 5 reports the 10-day volatility for various days using the data in Exhibit 1 and the formula for the variance given by equation (2). For the period 4/15/93 to 11/12/95, the 10-day volatility ranged from 0.16370% to 1.33006%.

---

[1] Jacques Longerstacey and Peter Zangari, *Five Questions about RiskMetrics*[TM], JP Morgan Research Publication 1995.

Exhibit 4: 10-Day Moving Daily Average for Treasury 30-Year Zero

10-Trading Days Ending	Daily Average (%)
24-Oct-95	−0.20324
25-Oct-95	−0.04354
26-Oct-95	0.07902
29-Oct-95	0.04396
30-Oct-95	0.00913
31-Oct-95	−0.04720
01-Nov-95	−0.06121
02-Nov-95	−0.09142
05-Nov-95	−0.11700
06-Nov-95	−0.01371
07-Nov-95	−0.11472
08-Nov-95	−0.15161
09-Nov-95	−0.02728
12-Nov-95	−0.11102

Exhibit 5: Moving Daily Standard Deviation Based on 10-Days of Observations

10-Trading Days Ending	Daily Standard Deviation (%)
24-Oct-95	0.75667
25-Oct-95	0.81874
26-Oct-95	0.58579
29-Oct-95	0.56886
30-Oct-95	0.59461
31-Oct-95	0.60180
01-Nov-95	0.61450
02-Nov-95	0.59072
05-Nov-95	0.57705
06-Nov-95	0.52011
07-Nov-95	0.59998
08-Nov-95	0.53577
09-Nov-95	0.54424
12-Nov-95	0.60003

In April 1995, the Basel Committee on Banking Supervision at the Bank for International Settlements proposed that volatility (as measured by the standard deviation) be calculated based on an equal weighting of daily historical observations using one year of observations.[2] Moreover, the committee proposed that volatility estimates should be updated at least quarterly.

Weighted Average Method

There is reason to suspect that market participants give greater weight to recent movements in yield or price when determining volatility. Moreover, what has been observed in several studies of the stock market is that high periods of volatility are followed by high periods of volatility.

To give greater importance to more recent information, observations further in the past should be given less weight. This can be done by revising the variance as given by equation (2) as follows:

$$\text{Variance} = \sum_{t=1}^{T} \frac{W_t X_t^2}{T-1} \tag{3}$$

where W_t is the weight assigned to observation t such that the sum of the weights is equal to 1 (i.e., $\sum W_t = 1$) and the further the observation from today, the lower the weight.

The weights should be assigned so that the forecasted volatility reacts faster to a recent major market movements and declines gradually as we move away from any major market movement. The approach by JP Morgan in RiskMetrics[TM] is to use an *exponential moving average*. The formula for the weight W_t in an exponential moving average is:

$$W_t = (1-\beta)\beta^t$$

where ß is a value between 0 and 1. The observations are arrayed so that the closest observation is t = 1, the second closest is t = 2, etc.

For example, if ß is 0.90, then the weight for the closest observation (t = 1) is:

$$W_1 = (1-0.90)(0.90)^1 = 0.09$$

For t = 5 and ß equal to 0.90, the weight is:

$$W_5 = (1-0.90)(0.90)^5 = 0.05905.$$

---

[2] The proposal, entitled "The Supervisory Treatment of Market Risks," is an amendment to the *1988 Basel Capital Accord*.

Exhibit 6 shows the weights that would be assigned to 76 observations for different values for ß. Notice that the smaller the value of ß, the lower the relative weight assigned to further observations. For example, for ß equal to 0.80, the weight assigned to the first observation is 16%. For the 16th observation, a weight of only 0.6% is assigned. In contrast, for ß equal to 0.95, the corresponding values for the first and 16th observations are 4.8% and 2.2%, respectively.

The parameter ß is measuring how quickly the information contained in past observations is "decaying" and hence is referred to as the "decay factor." The smaller the ß, the faster the decay. What decay factor to use depends on how fast the mean value for the random variable X changes over time. A random variable whose mean value changes slowly over time will have a decay factor close to 1. A discussion of how the decay factor should be selected is beyond the scope of this book.[3]

RiskMetrics^{TM} has a "Special Regulatory Dataset" that incorporates the 1-year moving average proposed by the Basel Committee. Rather than updating at least quarterly as proposed by the Basel Committee, the dataset is updated daily.

ARCH Method and Variants

A times series characteristic of return data of financial assets suggests that a period of high volatility is followed by a period of high volatility. Furthermore, a period of relative stability in returns appears to be followed by a period that can be characterized in the same way.

This suggests that volatility today may depend upon recent prior volatility. This can be modeled and used to forecast volatility. The statistical model to estimate this time series property of volatility is called an *autoregressive* conditional *heteroscedasticity* or ARCH model.[4] The term "conditional" means that the value of the variance depends on or is conditional on the value of the random variable. The term heteroscedasticity means that the variance is not equal for all values of the random variable.

The simplest ARCH model is

$$\sigma_t^2 = a + b(X_{t-1} - \overline{X})^2 \tag{4}$$

where

σ_t^2 = variance on day t

$X_{t-1} - \overline{X}$ = deviation from the mean on day t−1

and a and b are parameters.

The parameters a and b must be estimated statistically. The statistical technique of regression analysis that we explain in Chapter 7 is used to estimate the parameters.

---

[3] A technical description is provided in *RiskMetrics^{TM}—Technical Document*, pp. 77-79.

[4] See Robert F. Engle, "Autoregressive Conditional Heteroskedasticity with Estimates of Variance of U.K. Inflation," *Econometrica* 50 (1982), pp. 987-1008.

Exhibit 6: Weights for Exponential Weighted Moving Average for Various Values of ß

Observation	Assumed value for ß				
	0.99	0.95	0.90	0.85	0.80
1	0.00990	0.04750	0.09000	0.12750	0.16000
2	0.00980	0.04513	0.08100	0.10838	0.12800
3	0.00970	0.04287	0.07290	0.09212	0.10240
4	0.00961	0.04073	0.06561	0.07830	0.08192
5	0.00951	0.03869	0.05905	0.06656	0.06554
6	0.00941	0.03675	0.05314	0.05657	0.05243
7	0.00932	0.03492	0.04783	0.04809	0.04194
8	0.00923	0.03317	0.04305	0.04087	0.03355
9	0.00914	0.03151	0.03874	0.03474	0.02684
10	0.00904	0.02994	0.03487	0.02953	0.02147
11	0.00895	0.02844	0.03138	0.02510	0.01718
12	0.00886	0.02702	0.02824	0.02134	0.01374
13	0.00878	0.02567	0.02542	0.01814	0.01100
14	0.00869	0.02438	0.02288	0.01542	0.00880
15	0.00860	0.02316	0.02059	0.01310	0.00704
16	0.00851	0.02201	0.01853	0.01114	0.00563
17	0.00843	0.02091	0.01668	0.00947	0.00450
18	0.00835	0.01986	0.01501	0.00805	0.00360
19	0.00826	0.01887	0.01351	0.00684	0.00288
20	0.00818	0.01792	0.01216	0.00581	0.00231
21	0.00810	0.01703	0.01094	0.00494	0.00184
22	0.00802	0.01618	0.00985	0.00420	0.00148
23	0.00794	0.01537	0.00886	0.00357	0.00118
24	0.00786	0.01460	0.00798	0.00303	0.00094
25	0.00778	0.01387	0.00718	0.00258	0.00076
26	0.00770	0.01318	0.00646	0.00219	0.00060
27	0.00762	0.01252	0.00581	0.00186	0.00048
28	0.00755	0.01189	0.00523	0.00158	0.00039
29	0.00747	0.01130	0.00471	0.00135	0.00031
30	0.00740	0.01073	0.00424	0.00114	0.00025
31	0.00732	0.01020	0.00382	0.00097	0.00020
32	0.00725	0.00969	0.00343	0.00083	0.00016
33	0.00718	0.00920	0.00309	0.00070	0.00013
34	0.00711	0.00874	0.00278	0.00060	0.00010
35	0.00703	0.00830	0.00250	0.00051	0.00008
36	0.00696	0.00789	0.00225	0.00043	0.00006
37	0.00689	0.00749	0.00203	0.00037	0.00005

Exhibit 6 Concluded

	Assumed value for ß				
Observation	0.99	0.95	0.90	0.85	0.80
38	0.00683	0.00712	0.00182	0.00031	0.00004
39	0.00676	0.00676	0.00164	0.00027	0.00003
40	0.00669	0.00643	0.00148	0.00023	0.00003
41	0.00662	0.00610	0.00133	0.00019	0.00002
42	0.00656	0.00580	0.00120	0.00016	0.00002
43	0.00649	0.00551	0.00108	0.00014	0.00001
44	0.00643	0.00523	0.00097	0.00012	0.00001
45	0.00636	0.00497	0.00087	0.00010	0.00001
46	0.00630	0.00472	0.00079	0.00008	0.00001
47	0.00624	0.00449	0.00071	0.00007	0.00001
48	0.00617	0.00426	0.00064	0.00006	0.00000
49	0.00611	0.00405	0.00057	0.00005	0.00000
50	0.00605	0.00385	0.00052	0.00004	0.00000
51	0.00599	0.00365	0.00046	0.00004	0.00000
52	0.00593	0.00347	0.00042	0.00003	0.00000
53	0.00587	0.00330	0.00038	0.00003	0.00000
54	0.00581	0.00313	0.00034	0.00002	0.00000
55	0.00575	0.00298	0.00030	0.00002	0.00000
56	0.00570	0.00283	0.00027	0.00002	0.00000
57	0.00564	0.00269	0.00025	0.00001	0.00000
58	0.00558	0.00255	0.00022	0.00001	0.00000
59	0.00553	0.00242	0.00020	0.00001	0.00000
60	0.00547	0.00230	0.00018	0.00001	0.00000
61	0.00542	0.00219	0.00016	0.00001	0.00000
62	0.00536	0.00208	0.00015	0.00001	0.00000
63	0.00531	0.00197	0.00013	0.00001	0.00000
64	0.00526	0.00188	0.00012	0.00000	0.00000
65	0.00520	0.00178	0.00011	0.00000	0.00000
66	0.00515	0.00169	0.00010	0.00000	0.00000
67	0.00510	0.00161	0.00009	0.00000	0.00000
68	0.00505	0.00153	0.00008	0.00000	0.00000
69	0.00500	0.00145	0.00007	0.00000	0.00000
70	0.00495	0.00138	0.00006	0.00000	0.00000
71	0.00490	0.00131	0.00006	0.00000	0.00000
72	0.00485	0.00124	0.00005	0.00000	0.00000
73	0.00480	0.00118	0.00005	0.00000	0.00000
74	0.00475	0.00112	0.00004	0.00000	0.00000
75	0.00471	0.00107	0.00004	0.00000	0.00000
76	0.00466	0.00101	0.00003	0.00000	0.00000

Equation (4) states that the estimate of the variance on day t depends on how much the observation on day t−1 deviates from the mean. Thus, the variance on day t is "conditional" on the deviation from day t−1. The reason for squaring the deviation is that it is the magnitude, not the direction of the deviation, that is important for forecasting volatility.[5] By using the deviation on day t−1, recent information (as measured by the deviation) is being considered when forecasting volatility.

The ARCH model can be generalized in two ways. First, information for days prior to t−1 can be included into the model by using the squared deviations for several prior days. For example, suppose that four prior days are used. Then equation (4) can be generalized to:

$$\sigma_t^2 = a + b_1(X_{t-1} - \overline{X})^2 + b_2(X_{t-2} - \overline{X})^2 \tag{5}$$

$$+ b_3(X_{t-3} - \overline{X})^2 + b_4(X_{t-4} - \overline{X})^2$$

where a, b_1, b_2, b_3, and b_4 are parameters to be estimated statistically.

A second way to generalize the ARCH model is to include not only squared deviation's from prior days as a random variable that the variance is conditional on but also the estimated variance for prior days. For example, the following equation generalizes equation (4) for the case where the variance at time t is conditional on the deviation squared at time t−1 and the variance at time t−1:

$$\sigma_t^2 = a + b(X_{t-1} - \overline{X})^2 + c\sigma_{t-1}^2 \tag{6}$$

where a, b, and c are parameters to be estimated statistically.

Suppose that the variance at time t is assumed to be conditional on four prior periods of squared deviations and three prior variances, then equation (4) can be generalized as follows:

$$\sigma_t^2 = a + b_1(X_{t-1} - \overline{X})^2 + b_2(X_{t-2} - \overline{X})^2 \tag{7}$$

$$+ b_3(X_{t-3} - \overline{X})^2 + b_4(X_{t-4} - \overline{X})^2 + c_1\sigma_{t-1}^2 + c_2\sigma_{t-2}^2 + c_3\sigma_{t-3}^2$$

where the parameters to be estimated are a, the b_i's (1=1,2,3,4), and c_j's (j=1,2,3).

Equations (5), (6), and (7) are referred to as *generalized* ARCH or GARCH models. GARCH models are conventionally denoted as follows: GARCH(i,j) where i indicates the number of prior squared deviations included in the model and j the number of prior variances in the model. Equations (5), (6), and (7) would be denoted GARCH(4,0), GARCH(1,1), and GARCH(4,3), respectively.

---

[5] The variance for the unconditional variance (i.e., a variance that does not depend on the prior day's deviation) is $\sigma_t^2 = a/(1-b)$.

There have been further extensions of ARCH models but these extensions are beyond the scope of this chapter.[6]

HISTORICAL VERSUS IMPLIED VOLATILITY

Market participants estimate yield volatility in one of two ways. The first way is by estimating historical yield volatility. This is the method that we have thus far described in this chapter. The resulting volatility is called *historical volatility*. The second way is to estimate yield volatility based on the observed prices of interest rate options. Yield volatility calculated using this approach is called *implied volatility*.

The implied volatility is based on some option pricing model. One of the inputs to any option pricing model in which the underlying is a bond or bond futures contract is expected yield volatility. If the observed price of an option is assumed to be the fair price and the option pricing model is assumed to be the model that would generate that fair price, then the implied yield volatility is the yield volatility that when used as an input into the option pricing model would produce the observed option price.

There are several problems with using implied volatility. First, it is assumed the option pricing model is correct. Second, option pricing models typically assume that volatility is constant over the life of the option. Therefore, interpreting an implied volatility becomes difficult. Finally, there is not a liquid option market for all yields whose underlying depends on the yield of interest.

---

[6] For an excellent overview of these extensions as well as the GARCH models, see Robert F. Engle, "Statistical Models for Financial Volatility," *Financial Analysts Journal* (January-February 1993), pp. 72-78.

KEY POINTS

1. *The standard deviation is commonly used as a measure of volatility.*

2. *Yield volatility can be estimated from daily yield observations.*

3. *The observation used in the calculation of the standard deviation is the natural logarithm of the percentage change in yield between two days.*

4. *The selection of the number of observations and the time period can have a significant effect on the calculated daily standard deviation.*

5. *A daily standard deviation is annualized by multiplying it by the square root of the number of days in a year.*

6. *Typically, either 250 days, 260 days, or 365 days are used to annualize the daily standard deviation.*

7. *Assuming that the yield volatility is approximately normally distributed, the annual standard deviation can be used to construct a confidence interval for the yield one year from now.*

8. *In forecasting volatility, it is more appropriate to use an expectation of zero for the mean value.*

9. *The simplest method for forecasting volatility is weighting all observations equally.*

10. *The Basel Committee on Banking Supervision at the Bank for International Settlements proposed that the volatility (as measured by the standard deviation) be calculated based on an equal weighting of daily historical observations using one year of observations and updating the forecast at least quarterly.*

11. *A forecasted volatility can be obtained by assigning greater weight to more recent observations such that the forecasted volatility reacts faster to a recent major market movement and declines gradually as we move away from any major market movement.*

12. *JP Morgan's RiskMetrics^{TM} uses an exponential moving average to forecast volatility.*

13. *Generalized autoregressive conditional heteroscedasticity (GARCH) models can be used to capture the times series characteristic of yield volatility in which a period of high volatility is followed by a period of high volatility and a period of relative stability appears to be followed by a period that can be characterized in the same way.*

14. *Implied volatility can also be used to estimate yield volatility.*

15. *Implied volatility depends on the option pricing model employed.*

16. *There is not a liquid option market for all yields whose underlying depends on the yield of interest.*

Chapter 7

Correlation Analysis and Regression Analysis

In the previous two chapters we have dealt with a single random variable. In this chapter, we will look at the relationship between random variables. The two statistical analyses that we shall describe are correlation analysis and regression analysis.

The objectives of this chapter are to:

1. describe what is meant by the correlation coefficient between two random variables and how it is calculated;

2. describe what the covariance is and its relationship to the correlation coefficient;

3. describe how the variance of the return of a portfolio of assets is calculated and the important role that the correlation plays;

4. explain the role of correlation in selecting hedging instruments;

5. explain what regression analysis is and how to estimate a regression; and,

6. explain what the coefficient of determination of a regression measures.

CORRELATION ANALYSIS

The *correlation coefficient* measures the association between two random variables. No cause and effect are assumed when a correlation coefficient is computed. After we describe how the correlation between two random variables is calculated from historical data, we will look at the role played by this measure in risk management.

The formula for calculating the correlation coefficient, or simply correlation, between two random variables X and Y is:

$$\text{correlation} = \frac{T \sum_{t=1}^{T} X_t Y_t - \left(\sum_{t=1}^{T} X_t \right)\left(\sum_{t=1}^{T} Y_t \right)}{\sqrt{\left[T \sum_{t=1}^{T} X_t^2 - \left(\sum_{t=1}^{T} X_t \right)^2 \right]\left[T \sum_{t=1}^{T} Y_t^2 - \left(\sum_{t=1}^{T} Y_t \right)^2 \right]}}$$

where the subscript t denotes the t-th observation and T is the total number of observations.

The correlation can have a value between −1 and 1. A positive value means that the two random variables tend to move together. In this case, the two random variables are said to be *positively correlated*. A negative value means that the two random variables tend to move in the opposite direction. Two random variables that exhibit this characteristic are said to be *negatively correlated*. A correlation close to zero means that the two random variables tend not to track each other.

To illustrate how to use the above formula, we will calculate the correlation between the rate of return on two hypothetical assets: asset 1 and asset 2. Let:

$$X = \text{rate of return on asset 1}$$
$$Y = \text{rate of return on asset 2}$$

Sixty pairs of monthly returns for the two assets are provided in Exhibit 1. The last row of the exhibit indicates that

$$\sum_{t=1}^{60} X_t = -36.516 \qquad \sum_{t=1}^{60} Y_t = 123.288 \qquad \sum_{t=1}^{60} X_t Y_t = 627.3633$$

$$\sum_{t=1}^{60} X_t^2 = 3,479.3256 \qquad \sum_{t=1}^{60} Y_t^2 = 3,402.0807$$

Substituting these values into the formula:

$$\text{correlation} = \frac{60(627.3633) - (-36.516)(123.288)}{\sqrt{[60(3,479.3256) - (-36.516)^2][60(3,402.0807) - (123.288)^2]}}$$

$$= 0.21$$

Covariance

The covariance also measures how two random variables vary together. The covariance is related to the correlation coefficient as follows:

$$\text{covariance} = \text{std(X) std(Y) (correlation)}$$

Exhibit 1: Calculation of the Correlation Between the Monthly Rate of Return Between Asset 1 and Asset 2

X_t = monthly return on asset 1 (%)
Y_t = monthly return on asset 2 (%)

t	X_t	Y_t	X_t^2	Y_t^2	X_tY_t
1	7.1790	27.2730	51.5380	743.8165	195.7929
2	−6.1440	−8.6490	37.7487	74.8052	53.1395
3	−10.1850	1.4290	103.7342	2.0420	−14.5544
4	4.4670	8.4510	19.9541	71.4194	37.7506
5	−2.7760	8.5560	7.7062	73.2051	−23.7515
6	2.0520	1.8020	4.2107	3.2472	3.6977
7	2.7930	16.8170	7.8008	282.8115	46.9699
8	2.9000	−4.9620	8.4100	24.6214	−14.3898
9	−6.7240	−0.5330	45.2122	0.2841	3.5839
10	−8.2380	−7.2370	67.8646	52.3742	59.6184
11	−1.4110	3.3530	1.9909	11.2426	−4.7311
12	−3.5850	5.0560	12.8522	25.5631	−18.1258
13	4.7810	−11.4990	22.8580	132.2270	−54.9767
14	6.5500	−1.3290	42.9025	1.7662	−8.7050
15	2.1660	4.6180	4.6916	21.3259	10.0026
16	2.7090	−1.1760	7.3387	1.3830	−3.1858
17	11.2020	11.7860	125.4848	138.9098	132.0268
18	−2.0830	6.1480	4.3389	37.7979	−12.8063
19	−5.1060	0.7580	26.0712	0.5746	−3.8703
20	−7.5470	−8.3520	56.9572	69.7559	63.0325
21	4.4170	−1.3680	19.5099	1.8714	−6.0425
22	−0.9400	5.2760	0.8836	27.8362	−4.9594
23	8.9770	6.8180	80.5865	46.4851	61.2052
24	−0.5500	1.9850	0.3025	3.9402	−1.0918
25	12.1680	9.7330	148.0602	94.7313	118.4311
26	2.5330	11.2750	6.4161	127.1256	28.5596
27	−11.5530	7.6000	133.4718	57.7600	−87.8028
28	−9.5500	−2.6020	91.2025	6.7704	24.8491
29	4.2090	−0.4120	17.7157	0.1697	−1.7341
30	−8.4810	2.3080	71.9274	5.3269	−19.5741
31	4.2470	2.6320	18.0370	6.9274	11.1781
32	−3.1260	1.0700	9.7719	1.1449	−3.3448
33	6.9680	−6.9090	48.5530	47.7343	−48.1419
34	−5.1870	4.2970	26.9050	18.4642	−22.2885
35	−4.6210	−2.6070	21.3536	6.7964	12.0469
36	−3.7840	17.3750	14.3187	301.8906	−65.7470

Exhibit 1 Concluded

t	X_t	Y_t	X_t^2	Y_t^2	$X_t Y_t$
37	1.1240	−0.6580	1.2634	0.4330	−0.7396
38	−2.1280	−3.6290	4.5284	13.1696	7.7225
39	−3.8850	−1.0340	15.0932	1.0692	4.0171
40	8.6830	−6.6200	75.3945	43.8244	−57.4815
41	1.3330	−0.3580	1.7769	0.1282	−0.4772
42	7.8510	1.8800	61.6382	3.5344	14.7599
43	−3.1930	5.9040	10.1952	34.8572	−18.8515
44	−7.2980	7.3310	53.2608	53.7436	−53.5016
45	−6.7820	−0.3260	45.9955	0.1063	2.2109
46	−17.1830	5.2290	295.2555	27.3424	−89.8499
47	3.8650	10.0000	14.9382	100.0000	38.6500
48	−26.1900	−1.1330	685.9161	1.2837	29.6733
49	2.2330	−8.5960	4.9863	73.8912	−19.1949
50	6.6310	−1.8180	43.9702	3.3051	−12.0552
51	−6.4370	3.5260	41.4350	12.4327	−22.6969
52	−4.4230	−5.8820	19.5629	34.5979	26.0161
53	9.5940	12.8950	92.0448	166.2810	123.7146
54	−6.3980	−5.5560	40.9344	30.8691	35.5473
55	−9.8730	−6.8110	97.4761	46.3897	67.2450
56	3.3710	3.7210	11.3636	13.8458	12.5435
57	−8.1970	−3.8590	67.1908	14.8919	31.6322
58	9.5240	13.7120	90.7066	188.0189	130.5931
59	17.6630	−3.7180	311.9816	13.8235	−65.6710
60	4.8720	0.3070	23.7364	0.0942	1.4957
Total	−36.5160	123.2880	3,479.3256	3,402.0807	627.3633

Since the standard deviations are positive, the covariance will have the same sign as the correlation. Thus, if two random variables are positively correlated they will have a positive covariance. Similarly, the covariance will be negative if the two random variables are negatively correlated.

The covariance between the rates of return for asset 1 and asset 2 for the 60 month period reported in Exhibit 1 is found as follows. The standard deviation for the rate of return of asset 1 is 7.765. For asset 2 it is 7.305. The correlation is 0.21. Therefore, the covariance is

covariance = 7.675 (7.305) (0.21) = 11.77

Measuring the Variance of a Two-Asset Portfolio

As explained in previous chapters, the variance or standard deviation can be viewed as a measure of risk for an individual security. The risk of a portfolio or position in several assets is not simply the weighted average of the variance of the component assets. The basic principle of modern portfolio theory is that the variance of a portfolio of assets depends not only on the variance of the assets, but also their covariances.[1] Specifically, the variance of a two-asset portfolio is equal to

$$var(P) = W_X^2 \, var(X) + W_Y^2 \, var(Y) + 2 \, W_X \, W_Y \, cov(X,Y)$$

where

$$
\begin{aligned}
var(P) \;&=\; \text{variance of the rate of return of a portfolio comprised of} \\
&\quad\;\; \text{asset 1 and asset 2} \\
var(X) \;&=\; \text{variance of the rate of return of asset 1} \\
var(Y) \;&=\; \text{variance of the rate of return of asset 2} \\
cov(X,Y) \;&=\; \text{covariance between the rate of return on asset 1 and asset 2} \\
W_X \;&=\; \text{market value of asset 1/market value of portfolio} \\
W_Y \;&=\; \text{market value of asset 2/market value of portfolio}
\end{aligned}
$$

In words, the formula says that the variance of the portfolio return is the sum of the weighted variances of the two assets plus the weighted covariance between the two assets.

For our two hypothetical assets, suppose that 60% is invested in asset 1 and 40% in asset 2. Then the inputs for calculating the variance of a portfolio consisting of these two assets are:

$$
\begin{aligned}
var(X) \;&=\; (7.675)^2 \;=\; 58.9056 \\
var(Y) \;&=\; (7.305)^2 \;=\; 53.3630 \\
cov(X,Y) \;&=\; 11.77 \\
W_X \;&=\; 0.6 \\
W_Y \;&=\; 0.4
\end{aligned}
$$

Then,

$$
\begin{aligned}
var(P) \;&=\; (0.6)^2(58.9056) + (0.4)^2(53.3630) + 2(0.6)(0.4)(11.77) \\
&=\; 21.2060 + 8.5381 + 5.6496 \;=\; 35.3937
\end{aligned}
$$

The portfolio's standard deviation is then 5.9494 (the square root of 35.3937). Notice that the portfolio's standard deviation is less than that of the standard deviation of either asset.

The key in the risk of a portfolio or position as measured by the standard deviation or variance is the correlation (or covariance) between the two assets. Exhibit 2 shows the portfolio standard deviation for several assumed correlations and different weights for asset 1 and asset 2 in the portfolio. For a given allocation of the two assets in the portfolio, the more negatively correlated, the lower the portfolio standard deviation. The minimum variance (for a given allocation) occurs when the correlation is −1.

---

[1] Harry M. Markowitz, "Portfolio Selection," *Journal of Finance* (March 1952), pp. 71-91.

Exhibit 2: Portfolio Standard Deviation for Different Correlations and Weights for Asset 1 and Asset 2

Assumptions:

X = rate of return of asset 1 (%)
Y = rate of return of asset 2 (%)
W_X = weight of asset 1
W_Y = weight of asset 2
Standard deviation for asset 1 = 7.675
Standard deviation for asset 2 = 7.305

		W_X: 0.6	0.5	0.4	0.4877
Correlation	Covariance	W_Y: 0.4	0.5	0.6	0.5123
1.0	56.07	7.5270	7.4900	7.4530	7.4854
0.8	44.85	7.1605	7.1059	7.0827	7.1013
0.6	33.64	6.7743	6.6998	6.6920	6.6952
0.4	22.43	6.3646	6.2674	6.2770	6.2628
0.2	11.21	5.9268	5.8029	5.8325	5.7982
0.0	0.00	5.4538	5.2978	5.3512	5.2930
−0.2	−11.21	4.9358	4.7393	4.8222	4.7342
−0.4	−22.43	4.3565	4.1054	4.2274	4.0999
−0.6	−33.64	3.6874	3.3537	3.5339	3.3476
−0.8	−44.85	2.8661	2.3750	2.6658	2.3671
−1.0	−56.07	1.6830	0.1850	1.3130	0.0007

Consequently, for a manager seeking to measure and then control the risk of a portfolio or position in two assets, the correlation and the relative amounts of the two assets determines the standard deviation of the portfolio or position. It is critical to have a good estimate of the correlation to measure risk.

There is another point to note from the results reported in Exhibit 2. Suppose that a manager wants to hedge a position in asset 1. By hedging it is meant that the manager seeks to employ some hedging instrument such that the combined position of asset 1 and the hedging instrument will produce a portfolio standard deviation of zero. Look at the last column of Exhibit 2. If a hedging instrument, say asset 2, can be identified that has a −1 correlation with asset 1 and the manager takes a position in asset 2 such that the portfolio has 48.77% of asset 1 and 51.23% of asset 2, then the standard deviation of the portfolio will be approximately zero.

Consequently, hedging involves identifying one or more instruments that have a correlation of close to −1 with the position that the manager seeks to protect and selecting the appropriate amount of the hedging instrument. If the position in asset 1 is a long position, then this typically involves shorting a position in the hedging instrument, asset 2.

Measuring the Variance of a Portfolio
with More than Two Assets

Thus far we have given the portfolio variance and standard deviation for a portfolio consisting of two assets. The extension to three assets — asset 1, asset 2, and asset 3 — is as follows:

$$var(P) = W_X^2\, var(X) + W_Y^2\, var(Y) + W_Z^2\, var(Z) + 2\, W_X W_Y\, cov(X,Y)$$
$$+ 2\, W_X W_Z\, cov(X,Z) + 2\, W_Y W_Z\, cov(Y,Z)$$

$var(P)$ = variance of the rate of return of a portfolio comprised of assets 1, 2 and 3
$var(X)$ = variance of the rate of return of asset 1
$var(Y)$ = variance of the rate of return of asset 2
$var(Z)$ = variance of the rate of return of asset 3
$cov(X,Y)$ = covariance between the rate of return on asset 1 and asset 2
$cov(X,Z)$ = covariance between the rate of return on asset 1 and asset 3
$cov(Y,Z)$ = covariance between the rate of return on asset 2 and asset 3
W_X = market value of asset 1/market value of portfolio
W_Y = market value of asset 2/market value of portfolio
W_Z = market value of asset 3/market value of portfolio

In words, the portfolio's variance is the sum of the weighted variances of the individual assets plus the sum of the weighted covariances of the assets.

In general, for a portfolio with J assets, the portfolio variance is:

$$var(P) = \sum_{j=1}^{J} W_j^2 var(j) + \sum_{\substack{j=1 \\ for\, j \neq k}}^{J} \sum_{k=1}^{J} W_j W_k cov(j,k)$$

REGRESSION ANALYSIS

In correlation analysis, neither random variable is assumed to effect the other random variable. In some situations in managing risk it is necessary to estimate the relationship between two random variables in which it is assumed that one random variable affects the other random variable. *Regression analysis* is a statistical technique that can be used to estimate relationships between variables. Regression analysis will be explained with an illustration.

The Simple Linear Regression Model

Suppose that a manager believes that the return on asset 3 affects the return on asset 2 and wants to estimate the relationship. Assume that the manager believes that the relationship can be expressed as follows:

return on asset 2 = α + ß (return on asset 3)

The values α and ß are called the *parameters* of the model. The objective of regression analysis is to estimate the parameters.

There are several points to note about this relationship. First there are only two variables in the relationship — the return on asset 3 and the return on asset 2. Because there are only two variables and the relationship is linear, this regression model is called a *simple linear regression model*. Since the return on asset 2 is assumed to depend on the return on asset 3, the return on asset 2 is referred to as the *dependent variable*. The return on asset 3 is referred to as the *explanatory* or *independent variable* because it is used to explain the return on asset 2. Second, it is highly unlikely that the estimated relationship will describe the true relationship between the two returns exactly because other factors may influence the return on asset 2. Consequently, the relationship may be more accurately described by adding a random error term to the relationship. That is, the relationship can be expressed as follows:

return on asset 2 = α + ß (return on asset 3) + random error term

The expression can be simplified as follows:

$$Y = α + ß X + e$$

where

$$Y = \text{rate of return on asset 2}$$
$$X = \text{rate of return on asset 3}$$
$$e = \text{random error term}$$

Estimating the Parameters
of the Simple Linear Regression Model

In order to estimate the parameters of the simple linear regression model, historical information on the returns of asset 3 and asset 2 are needed. We will use the 60 monthly returns in Exhibit 3.

One possible way of estimating the relationship between the two returns is simply to plot the observations on a graph and then draw a line through the observations which it is believed best represent the relationship. Selecting two points on this line will determine the estimated relationship. The obvious pitfall is that there is no specified criterion for drawing the line, and hence different individuals would obtain different estimates of the relationship based on the same observations.

Exhibit 3: Worksheet for the Estimation of the Parameters of the Simple Linear Regression: Relationship Between Monthly Return on Asset 3 and Asset 2

X_t = monthly return on asset 3 (%)
Y_t = monthly return on asset 2 (%)

t	X_t	Y_t	X_tY_t	X_t^2	Y_t^2
1	7.2100	7.1790	51.7606	51.9841	51.5380
2	-2.5000	-6.1440	15.3600	6.2500	37.7487
3	2.3600	-10.1850	-24.0366	5.5696	103.7342
4	5.1300	4.4670	22.9157	26.3169	19.9541
5	4.0400	-2.7760	-11.2150	16.3216	7.7062
6	-0.5500	2.0520	-1.1286	0.3025	4.2107
7	8.9800	2.7930	25.0811	80.6404	7.8008
8	1.9300	2.9000	5.5970	3.7249	8.4100
9	-0.3900	-6.7240	2.6224	0.1521	45.2122
10	-2.3600	-8.2380	19.4417	5.5696	67.8646
11	2.0700	-1.4110	-2.9208	4.2849	1.9909
12	2.3900	-3.5850	-8.5682	5.7121	12.8522
13	-6.7200	4.7810	-32.1283	45.1584	22.8580
14	1.2900	6.5500	8.4495	1.6641	42.9025
15	2.6200	2.1660	5.6749	6.8644	4.6916
16	-2.4800	2.7090	-6.7183	6.1504	7.3387
17	9.7500	11.2020	109.2195	95.0625	125.4848
18	-0.6900	-2.0830	1.4373	0.4761	4.3389
19	-0.3200	-5.1060	1.6339	0.1024	26.0712
20	-9.0400	-7.5470	68.2249	81.7216	56.9572
21	-4.9200	4.4170	-21.7316	24.2064	19.5099
22	-0.3700	-0.9400	0.3478	0.1369	0.8836
23	6.4300	8.9770	57.7221	41.3449	80.5865
24	2.7500	-0.5500	-1.5125	7.5625	0.3025
25	4.3600	12.1680	53.0525	19.0096	148.0602
26	7.1500	2.5330	18.1110	51.1225	6.4161
27	2.4200	-11.5530	-27.9583	5.8564	133.4718
28	0.2400	-9.5500	-2.2920	0.0576	91.2025
29	4.3200	4.2090	18.1829	18.6624	17.7157
30	-4.5800	-8.4810	38.8430	20.9764	71.9274
31	4.6600	4.2470	19.7910	21.7156	18.0370
32	2.3700	-3.1260	-7.4086	5.6169	9.7719
33	-1.6700	6.9680	-11.6366	2.7889	48.5530
34	1.3400	-5.1870	-6.9506	1.7956	26.9050
35	-4.0300	-4.6210	18.6226	16.2409	21.3536
36	11.4400	-3.7840	-43.2890	130.8736	14.3187

Exhibit 3 Concluded

t	X_t	Y_t	$X_t Y_t$	X_t^2	Y_t^2
37	-1.8600	1.1240	-2.0906	3.4596	1.2634
38	1.3000	-2.1280	-2.7664	1.6900	4.5284
39	-1.9500	-3.8850	7.5758	3.8025	15.0932
40	2.9400	8.6830	25.5280	8.6436	75.3945
41	0.4900	1.3330	0.6532	0.2401	1.7769
42	-1.4900	7.8510	-11.6980	2.2201	61.6382
43	4.0900	-3.1930	-13.0594	16.7281	10.1952
44	-2.0500	-7.2980	14.9609	4.2025	53.2608
45	1.1800	-6.7820	-8.0028	1.3924	45.9955
46	0.3500	-17.1830	-6.0141	0.1225	295.2555
47	3.4100	3.8650	13.1797	11.6281	14.9382
48	1.2300	-26.1900	-32.2137	1.5129	685.9161
49	0.7300	2.2330	1.6301	0.5329	4.9863
50	1.3600	6.6310	9.0182	1.8496	43.9702
51	2.1500	-6.4370	-13.8396	4.6225	41.4350
52	-2.4200	-4.4230	10.7037	5.8564	19.5629
53	2.6800	9.5940	25.7119	7.1824	92.0448
54	0.2900	-6.3980	-1.8554	0.0841	40.9344
55	-0.4000	-9.8730	3.9492	0.1600	97.4761
56	3.7900	3.3710	12.7761	14.3641	11.3636
57	-0.7700	-8.1970	6.3117	0.5929	67.1908
58	2.0700	9.5240	19.7147	4.2849	90.7066
59	-0.9500	17.6630	-16.7799	0.9025	311.9816
60	1.2100	4.8720	5.8951	1.4641	23.7364
Total	72.0100	-36.5160	401.8848	909.5345	3,479.3256

The regression method specifies a logical criterion for estimating the relationship. To understand this criterion, first rewrite the simple linear regression so that it shows the estimated relationship for each observation. This is done as follows:

$$Y_t = \alpha + \beta X_t + e_t$$

where the subscript t denotes the observation for the t-th month. For example, for the fourth observation (t = 4), the above expression is

$$4.467 = \alpha + \beta (5.13) + e_4$$

For observation 18 (t = 18), the expression is

$$-2.083 = \alpha + \beta (-0.60) + e_{18}$$

The values for e_4 and e_{18} are referred to as the *observed error term for the obser-vation*. Note that the value of the observed error term for both observations will depend on the values selected for α and ß. This suggests a criterion for selecting the two parameters. The parameters should be estimated in such a way that the sum of the observed error terms for all observations is as small as possible.

Although this is a good standard, it presents one problem. Some observed error terms will be positive, and others will be negative. Consequently, positive and negative observed error terms will offset each other. To overcome this prob-lem, each error term could be squared. On the basis of that criterion, the objective would then be to select parameters so as to minimize the sum of the square of the observed error terms. This is precisely the criterion used to estimate the parame-ters in regression analysis. Because of this property, regression analysis is some-times referred to as the *method of least squares*.

The formulas that can be used to estimate the parameters on the basis of this criterion are derived using differential calculus. Their use will be illustrated. If a hat ($\wedge$) over the parameter denotes the estimated value and T denotes the total number of observations, then the estimated parameters for α and ß are computed from the observations using the following formulas:

$$\hat{\beta} = \frac{\sum_{t=1}^{T} X_t Y_t - \frac{1}{T} \sum_{t=1}^{T} X_t \sum_{t=1}^{T} Y_t}{\sum_{t=1}^{T} X_t^2 - \frac{1}{T} \left(\sum_{t=1}^{T} X_t \right)^2} \quad \text{and} \quad \hat{\alpha} = \frac{1}{T} \sum_{t=1}^{T} Y_t - \frac{1}{T} (\hat{\beta}) \sum_{t=1}^{T} X_t$$

Although the formulas look complicated, they are easy to apply. In actual problems with a large number of observations, there are regression analysis pro-grams that will compute the value of the parameters using the above formulas. Most electronic spread sheets are preprogrammed to perform simple linear regres-sion analysis.

The above formulas may be used to compute the estimated parameters on the basis of the 60 observations given in Exhibit 3. The worksheet for the sums needed to apply the formula is shown as Exhibit 3 and summarized below.

$$\sum_{t=1}^{60} X_t = 72.03 \qquad \sum_{t=1}^{60} Y_t = -36.516$$

$$\sum_{t=1}^{60} X_t Y_t = 401.8848 \qquad \sum_{t=1}^{60} X_t^2 = 909.5345$$

We then have:

$$\hat{\beta} = \frac{401.8848 - \frac{1}{60}(72.01)(-36.516)}{909.5345 - \frac{1}{60}(72.01)^2}$$

and

$$\hat{\alpha} = \frac{1}{60}(-36.516) - \frac{1}{60}(0.5415)(72.01) = -1.2585$$

The estimated relationship between the monthly return on asset 3 and asset 2 is then

$$Y = -1.2585 + 0.5415\,X$$

Goodness of Fit

The manager will be interested in knowing how "good" the estimated relationship is. Statistical tests determine in some sense how good the relationship is between the dependent variable and the explanatory variable. A measure of the "goodness of fit" of the relationship is the *coefficient of determination.*

The explanatory or independent variable X is being used to try to explain movements in the dependent variable Y. But what movements is it trying to explain? The variable X is trying to explain why the variable Y would deviate from its mean. It can be shown that if no explanatory variable is used to try to explain movements in Y, the method of least squares would give the mean of Y as the value estimate of Y. Thus the ability of X to explain deviations of Y from its mean is of interest. In regression analysis, when we refer to the variation in a variable we mean its deviation from its mean.

The coefficient of determination indicates the percentage of the variation of the dependent variable that is explained by the explanatory variable (i.e., explained by the regression).[2] That is,

$$\text{Coefficient of determination} = \frac{\text{Variation of Y explained by X}}{\text{Variation of Y}}$$

The coefficient of determination is commonly referred to as "R-squared" and denoted by R^2.

The coefficient of determination can take on a value between 0 and 1. If all the variation of Y is explained by X, then the coefficient of determination is 1. When none is explained by X, the coefficient of determination is 0. Hence, the closer the coefficient of determination is to 1, the stronger the relationship between the variables.

---

[2] In statistics textbooks, the terms "total sum of squares" and "explained sum of squares" are used instead of variation in Y and variation in Y explained by X.

Another interpretation of the coefficient of determination is that it measures how close the observed points are to the regression line. The closer the observed points are to the regression line, the closer the coefficient of determination will be to 1. On the other hand, the greater the scatter of the observed points from the regression line, the closer the coefficient of determination will be to 0.

Computation of the coefficient of determination is as follows: To compute variation of Y, the following formula is used:

$$\text{Variation of Y} = \sum_{t=1}^{T} Y_t^2 - \frac{1}{T}\left(\sum_{t=1}^{T} Y_t\right)^2$$

The variation of Y explained by X is computed using the following formula:

$$\text{Variance of Y explained by X} = \hat{\beta}\left(\sum_{t=1}^{T} X_t Y_t - \frac{1}{T}\sum_{t=1}^{T} X_t \sum_{t=1}^{T} Y_t\right)$$

The coefficient of determination is then found by dividing the variation of Y explained by X by the variation of Y.

From the worksheet shown as Exhibit 3,

$$\sum_{t=1}^{60} X_t = 72.03 \qquad \sum_{t=1}^{60} Y_t = -36.516$$

$$\sum_{t=1}^{60} X_t Y_t = 401.8848 \qquad \sum_{t=1}^{60} Y_t^2 = 3{,}479.326$$

then

$$\text{Variation of Y} = 3{,}479.326 - \frac{1}{60}(-36.516)^2 = 3{,}457.142362$$

and

Variation of Y explained by X =

$$(0.5415)\left[401.8848 - \frac{1}{60}(72.01)(-36.516)\right] = 241.3500215$$

The coefficient of determination is therefore

$$\text{Coefficient of determination} = \frac{241.3500215}{3{,}457.142362} = 0.07$$

A coefficient of determination of 0.07 means that approximately 7% of the variation in the monthly return of asset 2 is explained by the monthly return of asset 3.

There are tests that can be performed to determine whether the coefficient of determination is statistically significant. Alternatively, the statistical significance of the estimated ß parameter can be tested. The test involves determining whether the estimated ß is statistically different from zero. If there is no relationship between the two random variables, the estimated ß would not be statistically different from zero. A discussion of these tests is provided in statistics textbooks.

Extension of the Simple Linear Regression Model

In many applications, a dependent variable may be best explained by more than one explanatory variable. When such a relationship is estimated, it is referred to as a *multiple regression*. The computations for obtaining the parameters of a multiple regression are difficult to perform by hand. Fortunately, there are numerous multiple regression analysis programs for computing the parameters of a multiple regression.

The interpretation of the coefficient of determination is the same in a multiple regression as it is in a simple linear regression. In the latter case, it is the total sum of squares explained by the explanatory variable X. In a multiple regression, the coefficient of determination is the variation in Y explained by all the explanatory variables. By adding an explanatory variable to a regression model, the belief is that the new explanatory variable will significantly increase the variation in Y explained by the regression. For example, suppose that a simple linear regression is estimated and that the variation in Y is 1,000 and the variation explained by the single explanatory variable X is 600. Suppose that another explanatory variable is added to the regression model and that the inclusion of this explanatory variable increased the variation in Y explained from 600 to 750. Thus, it would increase the coefficient of determination from 60% to 75% (750/1,000). This new explanatory variable would appear to have contributed substantially to explaining the variation in Y. On the other hand, had the variation in Y explained by the regression increased from 600 to 610, the coefficient of determination would have increased from 60% to only 61%. Thus it appears that the new explanatory variable did not do much to help explain the dependent variable.

Relationship Between Correlation Coefficient and Coefficient of Determination

The coefficient of determination turns out to be equal to the square of the correlation coefficient. Thus, the square root of the coefficient determination is the correlation coefficient. Since the correlation coefficient can be between −1 and 1, the coefficient of determination will be between 0 and 1. The sign of the correlation coefficient will be the same as the sign of the slope of the regression, ß. For example, the coefficient of determination between the monthly return of asset 3 and asset 2 is 0.07. The correlation coefficient is therefore 0.26.

Key Points

1. *The correlation coefficient measures the association between two random variables with no cause and effect assumed.*

2. *The correlation coefficient can have a value between −1 and 1.*

3. *A positive value for the correlation coefficient means that the two random variables tend to move together and are said to be positively correlated.*

4. *A negative value for the correlation coefficient means that the two random variables tend to move in the opposite direction and are said to be negatively correlated.*

5. *The covariance is related to the correlation, being the product of the standard deviation of the random variables and their correlation.*

6. *The variance of a portfolio's return is not simply the weighted average of the variance of the return of the component assets.*

7. *The variance of a portfolio's return depends not only on the variance of the assets, but also upon the correlation between the assets.*

8. *The variance of a portfolio's return is reduced the lower the correlation, with the maximum reduction when the correlation is −1.*

9. *For a manager to measure the risk of a portfolio, it is critical to have a good estimate of the correlation of returns between each pair of assets in the portfolio.*

10. *The correlation is important in selecting hedging instruments.*

11. *Hedging involves identifying one or more instruments that have a correlation close to −1 with the position that the manager seeks to protect, and selecting the appropriate amount of the hedging instrument.*

12. *Regression analysis is a statistical technique that can be used to estimate relationships between variables.*

13. *In regression analysis, one random variable is assumed to be affected by one or more other random variables.*

14. *In a simple linear regression, there is one dependent variable and one explanatory variable.*

15. *In a multiple linear regression there is more than one explanatory variable.*

16. *The procedure for estimating the parameters of a regression is the method of least squares.*

17. *The coefficient of determination, or R-squared, is a measure of how good the relationship is between the dependent variable and the explanatory variables.*

18. *The coefficient of determination can take on a value between 0 and 1.*

19. *The coefficient of determination indicates the percentage of the variation in the dependent variable explained by the explanatory variables.*

20. *The coefficient of determination between two random variables is equal to the square of the correlation coefficient.*

Chapter 8
Futures and Forward Contracts

In this and the next three chapters we will discuss risk control instruments: futures, forwards, swaps, options, caps, and floors. For each of these instruments, popularly referred to as derivative instruments, we will discuss their basic features and how they are valued. Our coverage in this chapter is on futures and forward contracts.

The objectives of this chapter are to:

1. explain the basic features of interest rate futures and forward contracts;

2. explain the risk and return characteristics of futures/forward contracts;

3. describe the more popular interest rate futures contracts;

4. describe forward rate agreements;

5. demonstrate how the theoretical price of a futures/forward contract is determined; and,

6. explain the complications in extending the standard arbitrage pricing model to the valuation of several currently traded interest rate futures contracts.

FUTURES AND FORWARD CONTRACTS

Futures and *forward contracts* are agreements that require a party to the agreement either to buy or sell something at a designated future date at a predetermined price. That is, one party is agreeing to make delivery and the other is agreeing to take delivery. The price at which the parties agree to transact in the case of a futures contract is called the *futures price,* and in the case of a forward contract, the *forward price.* The designated date on which the parties must transact is called the *settlement* or *delivery date.*

Futures contracts are standardized agreements as to the delivery date (or month) and quality of the deliverable, and are traded on organized exchanges. The clearinghouse associated with the exchange where the contract is traded guarantees the performance of each party to a futures contract. Thus, counterparty risk is minimal. Unlike a futures contract, a forward contract is an over-the-counter instrument. As a result, forward contracts are usually non-standardized (that is, the terms of each contract are negotiated individually between buyer and seller), there is no clearinghouse, and secondary markets are often non-existent or extremely thin. Since there is no clearinghouse, both parties to a forward contract are exposed to counterparty risk.

MECHANICS OF FUTURES TRADING

Most futures contracts have settlement dates in the months of March, June, September, or December. This means that at a predetermined time in the contract settlement month the contract stops trading, and a price is determined by the exchange for settlement of the contract. The contract with the closest settlement date is called the *nearby futures contract*. The next futures contract is the one that settles just after the nearby contract. The contract farthest away in time from settlement is called the *most distant futures contract*.

A party to a futures contract has two choices as to how to liquidate a position. First, a position can be liquidated prior to the settlement date. For this purpose, the party must take an offsetting position in the same contract. For the buyer of a futures contract, this means selling the same number of identical futures contracts; for the seller of a futures contract, this means buying the same number of identical futures contracts. About 97% of futures contracts are liqidated in this manner.

The alternative is to wait until the settlement date. At that time the party purchasing a futures contract accepts delivery of the underlying at the futures settlement price; the party that sells a futures contract liquidates the position by delivering the underlying at the futures settlement price. For some interest rate futures contracts that we shall describe later, settlement is made in cash only. Such contracts are referred to as *cash settlement contracts*.

Associated with every futures exchange is a clearinghouse, which performs several functions. One of these functions is to guarantee that the two parties to the transaction will perform. When an investor takes a position in the futures market, the clearinghouse takes the opposite position and agrees to satisfy the terms set forth in the contract. Because of the clearinghouse, the investor need not worry about the financial strength and integrity of the party taking the opposite side of the contract. After initial execution of an order, the relationship between the two parties ends. The clearinghouse interposes itself as the buyer for every sale and the seller for every purchase. Thus investors are free to liquidate their positions without involving the other party in the original contract, and without worry that the other party may default. Besides its guarantee function, the clearinghouse makes it simple for parties to a futures contract to unwind their positions prior to the settlement date.

When a position is first taken in a futures contract, the investor must deposit a minimum dollar amount per contract as specified by the exchange. This amount is called *initial margin* and is required as deposit for the contract. The initial margin may be in the form of an interest-bearing security such as a Treasury bill. As the price of the futures contract fluctuates, the value of the investor's equity in the position changes. At the end of each trading day, the exchange determines the day's settlement price for the futures contract. This price is used to mark to market the investor's position, so that any gain or loss from the position is reflected in the investor's equity account.

Maintenance margin is the minimum level (specified by the exchange) by which an investor's equity position may fall as a result of an unfavorable price movement before the investor is required to deposit additional margin. The additional margin deposited is called *variation margin*, and it is an amount necessary to bring the equity in the account back to its initial margin level. Unlike initial margin, variation margin must be in cash, not interest-bearing instruments. Any excess margin in the account may be withdrawn by the investor. If a party to a futures contract who is required to deposit variation margin fails to do so within 24 hours, the futures position is closed out.

Although there are initial and maintenance margin requirements for buying securities on margin, the concept of margin differs for securities and futures. When securities are acquired on margin, the difference between the price of the security and the initial margin is borrowed from the broker. The security becomes the collateral for the loan, and the investor pays interest. For futures contracts, the initial margin, in effect, serves as "good faith" money, an indication that the investor will satisfy the obligation of the contract. Normally no money is borrowed by the investor.

Since futures contracts are marked to market at the end of each trading day, the investor is subject to interim cash flows as additional margin may be required in the case of adverse price movements, or as cash is withdrawn in the case of favorable price movements. Forward contracts may or may not be marked to market, depending on the wishes of the two parties. For a forward contract that is not marked to market, there are no interim cash flow effects because no additional margin is required.

Other than the differences described above between futures and forward contracts, most of what we say about futures contracts applies equally to forward contracts.

RISK AND RETURN CHARACTERISTICS OF FUTURES CONTRACTS

When an investor takes a position in the market by buying a futures contract, the investor is said to be in a *long position* or to be *long futures*. If, instead, the investor's opening position is the sale of a futures contract, the investor is said to be in a *short position* or *short futures*. The buyer of a futures contract will realize a profit if the futures price increases; the seller of a futures contract will realize a profit if the futures price decreases. This is summarized in Exhibit 1.

Exhibit 1: Effect of Rate Changes on Parties to a Futures Contract

Party	Interest rates	
	Decrease	Increase
Buyer (long)	Gains	Loses
Seller (short)	Loses	Gains

When a position is taken in a futures contract, the party need not put up the entire amount of the investment. Instead, only initial margin must be put up. Consequently, an investor can create a leveraged position by using futures.

At first, the leverage available in the futures market may suggest that the market benefits only those who want to speculate on price movements. This is not true. As we shall see, futures markets can be used to control risk. Without the leverage possible in futures transactions, the cost of reducing price risk using futures would be too high for many market participants.

EXCHANGE-TRADED INTEREST RATE FUTURES CONTRACTS

Interest rate futures contracts can be classified by the maturity of their underlying security. Short-term interest rate futures contracts have an underlying security that matures in less than one year. The maturity of the underlying security of long-term futures contracts exceeds one year. Below we describe the specifications of the more commonly used futures contracts.

Eurodollar CD Futures

Eurodollar certificates of deposit (CDs) are denominated in dollars but represent the liabilities of banks outside the United States. The rate paid on Eurodollar CDs is the London interbank offered rate (LIBOR). Eurodollar CD futures contracts are traded on both the International Monetary Market (IMM) of the Chicago Mercantile Exchange and the London International Financial Futures Exchange.

The 3-month Eurodollar CD is the underlying instrument for the Eurodollar CD futures contract. The contract is for $1 million face value and is traded on an index price basis. The index price basis in which the contract is quoted is equal to 100 minus the annualized futures LIBOR. For example, a Eurodollar CD futures price of 94.00 means a futures 3-month LIBOR of 6%.

The minimum price fluctuation (tick) for this contract is 0.01 (or 0.0001 in terms of LIBOR). This means that the price value of a basis point for this contract is $25, found as follows. The simple interest on $1 million for 90 days is equal to:

$$\$1,000,000 \times (LIBOR \times 90/360)$$

If LIBOR changes by one basis point (0.0001), then:

$$\$1,000,000 \times (0.0001 \times 90/360) = \$25$$

The Eurodollar CD futures contract is a cash settlement contract. That is, the parties settle in cash for the value of a Eurodollar CD based on LIBOR at the settlement date. For a terminating contract, the settlement rate for LIBOR used to determine the settlement price is determined by a survey of top-tier banks conducted by the exchange. The exchange conducts the survey in the last 90 minutes of trading.

The settlement date of a contract month is the second London bank business day preceding the third Wednesday in that month. If that Wednesday is a bank holiday in Chicago or New York, the settlement date is one day later. On the settlement date, the contract stops trading at 3:30 p.m. London time.

The Eurodollar CD futures contract is one of the most heavily traded futures contract in the world. It is frequently used to trade the short end of the yield curve, and many hedgers have found this contract to be the best hedging vehicle for a wide range of situations.

Treasury Bill Futures

The Treasury bill futures contract, which is traded on the IMM, is based on a 13-week (3-month) Treasury bill with a face value of $1 million. More specifically, the seller of a Treasury bill futures contract agrees to deliver to the buyer at the settlement date a Treasury bill with 13 weeks remaining to maturity and a face value of $1 million. The Treasury bill delivered can be newly issued or seasoned. The futures price is the price at which the Treasury bill will be sold by the short and purchased by the long. For example, a Treasury bill futures contract that settles in 9 months requires that 9 months from now the short deliver to the long $1 million face value of a Treasury bill with 13 weeks remaining to maturity. The Treasury bill could be a newly issued 13-week Treasury bill or a Treasury bill that was issued one year prior to the settlement date and therefore at the settlement has only 13 weeks remaining to maturity.

Treasury bills are quoted in the cash market in terms of the annualized yield on a bank discount basis, where

$$Y_d = \frac{D}{F} \times \frac{360}{t}$$

where

Y_d = annualized yield on a bank discount basis (expressed as a decimal)

D = dollar discount, which is equal to the difference between the face value and the price of a bill maturing in t days

F = face value

t = number of days remaining to maturity.

The dollar discount (D) is found by:

$$D = Y_d \times F \times \frac{t}{360}$$

In contrast, the Treasury bill futures contract is quoted not directly in terms of yield, but instead on an index basis that is related to the yield on a bank discount basis as follows:

$$\text{Index price} = 100 - (Y_d \times 100)$$

For example, if Y_d is 8%, the index price is

$$100 - (0.08 \times 100) = 92$$

Given the price of the futures contract, the yield on a bank discount basis for the futures contract is determined as follows:

$$Y_d = \frac{100 - \text{Index price}}{100}$$

To see how this works, suppose that the index price for a Treasury bill futures contract is 92.52. The yield on a bank discount basis for this Treasury bill futures contract is:

$$Y_d = \frac{100 - 92.52}{100} = 0.0748 \text{ or } 7.48\%$$

The invoice price that the buyer of $1 million face value of 13-week Treasury bills must pay at settlement is found by first computing the dollar discount, as follows:

$$D = Y_d \times \$1,000,000 \times \frac{t}{360}$$

where t is either 90 or 91 days.

Typically, the number of days to maturity of a 13-week Treasury bill is 91 days. The invoice price is then:

$$\text{Invoice price} = \$1,000,000 - D$$

For example, for the Treasury bill futures contract with an index price of 92.52 (and a yield on a bank discount basis of 7.48%), the dollar discount for the 13-week Treasury bill to be delivered with 91 days to maturity is:

$$D = 0.0748 \times \$1,000,000 \times \frac{91}{360} = \$18,907.78$$

The invoice price is:

Invoice price = $1,000,000 - $18,907.78 = $981,092.22

The minimum index price fluctuation or "tick" for this futures contract is 0.01. A change of 0.01 for the minimum index price translates into a change in the yield on a bank discount basis of 1 basis point (0.0001). A 1 basis point change results in a change in the invoice price as follows:

$$0.0001 \times \$1,000,000 \times \frac{t}{360}$$

For a 13-week Treasury bill with 91 days to maturity, the change in the dollar discount is:

$$0.0001 \times \$1,000,000 \times \frac{91}{360} = \$25.28$$

For a 13-week Treasury bill with 90 days to maturity, the change in the dollar discount would be $25. Despite the fact that a 13-week Treasury bill typically has 91 days to maturity, market participants commonly refer to the value of a basis point for this futures contract as $25.

Treasury Bond Futures

The Treasury bond futures contract is traded on the Chicago Board of Trade (CBT). The underlying instrument for a Treasury bond futures contract is $100,000 par value of a hypothetical 20-year 8% coupon bond. The futures price is quoted in terms of par being 100. Quotes are in 32nds of 1%. Thus a quote for a Treasury bond futures contract of 97-16 means 97 and $^{16}/_{32}$, or 97.50. So, if a buyer and seller agree on a futures price of 97-16, this means that the buyer agrees to accept delivery of the hypothetical underlying Treasury bond and pay 97.50% of par value and the seller agrees to accept 97.50% of par value. Since the par value is $100,000, the futures price that the buyer and seller agree to pay for this hypothetical Treasury bond is $97,500.

The minimum price fluctuation for the Treasury bond futures contract is a 32nd of 1%. The dollar value of a 32nd for a $100,000 par value (the par value for the underlying Treasury bond) is $31.25. Thus, the minimum price fluctuation is $31.25 for this contract.

We have been referring to the underlying as a hypothetical Treasury bond. The seller of a Treasury bond futures who decides to make delivery rather than liquidate his position by buying back the contract prior to the settlement date must deliver some Treasury bond. But what Treasury bond? The CBT allows the seller to deliver one of several Treasury bonds that the CBT declares acceptable for delivery. The specific bonds that the seller may deliver are published by the CBT prior to the initial trading of a futures contract with a specific settlement date. Exhibit 2 shows the Treasury issues that the seller can select from to deliver to the buyer for the September 1994 contract. The CBT makes its determination of the Treasury issues that are acceptable for delivery from all outstanding Treasury issues that meet the following criteria: an issue must have at least 15 years to maturity from the date of delivery if not callable; in the case of callable bonds, the issue must not be callable for at least 15 years from the first day of the delivery month.

The delivery process for the Treasury bond futures contract makes the contract interesting. At the settlement date, the seller of a futures contract (the short) is required to deliver the buyer (the long) $100,000 par value of an 8% 20-year Treasury bond. Since no such bond exists, the seller must choose from one of the acceptable deliverable Treasury bonds that the CBT exchange has specified. Suppose the seller is entitled to deliver $100,000 of a 6% 20-year Treasury bond to settle the futures contract. The value of this bond, of course, is less than the value of an 8% 20-year bond. If the seller delivers the 6% 20-year, this would be unfair to the buyer of the futures contract who contracted to receive $100,000 of an 8% 20-year Treasury bond. Alternatively, suppose the seller delivers $100,000 of a 10% 20-year Treasury bond. The value of a 10% 20-year Treasury bond is greater than that of an 8% 20-year bond, so this would be a disadvantage to the seller.

How can this problem be resolved? To make delivery equitable to both parties, the CBT introduced *conversion factors* for determining the invoice price of each acceptable deliverable Treasury issue against the Treasury bond futures contract. The conversion factor is determined by the CBT before a contract with a specific settlement date begins trading. Exhibit 2 shows for each of the acceptable Treasury issues the corresponding conversion factor.[1] The conversion factor is constant throughout the trading period of the futures contract.

The product of the settlement price and the conversion factor for a deliverable issue is called the *converted price*. The amount that the buyer must pay the seller when a Treasury bond is delivered is called the *invoice price*. The invoice price is the settlement futures price plus accrued interest. However, as just noted, the seller can deliver one of several acceptable Treasury issues. To make delivery fair to both parties, the invoice price must be adjusted based on the actual Treasury issue delivered. It is the conversion factors that are used to adjust the invoice price. The invoice price is:

$$\text{Invoice price} = \text{Contract size} \times \text{Futures contract settlement price}$$
$$\times \text{Conversion factor} + \text{Accrued interest}$$

Suppose the Treasury bond futures contract settles at 94-08 and that the short elects to deliver a Treasury issue with a conversion factor of 1.20. The futures contract settlement price of 94-08 means 94.25% of par value. As the contract size is $100,000, the invoice price the buyer pays the seller is:

$$\$100,000 \times 0.9425 \times 1.20 + \text{Accrued interest}$$
$$= \$113,100 + \text{Accrued Interest}$$

---

[1] The conversion factor is based on the price that a deliverable bond would sell for at the beginning of the delivery month if it were to yield 8%.

Exhibit 2: Treasury Issues Acceptable for Delivery to Satisfy the U.S. Treasury Bond Futures Contract for Settlement in September 1994 and Their Conversion Factor

Issue:		Conversion
Coupon	Maturity	Factor
7¼	05/15/16	0.923600
7½	11/15/16	0.948600
8¾	05/15/17	1.077700
8⅞	08/15/17	1.090800
9⅞	11/15/15	1.189200
8⅛	08/15/19	1.013200
8⅞	02/15/92	1.092800
9⅛	05/15/18	1.118400
8½	02/15/20	1.053700
9¼	02/15/16	1.126500
8¾	05/15/20	1.081100
10⅝	08/15/15	1.263400
8⅛	08/15/21	1.013500
11¼	02/15/15	1.323000
8	11/15/21	1.000000
7¼	08/15/22	0.916700
7⅝	11/15/22	0.958300
11¾	11/15/14	1.324200
7⅛	02/15/23	0.902400
9	11/15/18	1.106000
6¼	08/15/23	0.804000
8¾	08/15/20	1.081100
7⅞	02/15/21	0.986200
8⅛	05/15/21	1.013700

In selecting the issue to be delivered, the short will select from all the deliverable issues the one that will give the largest rate of return from a *cash and carry trade*. A cash and carry trade is one in which a cash bond that is acceptable for delivery is purchased and simultaneously the Treasury bond futures contract is sold. The bond purchased can be delivered to satisfy the short futures position. Thus, by buying the Treasury issue that is acceptable for delivery and selling the futures, an investor has effectively sold the bond at the delivery price (i.e., converted price).

A rate of return can be calculated for this trade. The rate of return is determined by:

1. the price plus accrued interest of the Treasury bond that could be purchased

2. the converted price plus the accrued interest that will be received upon delivery of that Treasury bond to satisfy the short futures position
3. the coupon payments that will be received between today and the delivery date
4. the reinvestment income that will be realized on the coupon payments between the time received and the delivery date.

The first three elements are known. The last element will depend on the reinvestment rate that can be earned. While the reinvestment rate is unknown, typically this is a small part of the rate of return and not much is lost by assuming that this rate can be predicted with certainty.

The general formula for the annualized rate of return is as follows:

$$\text{Annual return} = \frac{\text{Dollar return}}{\text{Dollar investment}} \times \frac{360}{\text{Days}}$$

where

Dollar return	=	converted price plus accrued interest received − purchase price plus accrued interest + coupon income + reinvestment income
Dollar investment	=	dollar amount invested in the trade
Days	=	number of days from the settlement date on the bond until the futures delivery date

The dollar amount invested in the trade is not simply the purchase price of the Treasury issue plus accrued interest that had to be paid at the inception of the cash and carry trade. The reason is that part of the investment is recovered by the coupon income plus reinvestment income. In practice, the dollar investment is calculated as follows:

$$\text{Dollar investment} = \text{Days}_1 \text{ (Purchase price plus accrued interest)} - \text{Days}_2 \text{ (Coupon payment received + reinvestment income)}$$

where

Days_1	=	number of days between settlement and actual delivery
Days_2	=	number of days between interim coupon and bond delivery

The annual rate of return calculated for an acceptable Treasury issue is called the *implied repo rate*. Market participants will seek to maximize the implied repo rate; that is, they will use the acceptable Treasury issue that gives the largest rate of return in the cash and carry trade. The issue that satisfied this criterion is referred to as the *cheapest-to-deliver issue*. It plays a key role in the pricing of this futures contract. This is depicted in Exhibit 3.

Exhibit 3: Determination of Cheapest-to-Deliver Issue Based on the Implied Repo Rate

Implied repo rate: Rate of return by buying an acceptable Treasury issue, shorting the Treasury bond futures, and delivering the issue at the settlement date.

Buy this issue:	Deliver this issue at futures price:	Calculate return (implied repo rate):
Acceptable Treasury issue #1	Deliver issue #1	Implied repo rate #1
Acceptable Treasury issue #2	Deliver issue #2	Implied repo rate #2
Acceptable Treasury issue #3	Deliver issue #3	Implied repo rate #3
. . .	. . .	. . .
Acceptable Treasury issue #N	Deliver issue #N	Implied repo rate #N

Cheapest-to-deliver issue is the issue that produces the maximum implied repo rate.

In addition to the choice of which acceptable Treasury issue to deliver — sometimes referred to as the *quality option* or *swap option* — the short position has three more options granted under CBT delivery guidelines. The first is related to the quality option. If a Treasury bond is auctioned prior to the settlement date, then the short can select this new issue. This option is referred to as the *new auction option*. The second option grants the short the right to decide when in the delivery month delivery actually will take place. This is called the *timing option*. The third option is the right of the short to give notice of intent to deliver up to 8:00 p.m. Chicago time after the closing of the exchange (3:15 p.m. Chicago time) on the date when the futures settlement price has been fixed. This option is referred to as the *wild card option*. The quality option, the new auction option, the timing option, and the wild card option (in sum referred to as the *delivery options*), mean that the long can never be sure which Treasury bond will be delivered or when it will be delivered. The delivery options are summarized in Exhibit 4.

Exhibit 4: Delivery Options Granted to the Short (Seller) of a CBT Treasury Bond Futures Contract

Delivery option	Description
Quality or swap option	Choice of which acceptable Treasury issue to deliver
New auction option	Choice of a newly issued Treasury bond to deliver
Timing option	Choice of when in delivery month to deliver
Wild card option	Choice to deliver after the day's settlement price for the futures contract is determined

For a short who wants to deliver, the delivery procedure involves three days. The first day is the *position day*. On this day, the short notifies the CBT that it intends to deliver. The short has until 8 p.m. central standard time to do so. The second day is the *notice day*. On this day, the short specifies which particular issue will be delivered. The short has until 2:00 p.m. central standard time to make this declaration. (On the last possible notice day in the delivery month, the short has until 3:00 p.m.) The CBT then selects the long to whom delivery will be made. This is the longest outstanding long position. The long is then notified by 4:00 p.m. that delivery will be made. The third day is the *delivery day*. By 10 a.m. on this day the short must have in its account the bond issue that it specified on the notice day and by 1:00 p.m. must deliver that bond to the long that was assigned by the CBT to accept delivery. The long pays the short the invoice price upon receipt of the bond.

Treasury Note Futures

There are three Treasury note futures contracts: 10-year, 5-year, and 2-year. All three contracts are modeled after the Treasury bond futures contract and are traded on the CBT. The underlying instrument for the 10-year Treasury note futures contract is $100,000 par value of a hypothetical 10-year 8% Treasury note. There are several acceptable Treasury issues that may be delivered by the short. An issue is acceptable if the maturity is not less than 6.5 years and not greater than 10 years from the first day of the delivery month. The delivery options granted to the short position and the minimum price fluctuation are the same as for the Treasury bond futures contract.

For the 5-year Treasury note futures contract, the underlying is $100,000 par value of a U.S. Treasury note that satisfies the following conditions: (1) an original maturity of not more than five years and three months, (2) a remaining maturity no greater then five years and three months, and (3) a remaining maturity not less than four years and three months. The minimum price fluctuation for this contract is a 64th of 1%. The dollar value of a 64th for a $100,000 par value is $15.625 and is therefore the minimum price fluctuation.

The underlying for the 2-year Treasury note futures contract is $200,000 par value of a U.S. Treasury note with a remaining maturity of not more than two years and not less than one year and nine months. Moreover, the original maturity of the note delivered to satisfy the 2-year futures cannot be more than five years and two months. The minimum price fluctuation for this contract is a 128th of a 1%. The dollar value of a 128th for a $200,000 par value is $15.625 and is therefore the minimum price fluctuation.

Bond Buyer's Municipal Bond Index Futures Contract

The municipal bond index futures contract is based on the value of the Bond Buyer Index (BBI) which consists of 40 municipal bonds. Unlike the Treasury bond futures contract, where the underlying to be delivered is $100,000 of a hypothetical 8% 20-year Treasury bond, the municipal bond index futures contract does not specify a par amount of the underlying index to be delivered. Instead, the dollar value of a futures contract is equal to the product of the futures price and $1,000. The settlement price on the last day of trading is equal to the product of the Bond Buyer Index value and $1,000. Since delivery on all 40 bonds in the index would be difficult, the contract is a cash settlement contract. This is unlike the Treasury bond futures contract which requires physical delivery of an acceptable Treasury bond issue.

The contract is quoted in 32nds. So a futures price of 102-21 means 102.65625. If the futures price is 102-21, then the dollar value of the futures contract is $102,656.25 ($1,000 × 102.65625).

The minimum price change, or tick, is a 32nd, which therefore has a dollar value of $31.25 ($\frac{1}{32}$ × $1,000). As with the Treasury bond futures contract, the settlement months are March, June, September, and December and delivery can take place during the month. The municipal bond index futures contract is no where as liquid as the Treasury bond futures contract.

In order to understand this futures contract, it is necessary to understand the nuances of how the BBI is constructed. The BBI consists of 40 actively traded general obligation and revenue bonds. To be included in the BBI, the following criteria must be satisfied: (1) the rating of the issue must have a Moody's rating of A or higher and/or an S&P rating of A− or higher, and (2) the size of the term portion of the issue must be at least $50 million ($75 million for housing issues). No more than two bonds of the same issuer may be included in the BBI. In addition, for an issue to be considered, it must meet the following three conditions: (1) have at least 19 years remaining to maturity, (2) have a first call date between 7 and 16 years, and (3) have at least one call at par prior to redemption.

The Bond Buyer serves as the index manager for the contract and prices each issue in the index based on prices received daily from at least four of six dealer-to-dealer brokers. After dropping the highest price and the lowest price obtained for each issue, the average of the remaining prices is computed. This price is then used to calculate the BBI as follows. First, the price for an issue is multiplied by a conversion factor designed to equate the bond to an 8% issue, just as in the case of the Treasury bond futures contract. This gives a converted price for each bond in the BBI. The converted prices for the bonds in the index are then summed and divided by 40, giving an average converted price for the BBI. That is,

Average converted price for BBI

$$= \frac{(\text{Converted price of issue 1} + ... + \text{Converted price of issue 40})}{40}$$

Finally, because the BBI is revised bimonthly when newer issues are added and older issues, or issues that no longer meet the criteria for inclusion in the index, are dropped, a smoothing coefficient is calculated on the index revision date so that the value of the BBI will not change due merely to the change in its composition. The average converted price for the BBI is multiplied by this coefficient to get the value of the BBI for a particular date. That is,

BBI = Average converted price × Coefficient

The coefficient is calculated is as follows:

$$\text{Coefficient} = \frac{\text{BBI value before issues are substituted}}{\text{BBI value with new issues before applying coefficient}}$$

For example, if the BBI value is 89 and several issues are substituted that would increase the BBI value to 100 before applying the coefficient adjustment mechanism, then the new coefficient would be:

$$\text{Coefficient} = \frac{89}{100} = 0.890$$

The nuances of this contract are important because it makes the use of the contract to control risk difficult.

FORWARD RATE AGREEMENTS

A *forward rate agreement* (FRA) is the over-the-counter equivalent of the exchange-traded futures contracts on short-term rates. Typically, the short-term rate is LIBOR.

The elements of an FRA are the contract rate, reference rate, settlement rate, notional amount, and settlement date. The parties to an FRA agree to buy and sell funds on the settlement date. The *contract rate* is the rate specified in the FRA at which the buyer of the FRA agrees to pay for funds and the seller of the FRA agrees to receive for investing funds. The reference rate is the interest rate used. For example, the *reference rate* could be 3-month LIBOR or 6-month LIBOR. The benchmark from which the interest payments are to be calculated is specified in the FRA and is called the *notional amount* (or notional principal amount). This amount is not exchanged between the two parties. The *settlement rate* is the value of the reference rate at the FRA's settlement date. The source for determining the settlement rate is specified in the FRA.

The buyer of the FRA is agreeing to pay the contract rate, or equivalently, to buy funds on the settlement date at the contract rate; the seller of the FRA is agreeing to receive the contract rate, or equivalently to sell funds on the settlement date at the contract rate. So, for example, if the FRA has a contract rate of 5% for 3-month LIBOR (the reference rate) and the notional amount is for $10 million, the buyer is agreeing to pay 5% to buy or borrow $10 million at the settlement date and the seller is agreeing to receive 5% to sell or lend $10 million at the settlement date.

If at the settlement date the settlement rate is greater than the contract rate, the FRA buyer benefits because the buyer can borrow funds at a below market rate. If the settlement rate is less than the contract rate, this benefits the seller who can lend funds at an above market rate. If the settlement rate is the same as the contract rate, neither party benefits. This is summarized below:

FRA buyer benefits if settlement rate   > contract rate
FRA seller benefits if contract rate   > settlement rate
Neither party benefits if settlement rate = contract rate

As with the Eurodollar CD futures contract, FRAs are cash settlement contracts. At the settlement date, the party that benefits based on the contract rate and settlement rate, must be compensated by the other. Assuming the settlement rate is not equal to the contract rate then:

buyer receives compensation if settlement rate   > contract rate
seller receives compensation if contract rate   > settlement rate

To determine the amount that one party must compensate the other, the following is first calculated assuming a 360 day count convention:

If settlement rate > contract rate:

Interest differential = (Settlement rate − Contract rate) ×
    (Days in contract period/360) × Notional amount

If contract rate > settlement rate:

Interest differential = (Contract rate − Settlement rate)
    × (Days in contract period/360) × Notional amount

The amount that must be exchanged at the settlement is not the interest differential. Instead, the present value of the interest differential is exchanged. The discount rate used to calculate the present value of the interest differential is the settlement rate. Thus, the compensation is determined as follows:

$$\text{Compensation} = \frac{\text{Interest differential}}{[1 + \text{Settlement rate} \times (\text{Days to contract period}/360)]}$$

Exhibit 5: Effect of Rate Changes on Parties to a FRA and Futures Contract

Party	Interest rates			
	Decrease		Increase	
	FRA	Futures	FRA	Futures
Buyer	Loses	Gains	Gains	Loses
Seller	Gains	Loses	Loses	Gains

To illustrate, assume the following terms for an FRA: reference rate is 3-month LIBOR, the contract rate is 5%, the notional amount is for $10 million, and the number of days to settlement is 91 days. Suppose the settlement rate is 5.5%. This means that the buyer benefits since the buyer can borrow at 5% (the contract rate) when the market rate (the settlement rate) is 5.5%. The interest differential is:

$$\text{Interest differential} = (0.055 - 0.05) \times (91/360) \times \$100,000,000$$
$$= \$12,638.89$$

The compensation or payment that the seller must make to the buyer is:

$$\text{Compensation} = \frac{\$12,638.89}{[1 + 0.055 \times (91/360)]}$$

$$= \frac{\$12,638.89}{1.0139027} = \$12,465.58$$

It is important to note the difference of who benefits when interest rates move in an FRA and a futures contract. The buyer of an FRA benefits if the reference rate increases and the seller benefits if the reference rate decreases. In a futures contract, the buyer benefits from a falling rate while the seller benefits from a rising rate. This is summarized in Exhibit 5. This is because the underlying for each of the two contracts is different. In the case of an FRA, the underlying is a rate. The buyer gains if the rate increases and loses if the rate decreases. The opposite occurs for the seller of an FRA. In contrast, in a futures contract the underlying is a fixed-income instrument. The buyer gains if the fixed-income instrument increases in value. This occurs when rates decline. The buyer loses when the fixed-income instrument decreases in value. This occurs when interest rates increase. The opposite occurs for the seller of a futures contract.

The liquid and easily accessible sector of the FRA market is for 3-month and 6-month LIBOR. Rates are widely available for settlement starting one month forward, and settling once every month thereafter out to about six months forward. Thus, for example, on any given day forward rates are available for both 3-month and 6-month LIBOR one month forward, covering, respectively, the interest period starting in one month and ending in four months and the interest period staring in one month and ending in seven months. These contracts are referred to as 1×4 and 1×7 contracts. On the same day there will be FRAs on 3-month and 6-month LIBOR for settlement two months forward. These are the 2×5 and 2×8 contracts. Similarly, settlements occur three months, four months, five months, and six months forward for both 3-month LIBOR and 6-month LIBOR. These contracts are also denoted by the beginning and ending of the interest period that they cover. Many banks are willing to quote a much wider variety of structures than the standard structures explained above.

On each subsequent day, contracts with the same type of structures are offered again (i.e., contracts with one month, two months, etc., to settlement date). Thus, although on any given day a relatively limited number of structures are widely offered, new contracts with new settlement dates are offered at the beginning of each day. This is quite different from the futures market where the same contracts with the same delivery dates trade day after day.

THEORETICAL FUTURES/FORWARD PRICE

To understand how futures contracts are valued, consider the following example. Suppose that a 12% 20-year bond is selling at par. Also suppose that this bond is the deliverable for a futures contract that settles in 3 months. If the current 3-month interest rate at which funds can be loaned or borrowed is 8% per year, what should be the price of this futures contract?

Suppose the price of the futures contract is 107. Consider the following strategy:

> Sell the futures contract at 107.
> Purchase the bond for 100.
> Borrow 100 for 3 months at 8% per year.

The borrowed funds are used to purchase the bond, resulting in no initial cash outlay for this strategy. Three months from now, the bond must be delivered to settle the futures contract and the loan must be repaid. These trades will produce the following cash flows:

From settlement of the futures contract:

$$
\begin{aligned}
\text{Flat price of bond} &= 107 \\
\text{Accrued interest (12\% for 3 months)} &= \underline{3} \\
\text{Total proceeds} &= 110
\end{aligned}
$$

From the loan:

$$
\begin{aligned}
\text{Repayment of principal of loan} &= 100 \\
\text{Interest on loan (8\% for 3 months)} &= \underline{2} \\
\text{Total outlay} &= 102
\end{aligned}
$$

$$
\text{Profit} = \text{Total proceeds} - \text{Total outlay} = 8
$$

This strategy will guarantee a profit of 8. Moreover, the profit is generated with no initial outlay because the funds used to purchase the bond are borrowed. The profit will be realized *regardless of the futures price at the settlement date*. Obviously, in a well-functioning market, arbitrageurs would buy the bond and sell the futures, forcing the futures price down and bidding up the bond price so as to eliminate this profit.

In contrast, suppose that the futures price is 92 instead of 107. Consider the following strategy:

> Buy the futures contract at 92.
> Sell (short) the bond for 100.
> Invest (lend) 100 for 3 months at 8% per year.

Once again, there is no initial cash outlay. Three months from now a bond will be purchased to settle the long position in the futures contract. That bond will then be used to cover the short position (i.e. to cover the short sale in the cash market). The outcome in 3 months would be as follows:

From settlement of the futures contract:

$$
\begin{array}{rcr}
\text{Flat price of bond} &=& 92 \\
\text{Accrued interest (12\% for 3 months)} &=& 3 \\ \hline
\text{Total outlay} &=& 95
\end{array}
$$

From the loan:

$$
\begin{array}{rcr}
\text{Principal received from maturing investment} &=& 100 \\
\text{Interest earned (8\% for 3 months)} &=& 2 \\ \hline
\text{Total proceeds} &=& 102
\end{array}
$$

$$\text{Profit = Total proceeds} - \text{Total outlay} \ = \ 7$$

The 7 profit is a pure arbitrage profit. It requires no initial cash outlay and will be realized regardless of the futures price at the settlement date.

However, there is a futures price that will eliminate the arbitrage profit. There will be no arbitrage if the futures price is 99. Let's look at what would happen if the two previous strategies are followed and the futures price is 99. First, consider the following strategy:

> Sell the futures contract at 99.
> Purchase the bond for 100.
> Borrow 100 for 3 months at 8% per year.

In 3 months, the outcome would be as follows:

From settlement of the futures contract:

$$
\begin{array}{rcr}
\text{Flat price of bond} &=& 99 \\
\text{Accrued interest (12\% for 3 months)} &=& 3 \\ \hline
\text{Total proceeds} &=& 102
\end{array}
$$

From the loan:

Repayment of principal of loan	=	100
Interest on loan (8% for 3 months)	=	2
Total outlay	=	102

Profit = Total proceeds − Total outlay =   0

There is no arbitrage profit in this case.

Next consider the following strategy:

Buy the futures contract at 99.
Sell (short) the bond for 100.
Invest (lend) 100 for 3 months at 8% per year.

The outcome in 3 months would be as follows:

From settlement of the futures contract:

Flat price of bond	=	99
Accrued interest (12% for 3 months)	=	3
Total outlay	=	102

From the loan:

Principal received from maturing investment	=	100
Interest earned (8% for 3 months)	=	2
Total proceeds	=	102

Total proceeds − Total outlay = Profit =   0

Thus neither strategy results in a profit. Hence the futures price of 99 is the theoretical price, because any higher or lower futures price will permit arbitrage profits.

Theoretical Futures Price Based on Arbitrage Model
Considering the arbitrage arguments just presented, the theoretical futures price can be determined on the basis of the following information:

1. The price of the bond in the cash market.
2. The coupon rate on the bond. In our example, the coupon rate is 12% per year.
3. The interest rate for borrowing and lending until the settlement date. The borrowing and lending rate is referred to as the financing rate. In our example, the financing rate is 8% per year.

We will let

r = annualized financing rate (%)

c = annualized current yield, or annual coupon rate divided by the cash market price (%)

P = cash market price

F = futures price

t = time, in years, to the futures delivery date

and then consider the following strategy that is initiated on a coupon date:

Sell the futures contract at F.

Purchase the bond for P.

Borrow P until the settlement date at r.

The outcome at the settlement date is

From settlement of the futures contract:

$$
\begin{array}{rcl}
\text{Flat price of bond} &=& F \\
\text{Accrued interest} &=& ctP \\
\hline
\text{Total proceeds} &=& F + ctP
\end{array}
$$

From the loan:

$$
\begin{array}{rcl}
\text{Repayment of principal of loan} &=& P \\
\text{Interest on loan} &=& rtP \\
\hline
\text{Total outlay} &=& P + rtP
\end{array}
$$

The profit will equal:

Profit = Total proceeds − Total outlay

$$\text{Profit} = F + ctP - (P + rtP)$$

In equilibrium the theoretical futures price occurs where the profit from this trade is zero. Thus to have equilibrium, the following must hold:

$$0 = F + ctP - (P + rtP)$$

Solving for the theoretical futures price, we have

$$F = P + Pt(r - c) \tag{1}$$

Alternatively, consider the following strategy:

Buy the futures contract at F.

Sell (short) the bond for P.

Invest (lend) P at r until the settlement date.

The outcome at the settlement date would be

> From settlement of the futures contract:

Flat price of bond	=	F
Accrued interest	=	ctP
Total outlay	=	F + ctP

> From the loan:

Proceeds received from maturing of investment	=	P
Interest earned	=	rtP
Total proceeds	=	P + rtP

The profit will equal:

Profit = Total proceeds – Total outlay

Profit = P + rtP – (F + ctP)

Setting the profit equal to zero so that there will be no arbitrage profit and solving for the futures price, we obtain the same equation for the futures price as equation (1).

Let's apply equation (1) to our previous example in which

$$r = 0.08$$
$$c = 0.12$$
$$P = 100$$
$$t = 0.25$$

Then the theoretical futures price is

$$F = 100 + 100 \times 0.25(0.08 - 0.12) = 100 - 1 = 99$$

The theoretical price may be at a premium to the cash market price (higher than the cash market price) or at a discount from the cash market price (lower than the cash market price), depending on (r – c). The term r – c is called the *net financing cost* because it adjusts the financing rate for the coupon interest earned. The net financing cost is more commonly called the *cost of carry*, or simply *carry*. *Positive carry* means that the current yield earned is greater than the financing cost; *negative carry* means that the financing cost exceeds the current yield. The relationships can be expressed as follows:

Carry	Theoretical Futures Price
Positive (c<r)	Will sell at a discount to cash price (F<P)
Negative (c>r)	Will sell at a premium to cash price (F>P)
Zero (c=r)	Will be equal to cash price (F=P)

In the case of interest rate futures, carry (the relationship between the short-term financing rate and the current yield on the bond) depends on the shape of the yield curve. When the yield curve is upward sloping, the short-term financing rate will be less than the current yield on the bond, resulting in positive carry. The theoretical futures price will then sell at a discount to the cash price for the bond. The opposite will hold true when the yield curve is inverted.

Adjustments to the Theoretical Pricing Model

Several assumptions were made to derive the theoretical futures price using the arbitrage argument. First, no interim cash flows due to variation margin or coupon interest payments were assumed in the model. However, we know that interim cash flows can occur for both of these reasons. Consider first variation margin. If interest rates rise, the short position in futures will receive margin as the futures price decreases; the margin can then be reinvested at a higher interest rate. If interest rates fall, there will be variation margin that must be financed by the short position; however, because interest rates have declined, financing will be possible at a lower cost. The same is true for a forward contract that is marked to market. Thus, whichever way rates move, those who are short futures or forwards that are marked to market gain relative to those who are short forwards that are not marked to market. Conversely, those who are long futures or forwards that are not marked to market lose relative to those who are long forwards that are marked to market. These facts account for the difference between futures prices and forward prices for non-marked-to-market contracts.

Incorporating interim coupon payments into the pricing model is not difficult. However, the value of the coupon payments at the settlement date will depend on the interest rate at which they can be reinvested. The shorter the maturity of the contract and the lower the coupon rate, the less important the reinvestment income is in determining the theoretical futures price.

The second assumption in deriving the theoretical futures price is that the borrowing and lending rates are equal. Typically, however, the borrowing rate is higher than the lending rate. As a result, there is not one theoretical futures price but rather there are lower and upper boundaries for the theoretical futures price.

The third assumption made to derive equation (1) is that only one instrument is deliverable. But as explained earlier, the futures contract on Treasury bonds and Treasury notes are designed to allow the short the choice of delivering one of a number of deliverable issues (the quality or swap option). Because there may be more than one deliverable, market participants track the price of each deliverable bond and determine which bond is the cheapest to deliver. The theoretical futures price will then trade in relation to the cheapest-to-deliver issue.

There is the risk that while an issue may be the cheapest to deliver at the time a position in the futures contract is taken, it may not be the cheapest to deliver after that time. A change in the cheapest to deliver can dramatically alter the futures price. Because the swap option is an option granted by the long to the short, the long will want to pay less for the futures contract than indicated by equation (1). Therefore, as a result of the quality option, the theoretical futures price as given by equation (1) must be adjusted as follows:

$$F = P + Pt(r - c) - \text{Value of quality option} \qquad (2)$$

Market participants have employed theoretical models in attempting to estimate the fair value of the quality option.

Finally, in deriving equation (1) a known delivery date is assumed. For Treasury bond and note futures contracts, the short has a timing and wild card option, so the long does not know when the securities will be delivered. The effect of the timing and wild card options on the theoretical futures price is the same as with the quality option. These delivery options result in a theoretical futures price that is lower than the one suggested in equation (1), as shown below:

$$F = P + Pt(r - c) - \text{Value of quality option} - \text{Value of new auction option}$$

$$- \text{Value of timing option} - \text{Value of wild card option} \qquad (3)$$

or alternatively,

$$F = P + Pt(r - c) - \text{Delivery options} \qquad (4)$$

Market participants attempt to value the delivery options in order to apply equation (4).

KEY POINTS

1. *A futures contract is an agreement between a buyer (seller) and an established exchange or its clearinghouse in which the buyer (seller) agrees to take (make) delivery of something at a specified price at the end of a designated period of time.*

2. *The parties to a futures contract are required to satisfy margin requirements.*

3. *A forward contract is an agreement for the future delivery of something at a specified price at the end of a designated period of time but differs from a futures contract in that it is non-standardized and traded in the over-the-counter market.*

4. *Parties to over-the-counter interest rate contracts are exposed to counterparty risk which is the risk that the counterparty will not satisfy its contractual obligations.*

5. *An investor who takes a long futures position realizes a gain when the futures price increases; an investor who takes a short futures position realizes a loss when the futures price decreases.*

6. *The Eurodollar CD futures contract is a cash settlement contract whose underlying is a 3-month Eurodollar CD and is one of the most heavily traded futures contract in the world.*

7. *For the Treasury bond futures contract the underlying instrument is $100,000 par value of a hypothetical 20-year 8% Treasury coupon bond.*

8. *Conversion factors are used to adjust the invoice price of a Treasury bond futures contract to make delivery equitable to both parties.*

9. *The short in a Treasury bond futures contract has several delivery options: quality option (or swap option), new auction option, timing option, and wild card option.*

10. *The cheapest-to-deliver issue is the acceptable Treasury bond issue that has the largest implied repo rate.*

11. *The 2-year, 5-year, and 10-year Treasury note futures contracts are modeled after the Treasury bond futures contract.*

12. *The municipal bond index futures contract is based on the value of the Bond Buyer Index.*

13. *A forward rate agreement is the over-the-counter equivalent of the exchange-traded futures contract on a short-term rate, typically LIBOR, and is a cash settlement contract.*

14. *The elements of an FRA are the contract rate, reference rate, settlement rate, notional amount, and settlement date.*

15. *The buyer of an FRA is agreeing to pay the contract rate and the seller of the FRA is agreeing to receive the contract rate.*

16. *The amount that must be exchanged at the settlement date is the present value of the interest differential.*

17. *In contrast to an interest rate futures contract, the buyer of an FRA benefits if the reference rate increases and the seller benefits if the reference rate decreases.*

18. *The theoretical price of a futures contract is equal to the cash or spot price plus the cost of carry.*

19. *The cost of carry is equal to the cost of financing the position less the cash yield on the underlying security.*

20. *The shape of the yield curve affects the cost of carry.*

21. *The standard arbitrage model must be modified to take into consideration the nuances of particular futures contracts.*

22. *For a Treasury bond futures contracts, the delivery options granted to the seller reduce the theoretical futures price below the theoretical futures price suggested by the standard arbitrage model.*

Chapter 9

Interest Rate Swaps

In this chapter we will look at our second derivative instrument, an interest rate swap. In an *interest rate swap*, two parties agree to exchange periodic interest payments. The dollar amount of the interest payments exchanged is based on some predetermined dollar principal, which is called the *notional principal amount*. The dollar amount each counterparty pays to the other is the agreed-upon periodic interest rate times the notional principal amount. The only dollars that are exchanged between the parties are the net interest payments, not the notional principal amount.

The objectives of this chapter are to:

1. *explain what a generic interest rate swap is;*

2. *describe the different types of transactions in the secondary market for swaps;*

3. *explain how a swap should be interpreted;*

4. *explain the risk and return relationship for an interest rate swap;*

5. *show the relationship between an interest rate swap, a futures contract, and a forward rate agreement;*

6. *explain how the dollar duration of a swap is calculated;*

7. *review the jargon used in the market to describe the position of the parties to an interest rate swap;*

8. *describe the several types of non-generic swaps;*

9. *demonstrate how the swap rate is determined; and,*

10. *show how the value of a swap is determined.*

GENERIC INTEREST RATE SWAP

In a generic or plain vanilla interest rate swap, one party agrees to pay the other party fixed interest payments at designated dates for the life of the contract. This party is referred to as the *fixed-rate payer*. The other party agrees to make interest rate payments that float based on some reference rate. This party is referred to as the *floating-rate payer*.

The reference rates that have been used for the floating rate in an interest rate swap are those on various money market instruments: Treasury bills, the London interbank offered rate (LIBOR), commercial paper, bankers acceptances, certificates of deposit, the federal funds rate, and the prime rate. The most common reference rate is LIBOR.

The date that the counterparties commit to the swap is called the *trade date*. The date that the swap begins accruing interest is called the *effective date*, while the date that the swap stops accruing interest is called the *maturity date*. The frequency with which the floating-rate is determined for the floating-rate payer is called the *reset frequency*.

To illustrate a generic interest rate swap, suppose that for the next five years party X agrees to pay party Y 10% per year, while party Y agrees to pay party X 6-month LIBOR (the reference rate). Party X is the fixed-rate payer, while party Y is the floating-rate payer. Assume that the notional principal amount is $50 million, and that payments are exchanged every six months for the next five years. This means that every six months, party X (the fixed-rate payer) will pay party Y $2.5 million (10% times $50 million divided by 2). The amount that party Y (the floating-rate payer) will pay party X will be 6-month LIBOR times $50 million divided by 2. If 6-month LIBOR is 7%, party Y will pay party X $1.75 million (7% times $50 million divided by 2). Note that we divide by two because one-half year's interest is being paid.

ENTERING INTO A SWAP AND COUNTERPARTY RISK

Interest rate swaps are over-the-counter instruments. This means that they are not traded on an exchange. An institutional investor wishing to enter into a swap transaction can do so through either a securities firm or a commercial bank that transacts in swaps.[1] These entities can do one of the following. First, they can arrange or broker a swap between two parties that want to enter into an interest rate swap. In this case, the securities firm or commercial bank is acting in a brokerage capacity.

---

[1] Don't get confused here about the role of commercial banks. A bank can use a swap in its asset/liability management, or a bank can engage in swap transactions with its clients to generate fee income. It is in the latter sense that we are discussing the role of a commercial bank in the swap market here.

The second way in which a securities firm or commercial bank can get an institutional investor into a swap position is by taking the other side of the swap. This means that the securities firm or commercial bank is a dealer rather than a broker in the transaction. Acting as a dealer, the securities firm or the commercial bank must hedge its swap position in the same way that it hedges its position in other securities that it holds. Also it means that the dealer (referred to as a swap dealer) is the counterparty to the transaction. Merrill Lynch, for example, is a swap dealer. If an institutional investor entered into a swap with Merrill Lynch, the institutional investor will look to Merrill Lynch to satisfy the obligations of the swap; similarly, Merrill Lynch looks to the institutional investor to fulfill its obligations as set forth in the swap. Today most swaps are transacted using a swap dealer.

The risk that each party takes on when it enters into a swap is that the other party will fail to fulfill its obligations as set forth in the swap agreement. That is, each party faces default risk. The default risk in a swap agreement is called *counterparty risk*. In fact, counterparty risk is more general than the default risk for only a swap agreement. In any agreement between two parties that must perform according to the terms of a contract, counterparty risk is the risk that the other party will default. With futures and exchange-traded options the counterparty risk is the risk that the clearing house established to guarantee performance of the contracts will default. Market participants view this risk as small. In contrast, counterparty risk in a swap can be significant.

Because of counterparty risk, not all securities firms and commercial banks can be swap dealers. Several securities firms have actually established subsidiaries that are separately capitalized so that they have a high credit rating which permits them to enter into swap transactions as a dealer.

Thus, it is imperative to keep in mind that any party who enters into a swap is subject to counterparty risk.

SECONDARY MARKET SWAP TRANSACTIONS

There are three general types of transactions in the secondary market for swaps. These include (1) a swap reversal, (2) a swap sale (or assignment), and (3) a swap buy-back (or close-out or cancellation).

In a *swap reversal*, the party that wants out of the transaction will arrange for a swap in which (1) the maturity on the new swap is equal to the time remaining for the original swap, (2) the reference rate is the same, and (3) the notional principal amount is the same. For example, suppose party X enters into a 5-year swap with a notional principal amount of $50 million in which it pays 10% and receives LIBOR, but that two years later X wants out of the swap. In a swap reversal, X would enter into a 3-year interest rate swap with a counterparty different from the original counterparty, let's say Z, in which the notional principal amount is $50 million, and X pays LIBOR and receives a fixed rate. The fixed rate that X receives from Z will depend on prevailing swap terms at the initiation of the 3-year swap.

While party X has effectively terminated the original swap in economic terms, there is a major drawback to this approach: party X is still liable to the original counterparty, Y, as well as to the new counterparty, Z. That is, party X now has two interest rate swaps on its books instead of one, and as a result it has increased its counterparty risk exposure.

The *swap sale* or *swap assignment* overcomes this drawback. In this secondary market transaction, the party that wishes to close out the original swap finds another party that is willing to accept its obligations under the swap. In our illustration, this means that X finds another party, say, A, that will agree to pay 10% to Y and receive LIBOR from Y for the next three years. A will have to be compensated to accept the position of X, or A will have to be willing to compensate X. The compensation depends on the value of the swap. If from X's perspective the swap has a positive value, that is the value A must pay to X. If, on the other hand, the value of the swap from X's perspective is negative, X must compensate A.

Once the transaction is completed, it is then A not X that is obligated to perform under the swap terms. In order to accomplish a swap sale, the original counterparty, Y in our example, must agree to the sale. A key factor in whether Y will agree is whether it is willing to accept the credit of A. For example, if A's credit rating is double-B while X's is double-A, Y would be unlikely to accept A as a counterparty.

A *swap buy-back* (or *close-out sale* or *cancellation*) involves the sale of the swap to the original counterparty. As in the case of a swap sale, one party might have to compensate the other, depending on how interest rates and swap spreads have changed since the inception of the swap.

RISK/RETURN CHARACTERISTICS OF AN INTEREST RATE SWAP

The value of an interest rate swap will fluctuate with market interest rates. To see how, let's consider our hypothetical swap. Suppose that interest rates change immediately after parties X and Y enter into the swap. First, consider what would happen if the market demanded that in any 5-year swap the fixed-rate payer must pay 11% in order to receive 6-month LIBOR. If party X (the fixed-rate payer) wants to sell its position to party A, then party A will benefit by having to pay only 10% (the original swap rate agreed upon) rather than 11% (the current swap rate) to receive 6-month LIBOR. Party X will want compensation for this benefit. Consequently, the value of party X's position has increased. Thus, if interest rates increase, the fixed-rate payer will realize a profit and the floating-rate payer will realize a loss.

Next, consider what would happen if interest rates decline to, say, 6%. Now a 5-year swap would require a new fixed-rate payer to pay 6% rather than 10% to receive 6-month LIBOR. If party X wants to sell its position to party B, the latter would demand compensation to take over the position. In other words, if interest rates decline, the fixed-rate payer will realize a loss, while the floating-rate payer will realize a profit.

Exhibit 1: Effect of Rate Changes on Interest Rate Swap Counterparties

Counterparty	Interest rates	
	decrease	increase
Floating-rate payer	Gains	Loses
Fixed-rate payer	Loses	Gains

The risk/return profile of the two positions when interest rates change is summarized in Exhibit 1.

INTERPRETING A SWAP POSITION

There are two ways that a swap position can be interpreted: (1) a package of forward/futures contracts, and (2) a package of cash flows from buying and selling cash market instruments.

Package of Forward Contracts

Contrast the positions of the counterparties in an interest rate swap summarized in Exhibit 1 to the positions of the long and short futures or a forward contract. (See Exhibit 1 of the previous chapter.) As emphasized in the previous chapter, we have to consider whether the underlying is an interest rate or a fixed-income instrument. Futures contracts have an underlying fixed-income instrument. A forward rate agreement (FRA) is one in which the underlying is a rate.

Consider first the FRA. As explained in the previous chapter, the buyer of an FRA gains if the reference rate rises above the contract rate at the settlement date (i.e., the settlement rate is greater than the contract rate) and loses if the reference rate falls below the contract rate at the settlement date (i.e., the settlement rate is less than the contract rate). The opposite is true for the seller of an FRA. Exhibit 2 compares the position of the swap parties and the parties to an FRA if rates increase and decrease. Consequently, the buyer of an FRA realizes the same effect when rates change as a fixed-rate payer and the seller of an FRA the same effect when rates change as a floating-rate payer.

A swap can be viewed as a package of FRAs. In fact, an FRA can be viewed as a special case of a swap in which there is only one settlement date.

Now let's compare a swap to a futures or forward contract where the underlying is a fixed-rate instrument such as a Eurodollar CD. The long futures position gains if interest rates decline and loses if interest rates rise; this is similar to the risk/return profile for a floating-rate payer. The risk/return profile for a fixed-rate payer is similar to that of a short futures position: a gain if interest rates increase and a loss if interest rates decrease. Exhibit 3 compares the counterparty positions for a swap, an FRA, and a forward/futures on a fixed-income instrument when rates change.

Exhibit 2: Effect of Rate Changes on Interest Rate Swap Counterparties and FRA Counterparties

Counterparty to		Interest rates	
Swap	FRA	decrease	increase
Floating-rate payer	Seller	Gains	Loses
Fixed-rate payer	Buyer	Loses	Gains

Exhibit 3: Effect of Rate Changes on Interest Rate Swap Counterparties, FRA Counterparties, and Futures and Forwards on Fixed-Income Instrument Counterparties

Counterparties to:			Interest rates	
Swap	FRA	Futures/forward on fixed-income instrument	decrease	increase
Floating-rate payer	Seller	Buyer	Gains	Loses
Fixed-rate payer	Buyer	Seller	Loses	Gains

Consequently, interest rate swaps can be viewed as a package of more basic interest rate control tools, such as futures and forwards. The pricing of an interest rate swap will then depend on the price of a package of forward/futures contracts with the same settlement dates in which the underlying for the forward/futures contract is the same reference rate.

While an interest rate swap may be nothing more than a package of forward/futures contracts, it is not a redundant contract for several reasons. First, maturities for forward or futures contracts do not extend out as far as those of an interest rate swap; an interest rate swap with a term of 15 years or longer can be obtained. Second, an interest rate swap is a more transactionally efficient instrument. By this we mean that in one transaction an entity can effectively establish a payoff equivalent to a package of forward contracts. The forward contracts would each have to be negotiated separately. Third, the interest rate swap market has grown in liquidity since its establishment in 1981; interest rate swaps now provide more liquidity than forward contracts, particularly long-dated (i.e., long-term) forward contracts.

Package of Cash Market Instruments
To understand why a swap can also be interpreted as a package of cash market instruments, consider an investor who enters into the transaction below:

- buy $50 million par of a 5-year floating-rate bond that pays 6-month LIBOR every six months

- finance the purchase by borrowing $50 million for five years on terms requiring a 10% annual interest rate paid every six months.

Exhibit 4: Cash Flow For the Purchase of a 5-Year Floating-Rate Bond Financed by Borrowing on a Fixed-Rate Basis

Transaction:
- Purchase $50 million of a 5-year floating-rate bond:
  floating rate = LIBOR, semiannual pay
- Borrow $50 million for five years:
  fixed rate = 10%, semiannual payments

Six Month Period	Cash Flow (In Millions of Dollars) From:		
	Floating-Rate Bond[*]	Borrowing Cost	Net
0	−$50	+$50.0	$0
1	+(LIBOR$_1$/2) × 50	−2.5	+(LIBOR$_1$/2) × 50 − 2.5
2	+(LIBOR$_2$/2) × 50	−2.5	+(LIBOR$_2$/2) × 50 − 2.5
3	+(LIBOR$_3$/2) × 50	−2.5	+(LIBOR$_3$/2) × 50 − 2.5
4	+(LIBOR$_4$/2) × 50	−2.5	+(LIBOR$_4$/2) × 50 − 2.5
5	+(LIBOR$_5$/2) × 50	−2.5	+(LIBOR$_5$/2) × 50 − 2.5
6	+(LIBOR$_6$/2) × 50	−2.5	+(LIBOR$_6$/2) × 50 − 2.5
7	+(LIBOR$_7$/2) × 50	−2.5	+(LIBOR$_7$/2) × 50 − 2.5
8	+(LIBOR$_8$/2) × 50	−2.5	+(LIBOR$_8$/2) × 50 − 2.5
9	+(LIBOR$_9$/2) × 50	−2.5	+(LIBOR$_9$/2) × 50 − 2.5
10	+(LIBOR$_{10}$/2) × 50 + 50	−52.5	+(LIBOR$_{10}$/2) × 50 − 2.5

[*] The subscript for LIBOR indicates the 6-month LIBOR as per the terms of the floating-rate bond at time t.

The cash flows for this transaction are set forth in Exhibit 4. The second column of the exhibit shows the cash flow from purchasing the 5-year floating-rate bond. There is a $50 million cash outlay and then ten cash inflows. The amount of the cash inflows is uncertain because they depend on future LIBOR. The next column shows the cash flow from borrowing $50 million on a fixed-rate basis. The last column shows the net cash flow from the entire transaction. As the last column indicates, there is no initial cash flow (no cash inflow or cash outlay). In all ten 6-month periods, the net position results in a cash inflow of LIBOR and a cash outlay of $2.5 million. This net position, however, is identical to the position of a fixed-rate payer.

It can be seen from the net cash flow in Exhibit 4 that a fixed-rate payer has a cash market position that is equivalent to a long position in a floating-rate bond and a short position in a fixed-rate bond — the short position being the equivalent of borrowing by issuing a fixed-rate bond.

What about the position of a floating-rate payer? It can be easily demonstrated that the position of a floating-rate payer is equivalent to purchasing a fixed-rate bond and financing that purchase at a floating-rate, where the floating rate is the reference rate for the swap. That is, the position of a floating-rate payer is equivalent to a long position in a fixed-rate bond and a short position in a floating-rate bond.

DURATION OF A SWAP

The duration of a swap follows from our interpretation of a swap position being a package of cash flows from buying and selling cash market instruments. From the perspective of the floating-rate payer, the position can be viewed as follows:

> long a fixed-rate bond + short a floating-rate bond

This means that the dollar duration of an interest rate swap from the perspective of a floating-rate payer is just the difference between the dollar duration of the two bond positions that comprise the swap. That is,

> Dollar duration of a swap = Dollar duration of a fixed-rate bond −
> Dollar duration of a floating-rate bond

Most of the interest rate sensitivity of a swap will result from the dollar duration of the fixed-rate bond since the dollar duration of the floating-rate bond will be small. The dollar duration of a floating-rate bond is smaller the closer the swap is to its reset date.

SWAP MARKET JARGON

One party to a generic swap is referred to as a fixed-rate payer or floating-rate receiver, and the other party a floating-rate payer or fixed-rate receiver. The terminology used to describe the positions in a swap combines cash market jargon and futures jargon, given that a swap position can be interpreted as a position in a package of cash market instruments or a package of futures/forward positions.

The fixed-rate payer is said to have bought a swap and is long a swap. The floating-rate payer is said to have sold a swap and is short a swap.

The fixed-rate payer position is sometimes said to be "short the bond market." This is because a fixed-rate payer benefits if interest rates rise, as does an investor who is short a bond. The floating-rate payer position is said to be "long the bond market," since a long bond position benefits from a decline in interest rates.

The fixed-rate payer is said to have established the price sensitivities of a longer term liability and a floating-rate asset. The floating-rate payer is said to have established the price sensitivities of a longer term asset and a floating-rate liability. These two descriptions of swap positions follow from our interpretation of a swap as a package of cash market instruments and the duration of a swap.

MARKET QUOTES

The convention that has evolved for quoting swaps levels is that a swap dealer sets the floating rate equal to the reference rate and then quotes the fixed rate that will apply. To illustrate this convention, consider the 10-year swap offered by a dealer that is shown in Exhibit 5.

Exhibit 5: Meaning of a "40-50" Quote for a 10-Year Swap when Treasuries Yield 8.35% (bid-offer spread of 10 basis points)

	Floating-rate payer	Fixed-rate payer
Pay	floating rate of 6-month LIBOR	fixed rate of 8.85%
Receive	fixed rate of 8.75%	floating rate of 6-month LIBOR

The offer price that the dealer would quote the fixed-rate payer would be to pay 8.85% and receive LIBOR "flat" ("flat" meaning with no spread to LIBOR). The bid price that the dealer would quote the floating-rate payer would be to pay LIBOR flat and receive 8.75%. The bid-offer spread is 10 basis points.

The fixed rate is some spread above the Treasury yield curve with the same term to maturity as the swap. In our illustration, suppose that the 10-year Treasury yield is 8.35%. Then the offer price that the dealer would quote to the fixed-rate payer is the 10-year Treasury rate plus 50 basis points versus receiving LIBOR flat. For the floating-rate payer, the bid price quoted would be LIBOR flat versus the 10-year Treasury rate plus 40 basis points. The dealer would quote such a swap as 40-50, meaning that the dealer is willing to enter into a swap to receive LIBOR and pay a fixed rate equal to the 10-year Treasury rate plus 40 basis points; and it would be willing to enter into a swap to pay LIBOR and receive a fixed rate equal to the 10-year Treasury rate plus 50 basis points. The difference between the Treasury rate paid and received is the bid-offer spread.

NON-GENERIC SWAPS

Non-generic or individualized swaps have evolved as a result of the asset/liability needs of borrowers and lenders. Several non-generic swaps are described below.

Amortizing, Step Up, and Roller Coaster Swaps
In a generic swap, the notional principal amount does not vary over the life of the swap. Thus, it is sometimes referred to as a *bullet swap*. In contrast, for amortizing, step up, and roller coaster swaps the notional principal amount varies over the life of the swap.

An *amortizing swap* is one in which the notional principal amount decreases in a predetermined way over the life of the swap. A *step up swap*, sometimes called an *accreting swap*, is one in which the notional principal amount increases in a predetermined way over time. In a *roller coaster swap*, the notional principal amount can rise or fall from period to period as specified in the contract.

Zero-Coupon Swaps
In a *zero-coupon swap*, one of the parties does not make any payments until the maturity date of the swap but does receive payments at regular payment dates. This type of swap exposes the party making payments over time to significant

credit risk because this party makes regular payments but does not receive any payments until the maturity date of the swap. A zero-coupon swap can be structured so that neither party makes payments until the maturity of the swap.

Prepaid Swaps

In a *prepaid swap* one party (typically the fixed-rate payer) pays the present value of the future payments at the initiation of the swap and then receives payments over the life of the swap. This is analogous to the purchase of an annuity.

Basis Rate Swap

The terms of a typical interest rate swap call for the exchange of fixed- and floating-rate payments. In a *basis rate swap*, both parties exchange floating-rate payments based on a different reference index. As an example, assume a commercial bank has a portfolio of loans in which the lending rate is based on the prime rate, but the bank's cost of funds is based on LIBOR. The risk the bank faces is that the spread between the prime rate and LIBOR will change. This is referred to as basis risk. The bank can use a basis rate swap to make floating-rate payments based on the prime rate and receive floating-rate payments based on LIBOR.

When the two reference rates are in the same sector of the market but differ only by maturity, the swap is called a *yield curve swap*. For example, a yield curve swap may require one party to pay the 3-month Treasury rate and receive the 10-year Treasury rate minus a certain number of basis points.

Forward Swaps

A *forward swap* is simply a forward contract on an interest rate swap. The terms of the swap are set today, but the parties agree that the swap will begin at a specified date in the future. A forward swap can be used to effectively extend the maturity of a swap.

CALCULATION OF THE SWAP RATE

At the initiation of an interest rate swap, the counterparties are agreeing to exchange future interest payments and no upfront payment by either party is made. This means that the swap terms must be such that the present value of the cash flows for the payments to be made by the counterparties must be equal. This is equivalent to saying that the present value of the cash flows of payments to be received by the counterparties must be equal. The equivalence of the cash flows is the principle in calculating the swap rate.

For the fixed-rate side, once a swap rate is determined, the payments of the fixed-rate payer are known. However, the floating-rate payments are unknown because they depend on the value of the reference rate at the reset dates. For a LIBOR-based swap, the Eurodollar CD futures contract can be used to establish the forward (or future) rate for 3-month LIBOR. Given the cash flow based on the forward rate for 3-month LIBOR, the swap rate is the rate that will make the present value of the payments on the fixed-rate side equal to the present value of the payments on the floating-rate side.

The next question is: what interest rate should be used to discount the payments? As explained in Chapter 2, the appropriate rate to discount any cash flow is the theoretical spot rate. Each cash flow should be discounted at a unique discount rate. Where do we get the theoretical spot rates? Recall from Chapter 2 that spot rates can be obtained from forward rates. It is the 3-month LIBOR forward rates derived from the Eurodollar CD futures contracts that can be used as the forward rates to obtain the theoretical spot rates.

Let's illustrate the procedure with an example. Consider the following hypothetical swap:

> Swap term: 3-years
> Notional amount: $100 million
> Fixed receiver: Actual/360 day count basis and quarterly payments
> Floating receiver: 3-month LIBOR, actual/360 day count basis, quarterly payments, and quarterly reset

Our worktable for calculating the swap rate is Exhibit 6. The first column lists the quarterly periods. There is a Eurodollar CD futures contract with a settlement date that corresponds to each period. The second column shows the number of days in the period for each Eurodollar CD futures contract. The third column shows the futures price for each contract. We know from the previous chapter that the future 3-month LIBOR is found by subtracting the futures price from 100. This is shown in Column (4) representing the forward rate.[2]

It is from the forward rates that the discount rates that will be used to discount the cash flows (payments) will be calculated. The discount factor (i.e., the present value of $1 based on the spot rate) is found as follows:[3]

$$\frac{\text{Discount factor in the previous period}}{[1 + (\text{Forward rate in previous period} \times \text{Number of days in period}/360)]}$$

The discount factors are shown in Column (5).

The floating cash flow is found by multiplying the forward rate and the notional amount. However, the forward rate must be adjusted for the number of days in the payment period. The formula to do so is:

$$\frac{\text{Forward rate in previous period} \times \text{Number of days in period}}{360} \times$$

Notional amount

---

[2] In practice, the forward rate is adjusted for the convexity of the Eurodollar CD futures contract.

[3] The formulas presented below are taken from Chapter 6 of Ravi E. Dattatreya, Raj E.S. Venkatesh, and Vijaya E. Venkatesh, *Interest Rate & Currency Swaps* (Chicago: Probus Publishing, 1994).

Exhibit 6: Determining the Swap Rate

Goal: Determination of swap rate

3-year swap, notional amount $100 million

Fixed receiver: Actual/360 day count basis, quarterly payments

Floating receiver: 3-month LIBOR, actual/360 day count basis, quarterly payments and reset

Swap rate is the rate that will produce a fixed cash flow whose present value will equal the present value of the floating cash flow: in illustration the swap rate is equal to 4.987551%.

(1) Period	(2) Day Count	(3) Futures Price ($)	(4) Forward Rate (%)	(5) Discount Factor	(6) Floating Cash Flow ($)	(7) PV of Floating CF ($)	(8) Fixed Cash Flow ($)	(9) PV of Fixed CF ($)
1	91		4.05	1.00000				
2	90	95.85	4.15	0.98998	1,012,500	1,002,351	1,246,888	1,234,390
3	91	95.45	4.55	0.97970	1,049,028	1,027,732	1,260,742	1,235,148
4	91	95.28	4.72	0.96856	1,150,139	1,113,978	1,260,742	1,221,104
5	91	95.10	4.90	0.95714	1,193,111	1,141,974	1,260,742	1,206,706
6	94	94.97	5.03	0.94505	1,279,444	1,209,137	1,302,305	1,230,741
7	91	94.85	5.15	0.93318	1,271,472	1,186,516	1,260,742	1,176,503
8	90	94.75	5.25	0.92132	1,287,500	1,186,201	1,246,888	1,148,784
9	91	94.60	5.40	0.90925	1,327,083	1,206,657	1,260,742	1,146,335
10	91	94.50	5.50	0.89701	1,365,000	1,224,419	1,260,742	1,130,899
11	91	94.35	5.65	0.88471	1,390,278	1,229,993	1,260,742	1,115,392
12	93	94.24	5.76	0.87198	1,459,583	1,272,732	1,288,451	1,123,507
13	91	94.10	5.79	0.85947	1,456,000	1,251,387	1,260,742	1,083,569
					Total	14,053,077		14,053,078

Explanation of columns:

Column (2): The day count refers to the number of days in the period.

Column (3): The Eurodollar CD futures price.

Column (4): Forward Rate = Futures Rate. The forward rate for LIBOR found from the futures price of the Eurodollar CD futures contract as follows: 100.00 − Futures price

Column (5): The discount factor is found as follows:

$$\frac{\text{Discount factor in the previous period}}{[1 + (\text{forward rate in previous period} \times \text{number of days in period}/360)]}$$

number of days in period is found in Column (2).

Column (6): The floating cash flow is found by multiplying the forward rate and the notional amount, adjusted for the number of days in the payment period. That is:

$$\frac{\text{Forward rate previous period} \times \text{number of days in period}}{360} \times \text{notional amount}$$

Column (7): Present value of floating cash flow, found by multiplying Column (5) and Column (6).

Column (8): This column is found by trial and error. In determining the fixed cash flow, the cash flow must be adjusted for the day count, as follows:

$$\frac{\text{Assumed swap rate} \times \text{number of days in period}}{360} \times \text{notional amount}$$

Column (9): Present value of fixed cash flow, found by multiplying Column (5) and Column (8).

These values represent the payments by the floating-rate payer and the receipts of the fixed-rate receiver. The values are shown in Column (6). The present value of each of these cash flows is shown in Column (7) using the discount factor shown in Column (5). The present value of the floating cash flow is $14,053,077.

In order for no other payments to be exchanged between the counterparties other than the interest payments, the swap rate must be set such that the present value of the fixed cash flows is equal to the same value, $14,053,077. This can only be found by trial and error. For our hypothetical swap, when a swap rate of 4.987551% is tried, the cash flow is as shown in Column (8). In determining the fixed cash flows, each cash flow must be adjusted for the day count, as follows:

$$\frac{\text{Assumed swap rate} \times \text{Number of days in period}}{360} \times \text{Notional amount}$$

Using the discount factors in Column (5), the present value of the fixed cash flows is equal to $14,053,078. Therefore, the swap rate is 4.987551%, since it is this rate that equates the present value of the floating and fixed cash flows.

Given the swap rate, the swap spread can be determined. For example, since this is a 3-year swap, the 3-year on-the-run Treasury rate would be used as the benchmark. If the yield on that issue is 4.587551%, the swap spread is then 40 basis points.

The calculation of the swap rate for all swaps follows the same principle: equating the present value of the cash flows.[4]

While our illustration assumes that the timing of the cash flows for both the fixed-rate payer and floating-rate payer will be the same, this is not necessarily the case in a swap. In fact, an agreement may call for the fixed-rate payer to make payments annually but the floating-rate payer to make payments more frequently (semiannually or quarterly). Also, the way in which interest accrues on each leg of the transaction differs, because there are several day count conventions in the fixed-income markets. Once again, the principle is the same.

VALUING A SWAP

Once a the swap transaction is completed, changes in market interest rates will change the cash flow of the floating rate side of the swap. The value of an interest rate swap is the difference between the present value of the cash flow of the two sides of the swap. The 3-month LIBOR forward rates from the current Eurodollar CD futures contracts are used to (1) calculate the floating cash flows and (2) determine the discount factors at which to calculate the present value of the fixed and floating cash flows.

---

[4] For a more detailed explanation of how this is done with more complicated swaps, see Chapter 6 of Dattatreya, Venkatesh, and Venkatesh, *Interest Rate & Currency Swaps*.

Exhibit 7: Determining the Value of a Swap

Goal: Determination of swap value after one year 2-year swap
Notional amount: $100 million
Fixed Receiver: Swap rate 4.987551%, actual/360 day count basis, quarterly payments
Floating receiver: 3-month LIBOR, actual 360 day count basis, quarterly payments and reset

(1)	(2)	(3)	(4)	(5)	(6)	(7)	(8)	(9)
					Floating	PV of	Fixed	PV of
	Day	Futures	Forward	Discount	Cash	Floating	Cash	Fixed
Period	Count	Price ($)	Rate (%)	Factor	Flow ($)	CF ($)	Flow ($)	CF ($)
1	91		5.25	1.000000				
2	94	94.27	5.73	0.987045	1,370,833	1,353,074	1,302,305	1,285,434
3	91	94.22	5.78	0.972953	1,448,417	1,409,241	1,260,742	1,226,642
4	90	94.00	6.00	0.958942	1,445,000	1,385,671	1,246,888	1,195,693
5	91	93.85	6.15	0.944615	1,516,667	1,432,667	1,260,742	1,190,916
6	91	93.75	6.25	0.929686	1,554,583	1,445,274	1,260,742	1,172,094
7	91	93.54	6.46	0.915227	1,579,861	1,445,931	1,260,742	1,153,865
8	93	93.25	6.75	0.900681	1,668,833	1,503,086	1,288,451	1,160,483
9	91	93.15	6.85	0.885571	1,706,250	1,511,005	1,260,742	1,116,476
					Total	11,485,949		9,501,603

PV of floating cash flow $11,485,949
PV of fixed cash flow $9,501,603
Value of swap $1,984,346

To illustrate this, consider the 3-year swap used to demonstrate how to calculate the swap rate. Suppose that one year later, interest rates change such that Column (3) in Exhibit 7 shows the prevailing futures price for the Eurodollar CD futures contract. Columns (4) and (5) then show the corresponding forward rates and discount factors. Column (6) shows the floating cash flow based on the forward rates in Column (4) and Column (7) shows the present value of the floating cash flow using the discount factors in Column (5). The present value of the floating cash flow is $11,485,949. This means that the floating-rate payer has agreed to make payments with a value of $11,485,949 and the fixed-rate payer will receive a cash flow with this value.

Now let's look at the fixed rate side. The swap rate is fixed over the life of the swap. The fixed cash flow is given in Column (8) and the present value based on the discount factors in Column (5) is shown in Column (9). The present value of the fixed cash flows is $9,501,601. This means that the fixed-rate payer has agreed to make payments with a value of $9,501,603 and the floating-rate payer will be receiving a cash flow with this value.

From the fixed-rate payer's perspective, a floating cash flow with a present value of $11,485,949 is going to be received and a fixed cash flow with a present value of $9,501,601 is going to be paid out. The difference between these two present values, $1,984,346, is the value of the swap. It is a positive value for the fixed-rate payer because the present value of what is to be received exceeds the present value of what is to be paid out.

From the floating-rate payer's perspective, a floating cash flow with a present value of $11,485,949 is going to be paid out and a fixed cash flow with a present value of $9,501,601 is going to be received. Once again, the difference between these two present values, $1,984,346, is the value of the swap. It is a negative value for the floating-rate payer because the present value of what is to be received is less than the present value of what is to be paid out. A negative value for a counterparty means a liability.

The same valuation principle applies to the non-generic swaps since once the cash flows are specified, the present value is calculated as described above.

KEY POINTS

1. *An interest rate swap is an agreement specifying that the parties exchange interest payments at designated times based on a notional principal amount.*

2. *In a generic or plain vanilla interest rate swap, one party agrees to make fixed-rate payments and receive floating-rate payments and the counterparty agrees to make floating-rate payments and receive fixed-rate payments.*

3. *The reference rates that have been used for the floating rate in an interest rate swap are those on various money market instruments, the most common being LIBOR.*

4. *Interest rate swaps are over-the-counter instruments.*

5. *An entity seeking to enter into a swap can use a swap dealer or a swap broker.*

6. *The default risk in a swap agreement is called counterparty risk.*

7. *The types of transactions in the secondary market for swaps are a swap reversal, a swap sale (or assignment), and a swap buy-back (or close-out or cancellation).*

8. *A swap position can be interpreted as either a package of forward/futures contracts or a package of cash flows from buying and selling cash market instruments.*

9. *An FRA can be viewed as a special case of a swap in which there is only one settlement date.*

10. *The value of an interest rate swap will fluctuate with market interest rates.*

11. *The risk/return profile for a fixed-rate payer is similar to that of a short futures position, while that of a floating-rate payer is similar to that of a long futures position.*

12. *A fixed-rate payer has a cash market position that is equivalent to a long position in a floating-rate bond and a short position in a fixed-rate bond — the short position being the equivalent of borrowing by issuing a fixed-rate bond.*

13. *The position of a floating-rate payer is equivalent to purchasing a fixed-rate bond and financing that purchase at a floating-rate, where the floating rate is the reference rate for the swap.*

14. *The dollar duration of an interest rate swap from the perspective of a floating-rate payer is just the difference between the dollar duration of a fixed-rate bond and the dollar duration of a floating rate-bond.*

15. *The convention for quoting swap levels is that a swap dealer sets the floating rate equal to the reference rate and then quotes the fixed rate that will apply.*

16. *The swap spread is the spread over the Treasury rate specified at the initiation of the swap that the fixed-rate payer must pay.*

17. *Non-generic swaps include amortizing, step up, roller coaster, zero-coupon, prepaid, basis rate, and forward swaps.*

18. *The swap rate is determined by finding the rate that will make the present value of the cash flow of both sides of the swap equal.*

19. *In a LIBOR-based swap, the cash flow for the floating-rate side is determined from the Eurodollar CD futures contract.*

20. *The discount rates to calculate the present value of the cash flow in a swap are the spot rates.*

21. *The value of an existing swap is equal to the difference in the present value of the two payments.*

Chapter 10
Exchange-Traded Options

In this chapter we look at a different type of derivative instrument called an option. It is different from the derivative instruments previously discussed (futures, forwards, and swaps) in terms of its risk and return characteristics. As a result, an option can be used to control interest rate risk in ways that are either not possible or too difficult to achieve using futures, forwards, or swaps.

Options, like other financial instruments, may be traded either on an organized exchange or in the over-the-counter market. Our focus in this chapter is on exchange-traded options. The most popular form of an exchange-traded option is an option on a futures contract. In the next chapter we look at over-the-counter options and other derivative products with option-like features.

The objectives of this chapter are to:

1. describe the basic features of options contracts;

2. explain the differences between options and futures;

3. describe what futures options are, their trading mechanics, and the reasons for their popularity;

4. review the various futures options currently traded;

5. explain the risk and return characteristics for basic option positions;

6. explain the two components of the option price and the factors that affect the value of an option;

7. discuss the limitations of applying the Black-Scholes pricing model to value futures options and options on fixed-income instruments;

8. explain how to measure the sensitivity of an option to changes in the factors that affect its value; and,

9. explain how to estimate the duration of an option.

THE BASIC OPTION CONTRACT

An *option* is a contract in which the writer of the option grants the buyer of the option the right, but not the obligation, to purchase from or sell to the writer something at a specified price within a specified period of time (or at a specified date). The *writer*, also referred to as the *seller*, grants this right to the buyer in exchange for a certain sum of money, which is called the *option price* or *option premium*. The price at which the underlying may be bought or sold is called the *exercise* or *strike price*. The date after which an option is void is called the *expiration date*. Our focus in this chapter is on options where the "something" underlying the option is a interest rate instrument.

When an option grants the buyer the right to purchase the designated instrument from the writer (seller), it is referred to as a *call option*, or *call*. When the option buyer has the right to sell the designated instrument to the writer, the option is called a *put option*, or *put*.

An option is also categorized according to when the option buyer may exercise the option. There are options that may be exercised at any time up to and including the expiration date. Such an option is referred to as an *American option*. There are options that may be exercised only at the expiration date. An option with this feature is called a *European option*.

The maximum amount that an option buyer can lose is the option price. The maximum profit that the option writer can realize is the option price. The option buyer has substantial upside return potential, while the option writer faces substantial downside risk. We'll investigate the risk and reward profile for option positions later.

There are no margin requirements for the buyer of an option once the option price has been paid in full. Because the option price is the maximum amount that the investor can lose, no matter how adverse the price movement of the underlying instrument, there is no need for margin. Because the writer of an option has agreed to accept all of the risk (and none of the reward) of the position in the underlying instrument, the writer is generally required to put up the option price received as margin. In addition, as price changes occur that adversely affect the writer's position, the writer is required to deposit additional margin (with some exceptions) as the position is marked to market.

DIFFERENCES BETWEEN OPTIONS AND FUTURES CONTRACTS

Notice that unlike in a futures contract, one party to an option contract is not obligated to transact. Specifically, the option buyer has the right but not the obligation to transact. The option writer does have the obligation to perform. In the case of a futures contract, both buyer and seller are obligated to perform. Of course, the buyer of a futures contract does not pay the seller to accept the obligation, while an option buyer pays the seller the option price.

Consequently, the risk and reward characteristics of the two contracts are also different. In the case of a futures contract, the buyer of the contract realizes a dollar-for-dollar gain when the price of the futures contract increases and suffers a dollar-for-dollar loss when the price of the futures contract drops. The opposite occurs for the seller of a futures contract. Options do not provide this symmetric risk and reward characteristic. The most that the buyer of an option can lose is the option price. While the buyer of an option retains all the potential benefits, the gain is always reduced by the amount of the option price. The maximum profit that the writer may realize is the option price; this is offset against substantial downside risk. This difference is extremely important because managers can use futures to protect against symmetric risk and options to protect against asymmetric risk.

EXCHANGE-TRADED VERSUS OTC OPTIONS

There are exchange-traded options and over-the-counter options. Exchange-traded options have two advantages. First, the exercise price and expiration date of the contract are standardized. Second, as in the case of futures contracts, the direct link between buyer and seller is severed after the order is executed because of the interchangeability of exchange-traded options. The clearinghouse associated with the exchange where the option trades performs the same function in the options market that it does in the futures market.

OTC options are used in the many situations where an institutional investor needs to have a tailor-made option because the standardized exchange-traded option does not satisfy its investment objectives. Investment banking firms and commercial banks act as principals as well as brokers in the OTC options market.

OTC options can be customized in any manner sought by an institutional investor. There are plain vanilla options such as options on a specific Treasury issue. The more complex OTC options created are called *exotic options*. Examples of OTC options are given in the next chapter. While an OTC option is less liquid than an exchange-traded option, this is typically not of concern since institutional investors who use OTC options as part of a hedging or asset/liability strategy intend to hold them to expiration.

In the absence of a clearinghouse the parties to any over-the-counter contract are exposed to counterparty risk. In the case of a forward contract (an OTC contract) both parties face counterparty risk since both parties are obligated to perform. Thus, there is bilateral counterparty risk. In contrast, for an OTC option, once the option buyer pays the option price, it has satisfied its obligation. It is only the seller that must perform if the option is exercised. Thus, the option buyer is exposed to unilateral counterparty risk — the risk that the option seller will fail to perform.

FUTURES OPTIONS

The underlying for an interest rate option can be a fixed-income security or an interest rate futures contract. The former options are called *options on physicals*. In the United States, there are no actively exchange-traded options on physicals. Options on interest rate futures are called *futures options*. The actively traded interest rate options on exchanges are futures options.

The Basics of Futures Options

A futures option gives the buyer the right to buy from or sell to the writer a designated futures contract at the strike price at any time during the life of the option. If the futures option is a call option, the buyer has the right to purchase one designated futures contract at the strike price. That is, the buyer has the right to acquire a long futures position in the designated futures contract. If the buyer exercises the call option, the writer acquires a corresponding short position in the futures contract.

A put option on a futures contract grants the buyer the right to sell a designated futures contract to the writer at the strike price. That is, the option buyer has the right to acquire a short position in the designated futures contract. If the put option is exercised, the writer acquires a corresponding long position in the designated futures contract.

As the parties to the futures option will realize a position in a futures contract when the option is exercised, the question is: what will the futures price be? That is, at what price will the long be required to pay for the instrument underlying the futures contract, and at what price will the short be required to sell the instrument underlying the futures contract?

Upon exercise, the futures price for the futures contract will be set equal to the strike price. The position of the two parties is then immediately marked-to-market in terms of the then-current futures price. Thus, the futures position of the two parties will be at the prevailing futures price. At the same time, the option buyer will receive from the option seller the economic benefit from exercising. In the case of a call futures option, the option writer must pay the difference between the current futures price and the strike price to the buyer of the option. In the case of a put futures option, the option writer must pay the option buyer the difference between the strike price and the current futures price.

For example, suppose an investor buys a call option on some futures contract in which the strike price is 85. Assume also that the futures price is 95 and that the buyer exercises the call option. Upon exercise, the call buyer is given a long position in the futures contract at 85 and the call writer is assigned the corresponding short position in the futures contract at 85. The futures positions of the buyer and the writer are immediately marked-to-market by the exchange. Because the prevailing futures price is 95 and the strike price is 85, the long futures position (the position of the call buyer) realizes a gain of 10, while the short futures position (the position of the call writer) realizes a loss of 10. The call writer pays the exchange 10 and the call buyer receives from the exchange 10. The call buyer, who now has a long futures position at 95, can either liquidate the futures position at 95 or maintain a long futures position. If the former course of action is taken, the call buyer sells a futures contract at the prevailing futures price of 95. There is no gain or loss from liquidating the position. Overall, the call buyer realizes a gain of 10. The call buyer who elects to hold the long futures position will face the same risk and reward of holding such a position, but still realizes a gain of 10 from the exercise of the call option.

Suppose instead that the futures option is a put rather than a call, and the current futures price is 60 rather than 95. Then if the buyer of this put option exercises it, the buyer would have a short position in the futures contract at 85; the option writer would have a long position in the futures contract at 85. The exchange then marks the position to market at the then-current futures price of 60, resulting in a gain to the put buyer of 25 and a loss to the put writer of the same amount. The put buyer who now has a short futures position at 60 can either liquidate the short futures position by buying a futures contract at the prevailing futures price of 60 or maintain the short futures position. In either case the put buyer realizes a gain of 25 from exercising the put option.

There are no margin requirements for the buyer of a futures option once the option price has been paid in full. Because the option price is the maximum amount that the buyer can lose, regardless of how adverse the price movement of the underlying instrument, there is no need for margin.

Because the writer (seller) of an option has agreed to accept all of the risk (and none of the reward) of the position in the underlying instrument, the writer (seller) is required to deposit not only the margin required on the interest rate futures contract position, but also (with certain exceptions) the option price that is received for writing the option. In addition, as prices adversely affect the writer's position, the writer would be required to deposit variation margin as it is marked to market.

Exchange-Traded Futures Options

In Chapter 8 we discussed the various futures contracts traded on the Chicago Board of Trade (CBT) and the International Monetary Market (IMM) of the Chicago Mercantile Exchange. Options on Treasury bond and note futures are traded on the CBT and options on the Eurodollar CD futures are traded on the IMM. All futures options are of the American type. If the option buyer elects to exercise early, he or she must notify the clearing corporation which then randomly selects a clearing member that must select a short from amongst its customers.

The CBT's Treasury bond futures contracts have delivery months of March, June, September, and December. In Chapter 8 we described the delivery process and the choices granted to the short. There are futures options that expire in the next three regular quarterly expiration months. Trading of futures options on Treasury bonds stops in the month prior to the underlying futures contract's delivery month. The day in that month in which the futures options stop trading is the first Friday preceding, by at least five days, the first notice day for the Treasury bond futures contract. The CBT also lists futures options for the current front month.

In an attempt to compete with the OTC option market, the CBT introduced in 1994 the *flexible Treasury futures options*. These futures options allow counterparties to customize options within certain limits. Specifically, the strike price, expiration date, and type of exercise (American or European) can be customized subject to CBT constraints. One key constraint is that the expiration date of a flexible contract cannot exceed that of the longest standard option traded on the CBT. Unlike an OTC option, where the option buyer is exposed to counterparty risk, a flexible Treasury futures option is guaranteed by the clearing house. The minimum size requirement for the launching of flexible futures option is 100 contracts.

The price of a futures option on a Treasury bond is quoted in a 64th of 1% of par value. For example, a price of 24 means $^{24}/_{64}$th of 1% of par value. Since the par value of a Treasury bond futures contract is $100,000, an option price of 24 means:

$$[(^{24}/_{64})/100] \times \$100,000 = \$375$$

In general, the price of a futures option on a Treasury bond quoted at Q is equal to:

$$\text{Option price} = [(Q/64)/100] \times \$100,000$$

For options on the Eurodollar CD futures contract traded on the IMM, options are listed for the six nearest futures contracts in the regular March quarterly cycle and for two serial expirations. Futures and futures options expire on the same day. The IMM now offers mid-curve options on Eurodollar CD futures. These are options on deferred Eurodollar CD futures. As with the Eurodollar CD futures contract, the Eurodollar CD futures option is quoted in hundredths of an index point. Thus, the minimum fluctuation for the price of a Eurodollar CD futures option is $25.

RISK AND RETURN CHARACTERISTICS OF OPTIONS

Here we illustrate the risk and return characteristics of the four basic option positions — buying a call option, selling a call option, buying a put option, and selling a put option. The illustrations assume that each option position is held to the expiration date and not exercised early. In our illustrations we will use an option on a physical since the principles apply equally to futures options. To keep the illustration simple, we ignore transactions costs.

Buying Call Options
The purchase of a call option creates a financial position referred to as a *long call position*. To illustrate this position, assume that there is a call option on Asset

XYZ that expires in one month and has a strike price of $100. The option price is $3. Suppose that the current price of Asset XYZ is $100. For an investor who purchases this call option, the profit or loss at the expiration date is shown in the second column of Exhibit 1. The maximum loss is the option price and there is substantial upside potential.

It is worthwhile to compare the profit and loss profile of the call option buyer to taking a long position in one unit of Asset XYZ. The payoff from the position depends on Asset XYZ's price at the expiration date. Exhibit 1 compares the long call position and the long position in Asset XYZ. This comparison clearly demonstrates the way in which an option can change the risk/return profile. An investor who takes a long position in Asset XYZ realizes a profit of $1 for every $1 increase in Asset XYZ's price. As Asset XYZ's price falls, however, the investor loses dollar-for-dollar. If the price drops by more than $3, the long position in Asset XYZ results in a loss of more than $3. The long call position, in contrast, limits the loss to only the option price of $3 but retains the upside potential, which will be $3 less than for the long position in Asset XYZ.

Writing (Selling) Call Options

The writer of a call option is said to be in a *short call position*. To illustrate the option seller's (writer's) position, we use the same call option we used to illustrate buying a call option. The profit and loss profile of the short call position (that is, the position of the call option writer) is the mirror image of the profit and loss profile of the long call position (the position of the call option buyer). That is, the profit of the short call position for any given price for Asset XYZ at the expiration date is the same as the loss of the long call position. Consequently, the maximum profit that the short call position can produce is the option price. The maximum potential loss is the highest price realized by Asset XYZ on or before the expiration date, less the option price; this price can be indefinitely high.

Buying Put Options

The buying of a put option creates a financial position referred to as a *long put position*. To illustrate this position, we assume a hypothetical put option on one unit of Asset XYZ with one month to maturity and a strike price of $100. Assume the put option is selling for $2. The current price of Asset XYZ is $100. The profit or loss for this position at the expiration date depends on the market price of Asset XYZ. The profit and loss profile for the long put position is shown in the second column of Exhibit 2.

As with all long option positions, the loss is limited to the option price. The profit potential, however, is substantial: the theoretical maximum profit is generated if Asset XYZ's price falls to zero. Contrast this profit potential with that of the buyer of a call option. The theoretical maximum profit for a call buyer cannot be determined beforehand because it depends on the highest price that can be reached by Asset XYZ before or at the option expiration date.

Exhibit 1: Comparison of Long Call Position and Long Asset Position

Assumptions: Price of Asset XYZ = $100
Option price = $3
Strike price = $100
Time to expiration = 1 month

Price of Asset XYZ at Expiration Date	Net Profit/Loss for	
	Long Call[*]	Short Asset XYZ[**]
$150	$47	$50
140	37	40
130	27	30
120	17	20
115	12	15
114	11	14
113	10	13
112	9	12
111	8	11
110	7	10
109	6	9
108	5	8
107	4	7
106	3	6
105	2	5
104	1	4
103	0	3
102	−1	2
101	−2	1
100	−3	0
99	−3	−1
98	−3	−2
97	−3	−3
96	−3	−4
95	−3	−5
94	−3	−6
93	−3	−7
92	−3	−8
91	−3	−9
90	−3	−10
89	−3	−11
88	−3	−12
87	−3	−13
86	−3	−14
85	−3	−15
80	−3	−20
70	−3	−30
60	−3	−40

* Price at expiration – $100 – $3, Maximum loss = $3
** Price at expiration – $100

Exhibit 2: Profit/Loss Profile for a Long Put Position and Comparison with a Short Asset Position

Assumptions: Price of Asset XYZ = $100
Option price = $2
Strike price = $100
Time to expiration = 1 month

Price of Asset XYZ	Net Profit/Loss for	
at Expiration Date ($)	Long Put ($)*	Short Asset XYZ ($)**
150	−2	−50
140	−2	−40
130	−2	−30
120	−2	−20
115	−2	−15
110	−2	−10
105	−2	−5
100	−2	0
99	−1	1
98	0	2
97	1	3
96	2	4
95	3	5
94	4	6
93	5	7
92	6	8
91	7	9
90	8	10
89	9	11
88	10	12
87	11	13
86	12	14
85	13	15
84	14	16
83	15	17
82	16	18
81	17	19
80	18	20
75	23	25
70	28	30
65	33	35
60	38	40

* $100 − Price at expiration − $2, Maximum loss = $2
** $100 − Price at expiration

To see how an option alters the risk and return profile we again compare it to a position in Asset XYZ. The long put position is compared to taking a short position in Asset XYZ because this is the position that would realize a profit if the price of the asset falls. Suppose an investor sells Asset XYZ short for $100. Exhibit 2 compares the profit and loss profile for the long put position and short position in Asset XYZ.

While the investor who takes a short position in Asset XYZ faces all the downside risk as well as the upside potential, the long put position limits the downside risk to the option price while still maintaining upside potential (reduced only by an amount equal to the option price).

Writing (Selling) Put Options

Writing a put option creates a financial position referred to as a *short put position*. The profit and loss profile for a short put option is the mirror image of the long put option. The maximum profit from this position is the option price. The theoretical maximum loss can be substantial should the price of the underlying asset fall; at the outside, if the price were to fall all the way to zero, the loss would be as large as the strike price less the option price.

To summarize, buying calls or selling puts allows the investor to gain if the price of the underlying asset rises. Selling calls and buying puts allows the investor to gain if the price of the underlying asset falls.

VALUATION OF OPTIONS

In this section we will look at how to value an option and discuss models for valuing futures options. In the next chapter, we will look at models for valuing options on physicals.

Basic Components of the Option Price

The option value is a reflection of the option's *intrinsic value* and any additional amount over its intrinsic value. The premium over intrinsic value is often referred to as the *time value*. The intrinsic value of an option is its economic value if it is exercised immediately. If no positive economic value would result from exercising the option immediately, then the intrinsic value is zero.

For a call option, the intrinsic value is positive if the current price of the underlying security is greater than the strike price. The intrinsic value is then the difference between the two prices. If the strike price of a call option is greater than or equal to the current price of the security, the intrinsic value is zero. For example, if the strike price for a call option is 100 and the current price for the security is 105, the intrinsic value is 5. That is, an option buyer exercising the option and simultaneously selling the underlying security would realize 105 from the sale of the security, which would be covered by acquiring the security from the option writer for 100, thereby netting a 5 gain.

Exhibit 3: Relationship Between Security Price, Strike Price, and Intrinsic Value

If Security price > Strike price	Call option	Put Option
Intrinsic value	Security price – Strike price	Zero
Jargon	In-the-money	Out-of-the money
If Security price < Strike price	**Call option**	**Put Option**
Intrinsic value	Zero	Security price – Stock price
Jargon	Out-of-the-money	In-the-money
If Security price = Strike price	**Call option**	**Put Option**
Intrinsic value	Zero	Zero
Jargon	At-the-money	At-the-money

When an option has intrinsic value, it is said to be *in the money*. When the strike price of a call option exceeds the current price of the security, the call option is said to be *out of the money*; it has no intrinsic value. An option for which the strike price is equal to the current price of the security is said to be *at the money*. Both at-the-money and out-of-the-money options have an intrinsic value of zero because they are not profitable to exercise.

For a put option, the intrinsic value is equal to the amount by which the current price of the security is below the strike price. For example, if the strike price of a put option is 100 and the current price of the security is 92, the intrinsic value is 8. The buyer of the put option who exercises it and simultaneously buys the underlying security will net 8 by exercising this option since the security will be sold to the writer for 100 and purchased in the market for 92. The intrinsic value is zero if the strike price is less than or equal to the current market price.

For our put option with a strike price of 100, the option would be: (1) in the money when the security's price is less than 100, (2) out of the money when the security's price exceeds 100, and (3) at the money when the security's price is equal to 100.

The relations above are summarized in Exhibit 3.

The time value of an option is the amount by which the option price exceeds its intrinsic value. The option buyer hopes that, at some time prior to expiration, changes in the market price of the underlying security will increase the value of the rights conveyed by the option. For this prospect, the option buyer is willing to pay a premium above the intrinsic value.

For example, if the price of a call option with a strike price of 100 is 9 when the current price of the security is 105, the time value of this option is 4 (9 minus its intrinsic value of 5). Had the current price of the security been 90 instead of 105, then the time value of this option would be the entire 9 because the option has no intrinsic value.

Factors that Influence the Value of an Option on a Fixed-Income Instrument

There are six factors that influence the value of an option in which the underlying is a fixed-income instrument:

Exhibit 4: Summary of Factors that Affect the Price of an Option on a Fixed-Income Instrument

Increase in factor with all other factors held constant	Effect on call option	Effect on put option
Current price of underlying security	increase	decrease
Strike price	decrease	increase
Time to expiration (American options)	increase	increase
Expected yield volatility	increase	increase
Short-term risk-free rate	increase	decrease
Coupon interest payments	decrease	increase

1. current price of the underlying security;
2. strike price;
3. time to expiration of the option;
4. expected yield volatility over the life of the option;
5. short-term risk-free interest rate over the life of the option; and,
6. coupon interest payment over the life of the option.

The impact of each of these factors may depend on whether (1) the option is a call or a put, and (2) the option is an American option or a European option. A summary of the effect of each factor on put and call option prices is presented in Exhibit 4.

Current Price of the Underlying Security The option price will change as the price of the underlying security changes. For a call option, as the price of the underlying security increases (holding all other factors constant), the option price increases. The opposite holds for a put option: as the price of the underlying security increases, the price of a put option decreases.

Strike Price All other factors equal, the lower the strike price, the higher the price of a call option. For put options, the higher the strike price, the higher the option price.

Time to Expiration An option is a "wasting asset." That is, after the expiration date passes the option has no value. Holding all other factors equal, the longer the time to expiration of the option, the greater the option price. This is because, as the time to expiration decreases, less time remains for the underlying security's price to rise (for a call buyer) or to fall (for a put buyer) and, therefore, the probability of a favorable price movement decreases. Consequently, for American options, as the time remaining until expiration decreases, the option price approaches its intrinsic value.

Expected Yield Volatility All other actors equal, the greater the expected yield volatility (as measured by the standard deviation or variance), the more an investor would be willing to pay for the option, and the more an option writer would demand for it. This is because the greater the yield volatility, the greater the probability that the price of the underlying security will move in favor of the option buyer at some time before expiration.

Short-Term Risk-Free Interest Rate Buying the underlying security ties up one's money. Buying an option on the same quantity of the underlying security makes the difference between the security price and the option price available for investment at the risk-free rate. All other factors constant, the higher the short-term risk-free interest rate, the greater the cost of buying the underlying security and carrying it to the expiration date of the call option. Hence, the higher the short-term risk-free interest rate, the more attractive the call option will be relative to the direct purchase of the underlying security. As a result, the higher the short-term risk-free interest rate, the greater the price of a call option. The reverse is true for a put option.

Coupon Payments Coupon interest payments on the underlying security tend to decrease the price of a call option because they make it more attractive to hold the underlying security than to hold the option. For put options, coupon interest payments on the underlying security tend to increase their price.

Factors that Influence the Value of a Futures Option
There are five factors that influence the value of an option in which the underlying is a futures contract:

> 1. current futures price;
> 2. strike price;
> 3. time to expiration of the option;
> 4. expected yield volatility over the life of the option; and,
> 5. short-term risk-free interest rate over the life of the option.

These are the same factors that affect the value of an option on a fixed-income instrument. Notice that the coupon payment is not a factor since the underlying is a futures contract.

Exhibit 5 summarizes how each factor affects the value of a futures option. The primary difference between factors that influence the price of a futures option and an option on a fixed-income instrument is the short-term risk-free rate. For both a call and a put, the option price decreases when the short-term risk-free rate increases.

Option Pricing Model
At any time, the intrinsic value of an option can be determined. The question is, what is the time value of an option worth. To answer this question, option pricing models have been developed.

Exhibit 5: Summary of Factors that Affect the Price of a Futures Option

Increase in factor with all other factors held constant	Effect on call option	Effect on put option
Current futures price	increase	decrease
Strike price	decrease	increase
Time to expiration	increase	increase
Expected yield volatility	increase	increase
Short-term risk-free rate	decrease	decrease

The most popular model for the pricing of equity options is the Black-Scholes option pricing model.[1] By imposing certain assumptions and using arbitrage arguments, the Black-Scholes option pricing model computes the fair (or theoretical) price of a European call option on a non-dividend-paying stock.

There are problems with using the model to value an option on a fixed-income instrument and a futures option due to its underlying assumptions. The Black-Scholes model would price a call option on a zero-coupon bond with a strike price of $103 at some positive value. Such an option will always be worthless since the price of a zero-coupon bond will never exceed $100.

There are three assumptions underlying the Black-Scholes model that limit its use in pricing options on fixed-income instruments. First, the probability distribution for the prices assumed by the Black-Scholes option pricing model permits some probability — no matter how small — that the price can take on any positive value. But in the case of a zero-coupon bond, the price cannot take on a value above $100. In the case of a coupon bond, we know that the price cannot exceed the sum of the coupon payments plus the maturity value. For example, for a 5-year 10% coupon bond with a maturity value of $100, the price cannot be greater than $150 (five coupon payments of $10 plus the maturity value of $100). Thus, unlike stock prices, bond prices have a maximum value. The only way that a bond's price can exceed the maximum value is if negative interest rates are permitted. This is not likely to occur, so any probability distribution for prices assumed by an option pricing model that permits bond prices to be higher than the maximum bond value could generate nonsensical option prices. The Black-Scholes model does allow bond prices to exceed the maximum bond value (or, equivalently, allows negative interest rates).

The second assumption of the Black-Scholes option pricing model is that the short-term interest rate is constant over the life of the option. Yet the price of an interest rate option will change as interest rates change. A change in the short-term interest rate changes the rates along the yield curve. Therefore, to assume that the short-term rate will be constant is inappropriate for interest rate options. The third assumption is that the variance of prices is constant over the life of the option. As a

---

[1] Fischer Black and Myron Scholes, "The Pricing of Corporate Liabilities," *Journal of Political Economy* (May-June 1973), pp. 637-659.

bond moves closer to maturity its price volatility declines. Therefore, the assumption that price variance is constant over the life of the option is inappropriate.[2]

The more commonly used model for valuing futures options is the Black model.[3] The model was developed to value European options on futures contracts. There are two problems with this model. First, the Black model does not overcome the problems cited earlier for the Black-Scholes model. Failing to recognize the yield curve means that there will not be a consistency between pricing bond futures and options on bond futures. Second, the Black model was developed for pricing European options on futures contracts. Futures options, however, are American options.

The second problem can be overcome. The Black model was extended by Barone-Adesi and Whaley to American options on futures contracts.[4] This is the model used by the CBT to settle the flexible Treasury futures options. However, this model was also developed for equities and is subject to the first problem noted above.

In the next chapter we will look at a model that overcomes the first problem.

Sensitivity of Option Price to Change in Factors

The use options to control risk, a manager would like to know how sensitive the price of an option is to a change in every factor that affects its price. Here we look at the sensitivity of a call option's price to changes in the price of the underlying bond, the time to expiration, and expected yield volatility.

The Call Option Price and the Price of the Underlying Bond
Exhibit 6 shows the theoretical price of a call option based on the price of the underlying bond. The horizontal axis is the price of the underlying bond at any point in time. The vertical axis is the call option price. The shape of the curve representing the theoretical price of a call option, given the price of the underlying bond, would be the same regardless of the actual option pricing model used. In particular, the relationship between the price of the underlying bond and the theoretical call option price is convex. Thus, option prices also exhibit convexity.

The line from the origin to the strike price on the horizontal axis in Exhibit 6 is the intrinsic value of the call option when the price of the underlying bond is less than the strike price, since the intrinsic value is zero. The 45-degree line extending from the horizontal axis is the intrinsic value of the call option once the price of the underlying bond exceeds the strike price. The reason is that the intrinsic value of the call option will increase by the same dollar amount as the increase in the price of the underlying bond.

---

[2] While we have discussed the problems of using the Black-Scholes model to price interest rate options, it can also be shown that the binomial option pricing model based on the price distribution of the underlying bond suffers from the same problems.

[3] Fischer Black, "The Pricing of Commodity Contracts," *Journal of Financial Economics* (March 1976), pp. 161-179.

[4] Giovanni Barone-Adesi and Robert E. Whaley, "Efficient Analytic Approximation of American Option Values," *Journal of Finance* (June 1987), pp. 301-320.

Exhibit 6: Theoretical Call Price and Price of Underlying Bond

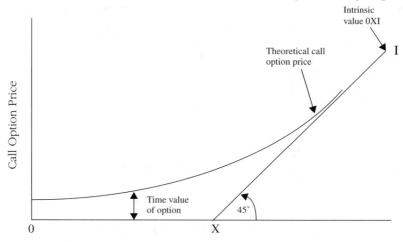

X= Strike price

For example, if the strike price is $100 and the price of the underlying bond increases from $100 to $101, the intrinsic value will increase by $1. If the price of the bond increases from $101 to $110, the intrinsic value of the option will increase from $1 to $10. Thus, the slope of the line representing the intrinsic value after the strike price is reached is 1.

Since the theoretical call option price is shown by the convex curve, the difference between the theoretical call option price and the intrinsic value at any given price for the underlying bond is the time value of the option.

Exhibit 7 shows the theoretical call option price, but with a tangent line drawn at the price of p^*. The tangent line in the figure can be used to estimate what the new option price will be (and therefore what the change in the option price will be) if the price of the underlying bond changes. Because of the convexity of the relationship between the option price and the price of the underlying bond, the tangent line closely approximates the new option price for a small change in the price of the underlying bond. For large changes, however, the tangent line does not provide as good an approximation of the new option price.

The slope of the tangent line shows how the theoretical call option price will change for small changes in the price of the underlying bond. The slope is popularly referred to as the *delta* of the option. Specifically,

$$\text{Delta} = \frac{\text{Change in price of call option}}{\text{Change in price of underlying bond}}$$

For example, a delta of 0.4 means that a $1 change in the price of the underlying bond will change the price of the call option by approximately $0.40.

Exhibit 7: Estimating the Theoretical Option Price with a Tangent Line

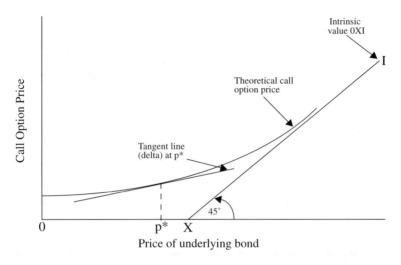

X = Strike price

Exhibit 8 shows the curve of the theoretical call option price with three tangent lines drawn. The steeper the slope of the tangent line, the greater the delta. When an option is deep out of the money (that is, the price of the underlying bond is substantially below the strike price), the tangent line is nearly flat (see Line 1 in Exhibit 8). This means that delta is close to zero. To understand why, consider a call option with a strike price of $100 and two months to expiration. If the price of the underlying bond is $20, its price would not increase by much, if anything, should the price of the underlying bond increase by $1, from $20 to $21.

For a call option that is deep in the money, the delta will be close to one. That is, the call option price will increase almost dollar for dollar with an increase in the price of the underlying bond. In terms of Exhibit 8, the slope of the tangent line approaches the slope of the intrinsic value line after the strike price. As we stated earlier, the slope of that line is 1.

Thus, the delta for a call option varies from zero (for call options deep out of the money) to one (for call options deep in the money). The delta for a call option at the money is approximately 0.5.

The curvature of the convex relationship can also be approximated. This is the rate of change of delta as the price of the underlying bond changes. The measure is commonly referred to as *gamma* and is defined as follows:

$$\text{Gamma} = \frac{\text{Change in delta}}{\text{Change in price of underlying bond}}$$

Exhibit 8: Theoretical Option Price with Three Tangents

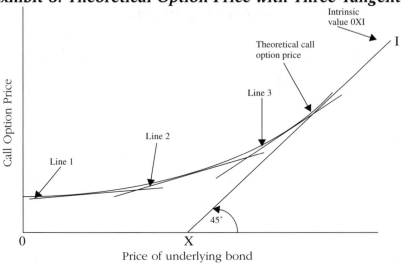

X = Strike price

The Call Option Price and Time to Expiration

All other factors constant, the longer the time to expiration, the greater the option price. Since each day the option moves closer to the expiration date, the time to expiration decreases. The *theta* of an option measures the change in the option price as the time to expiration decreases, or equivalently, it is a measure of *time decay*. Theta is measured as follows:

$$\text{Theta} = \frac{\text{Change in price of option}}{\text{Decrease in time to expiration}}$$

Assuming that the price of the underlying bond does not change (which means that the intrinsic value of the option does not change), theta measures how quickly the time value of the option changes as the option moves towards expiration.

Buyers of options prefer a low theta so that the option price does not decline quickly as it moves toward the expiration date. An option writer benefits from an option that has a high theta.

The Call Option Price and Expected Yield Volatility

All other factors constant, a change in the expected yield volatility will change the option price. The *kappa* of an option measures the dollar price change in the price of the option for a 1% change in expected yield volatility. That is,

$$\text{Kappa} = \frac{\text{Change in option price}}{1\% \text{ change in expected yield volatility}}$$

Duration of an Option

The duration of an option measures the price sensitivity of the option to changes in interest rates and can be shown to be equal to:

$$\text{Duration for an option } = \text{ Duration of underlying instrument } \times$$

$$\text{Delta} \times \frac{\text{Price of underlying instrument}}{\text{Price of option}}$$

As expected, the duration of an option depends on the duration of the underlying bond. It also depends on the price responsiveness of the option to a change in the underlying instrument, as measured by the option's delta. The leverage created by a position in an option comes from the last ratio in the formula. The higher the price of the underlying instrument relative to the price of the option, the greater the leverage (i.e., the more exposure to interest rates for a given dollar investment).

It is the interaction of all three factors that affects the duration of an option. For example, a deep out-of-the-money option offers higher leverage than a deep-in-the-money option, but the delta of the former is less than that of the former.

Since the delta of call option is positive, the duration of an interest rate call option will be positive. Thus, when interest rates decline, the value of an interest rate call option will rise. A put option, however, has a delta that is negative. Thus, duration is negative. Consequently, when interest rates rise, the value of a put option rises.

KEY POINTS

1. An option is a contract in which the writer of the option grants the buyer the right, but not the obligation, to purchase from or sell to the writer something at a specified price within a specified period of time (or on a specified date).

2. The option buyer pays the option writer (seller) a fee, called the option price.

3. A call option allows the option buyer to purchase the underlying from the option writer at the strike price; a put option allows the option buyer to sell the underlying to the option writer at the strike price.

4. Interest rate options include options on fixed-income securities and options on interest rate futures contracts, called futures options.

5. There are exchange-traded options and over-the-counter options.

6. The only actively-traded exchange-traded options are futures options.

7. Futures options are American-type options.

8. The Chicago Board of Trade has introduced customized futures options called flexible Treasury futures options.

9. The value of an option is composed of its intrinsic value and its time value.

10. The six factors that affect the value of an option on a fixed-income instrument are the current price of the underlying security, the strike price, the time to expiration of the option, the expected yield volatility over the life of the option, the short-term risk-free interest rate over the life of the option, and the coupon interest payment over the life of the option.

11. With the exception of the coupon interest payment, the value of a futures option is affected by the same factors that affect an option on a fixed-income instrument.

12. With the exception of the short-term risk-free interest rate, how an option changes when one of the factors changes is the same for futures options and options on fixed-income instruments.

13. Several assumptions underlying the Black-Scholes model limit its use in pricing options on interest rate instruments and futures options.

14. *The Black model is used for valuing futures options but is limited because it deals with European-type options.*

15. *The Black model was extended by Adesi-Barone and Whaley to futures options that are of the American type.*

16. *The Black model and the Adesi-Barone and Whaley model were originally developed for equities and as a result did not take into account the Treasury yield curve.*

17. *Failure to take into account the yield curve can result in an inconsistent valuation of bonds, bond futures, and futures options.*

18. *Managers need to know how sensitive an option's value is to changes in the factors that affect the value of an option.*

19. *The delta of an option measures how sensitive the option price is to changes in the price of the underlying bond and varies from zero (for call options deep out of the money) to one (for call options deep in the money).*

20. *The gamma of an option measures the rate of change of delta as the price of the underlying bond changes.*

21. *The theta of an option measures the change in the option price as the time to expiration decreases.*

22. *The kappa of an option measures the dollar price change in the price of the option for a 1% change in expected yield volatility.*

23. *The duration of an interest rate option is a measure of its price sensitivity to small changes in interest rates and depends on the option's delta, the option's leverage, and the duration of the underlying bond.*

Chapter 11
OTC Options and Related Products

As explained in the previous chapter, there are exchange-traded and over-the-counter (OTC) interest rate options. The product traded on exchanges is a futures option which we described in the previous chapter. In this chapter we focus on OTC options. We also look at option-related products. These include compound options, caps, floors, and options on swaps. With all of these products there is counterparty risk faced by the buyer of the option or option-related product.

The objectives of this chapter are to:

1. describe the different types of OTC options and how they can be structured;

2. demonstrate how to value an option on a fixed-income security using the binomial model;

3. explain how the binomial model can be extended to value futures options;

4. describe what a compound option is;

5. describe what a cap and a floor are and how they can be used to create a collar;

6. demonstrate how caps and floors can be valued using the binomial model; and,

7. describe what an option on a swap is.

OVER-THE-COUNTER INTEREST RATE OPTIONS

OTC interest rate options are created by commercial banks and investment banks for their clients. Dealers can customize the expiration date, the underlying, and the type of exercise. For example, the underlying could be a specific fixed-income security or a spread between yields in two sectors of the fixed-income market.

In addition to American- and European-type options, an OTC option can be created in which the buyer may exercise prior to the expiration date but only on designated dates. Such options are referred to as *modified American* or *Atlantic* or

Bermuda options. With an OTC option, the buyer need not pay the option price at the time of purchase. Instead, the option price can be paid at the expiration or exercise date. For such options, the option writer is exposed to counterparty risk in addition to the option buyer.

In the OTC option market there are plain vanilla and exotic options. Plain vanilla options are options on specific securities or on the spread between two sectors of the bond market. Exotic options have more complicated payoffs and we do not review these in this chapter.

Options on a Specific Security

Institutional investors who want to purchase an option on a specific Treasury security or a Ginnie Mae passthrough can do so on an over-the-counter basis. There are government and mortgage-backed securities dealers who make a market in options on specific securities. Over-the-counter (or dealer) options typically are purchased by institutional investors or mortgage bankers who want to hedge the risk associated with a specific security. Typically, the maturity of the option coincides with the time period over which the buyer of the option wants to hedge, so the buyer is usually not concerned with the option's liquidity.

A popular option used by mortgage originators for hedging forward delivery is an option on a specific mortgage-backed security (MBS). Typically, the underlying security is a TBA (pools to be arranged) agency passthrough security (Ginnie Mae, Fannie Mae, or Freddie Mac). The settlement process in the MBS market is forward delivery. The exercise of a mortgage option means the delivery of that security in the month specified in the option. Options are of the European type.

Spread Options

Some institutional investors may have exposure not only to the level of rates but the spread between two yields. It is difficult to hedge against spread risk with current exchange-traded options. As a result, several dealer firms have developed proprietary products for such purpose. These options can be structured with a payoff in one of the following ways should the option expire in the money. First, there could be a cash settlement based on the amount that the option expires in the money. Second, there could be an exchange of ownership of the two securities underlying the option. It is difficult to structure options with a settlement based on an exchange of securities, but there are institutional investors who desire this type of structure.[1]

Below we discuss two types of spread options — an option on the yield curve and an option on the spread between mortgage-backed securities (MBS) and Treasury securities.[2]

---

[1] Goldman Sachs refers to such structures as dual exercise options (DUOPs).

[2] For a discussion of the various Goldman Sachs spread options, see Scott McDermott, "A Survey of Spread Options for Fixed-Income Investors," Chapter 4 in Frank J. Fabozzi (ed.), *The Handbook of Fixed-Income Options* (Burr Ridge, IL: Irwin Professional Publishing, 1996).

Yield Curve Spread Option The reason for the popularity of yield curve spread options is that there are many institutional investors whose performance is affected by a change in the shape of the yield curve. We discussed yield curve risk in Chapter 4. As an example of a yield curve spread option, consider the Goldman Sachs' product called SYCURVE. This option represents the right to buy (in the case of a call option) or sell (in the case of a put option) specific segments of the yield curve. "Buying the curve" means buying the shorter maturity and selling the longer maturity; "selling the curve" means selling the shorter maturity and buying the longer maturity. The curve is defined by the spread between two specific maturities. They could be the 2-year/10-year spread, the 2-year/30-year spread, or the 10-year/30-year spread. The strike is quoted in basis points.

The yield spread is measured by the long maturity yield minus the short maturity yield. For a call option to be in the money at the expiration date, the yield spread must be positive; for a put option to be in the money at the expiration date, the yield spread must be negative. For example, a 25 basis point call option on the 2-year/10-year spread will be in the money at the expiration date if:

10-year yield − 2-year yield > 25 basis points

A 35 basis point put option on the 10-year/30-year spread will be in the money at the expiration date if:

30-year yield − 10-year yield < 35 basis points

Yield curve options such as the SYCURVE are cash settlement contracts. In the case of the SYCURVE, if the option expires in the money, the option buyer receives $0.01 per $1 of notional amount, per in-the-money basis point at exercise. That is:

amount option expires in money (in bp) × $0.01 × notional amount

For example, suppose that $10 million notional amount of a 2-year/10-year call is purchased with a strike of 25 basis points. Suppose at the expiration date the yield spread is 33 basis points. Then the option expires 8 basis points in the money. The cash payment to the buyer of this option is

8 × $0.01 × $10,000,000 = $800,000

From this amount, the option premium must be deducted.

MBS/Treasury Spread Option Some institutional investors seek to control the spread risk between the yield on MBS and Treasuries. One example of an option on this spread is Goldman Sachs' MOTTO (mortgages over Treasury) option. The buyer of a MOTTO call option benefits if MBS outperform Treasuries; the buyer of a MOTTO put option benefits if Treasuries outperform MBS.

As noted earlier in discussing MBS options, the structuring of MOTTO options is complicated by the nuances of the MBS market. For the particular Treasury, the calculation of its yield at the expiration date is straightforward given its price at the expiration date. On the other hand, at the expiration date while the market price of a generic agency MBS with a given coupon rate is known, its yield is not uniquely determined. The yield depends on the prepayment assumption which determines the particular security's cash flow. This yield is called the *cash flow yield* and the prepayment assumption is commonly called the *prepayment speed*. Each MBS dealer has a proprietary prepayment model to project the speed. One important factor in a prepayment model is the yield level relative to the coupon rate paid on the mortgages in the underlying mortgage pool. Thus, the yield on an MBS depends on the prepayment speed which, in turn, depends on the yield level.

One possible way to handle this problem is to specify at the outset of the option the prepayment speed that should be used to determine the yield on an MBS given the Treasury yield at the expiration date. Specifically, the higher the Treasury yield, the lower the prepayment speed. However, it is not only the yield level but also the shape of the yield curve that affects the prepayment speed. Structuring a MOTTO such that the prepayment speed for all possible combinations of yield curves and yield levels would be difficult. Consequently, a MOTTO is structured so that an in-the-money option at the expiration date is settled by the exchange of the two underlying securities.

Valuation of Options on Fixed-Income Securities

In the previous chapter, we discussed two models used for valuing futures options. The problem with these models is that they are not arbitrage free. The proper way to value options on a fixed-income security is to use an arbitrage-free model that takes into account the yield curve. In Chapter 2, an arbitrage-free binomial model was introduced and used to value a fixed-income security. The same model can be used to value an option on a fixed-income security. Thus, there will be consistency in the pricing of cash market instruments and options on those instruments. The most popular model employed by dealer firms is the Black-Derman-Toy model.[3]

We have already developed the basic principles for employing this model. In Chapter 2, we explained how to construct a binomial interest rate tree such that the tree would be arbitrage free. We used the interest rate tree to value bonds (both option-free and bonds with embedded options). But the same tree can be used to value a stand-alone option on a bond.

---

[3] Fischer Black, Emanuel Derman, and William Toy, "A One-Factor Model of Interest Rates and Its Application to Treasury Bond Options," *Financial Analysts Journal* (January-February 1990), pp. 24-32.

Exhibit 1: Valuing a Treasury Bond with Four Years to Maturity and a Coupon Rate of 6.5% (10% Volatility Assumed)

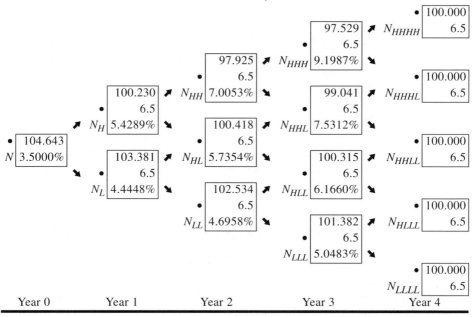

| Year 0 | Year 1 | Year 2 | Year 3 | Year 4 |

Valuing a Treasury Call Option To illustrate how this is done, let's consider a 2-year call option on a 6.5% 4-year Treasury bond with a strike price of 100.25. We will assume that the yield for the on-the-run Treasuries is the one in Chapter 2 and that the volatility assumption is 10% per year. Exhibit 10 in Chapter 2 repeated here as Exhibit 1 shows the binomial interest rate tree along with the value of the Treasury bond at each node.

It is a portion of Exhibit 1 that we use to value the call option. Specifically, Exhibit 2 shows the value of our Treasury bond (excluding coupon interest) at each node at the end of year 2. There are three values shown: 97.925, 100.418, and 102.534. Given these three values, the value of a call option struck at 100.25 can be determined at each node. For example, if at the end of year 2 the price of this Treasury bond is 97.925, then since the strike price is 100.25, the value of the call option would be zero. In the other two cases, since the price at the end of year 2 is greater than the strike price, the value of the call option is the difference between the price of the bond and 100.25.

Exhibit 2 shows the value of the call option at the end of year 2 (the option expiration date) for each of the three nodes. (The values are shown to four decimal places.) Given these values, the binomial interest rate tree is used to find the present value of the call option. The backward induction procedure is used. The discount rates are those from the binomial interest rate tree. For years 0 and

1, the discount rate is the second number shown at each node. The first number at each node for year 1 is the average present value found by discounting the call option value of the two nodes to the right using the discount rate at the node. The value of the option is the first number shown at the root, 0.6056.

Valuing a Treasury Put Option The same procedure is used to value a put option. This is illustrated in Exhibit 3 assuming that the put option has two years to expiration and that the strike price is 100.25. The value of the put option at the end of year 2 is shown at each of the three nodes.

Put-Call Parity Relationship There is a relationship between the price of a call option and the price of a put option on the same underlying instrument, with the same strike price and the same expiration date. This relationship is commonly referred to as the *put-call parity relationship*. For European options on coupon bearing bonds, the relationship is:

> Put price = Call price + Present value of strike price
> + Present value of coupon payments – Price of underlying bond

To demonstrate that the arbitrage-free binomial model satisfies the put-call parity relationship for European options, let's use the values from our illustration. We just found that the put price is 0.6056 and the call price is 0.5327. In Chapter 2, we showed that the theoretical price for the 6.5% 4-year option-free bond is 104.643. In the same chapter we showed the spot rates for each year. The spot rate for year 2 is 4.2147%. Therefore,

$$\text{Present value of strike price } = \frac{100.25}{(1.042147)^2} = 92.3053$$

The present value of the coupon payments are found by discounting the two coupon payments of 6.5 by the spot rates. As just noted, the spot rate for year 2 is 4.2147%; the spot rate for year 1 is 3.5%. Therefore,

$$\text{Present value of coupon payments } = \frac{6.5}{(1.035)^1} + \frac{6.5}{(1.042147)^2} = 12.2650$$

Substituting the values into the right-hand side of the put-parity relationship we find:

$$0.6056 + 92.3053 + 12.2650 - 104.643 = 0.5319$$

The put value that we found is 0.5327. The discrepancy is due simply to rounding error. Therefore, put-call parity holds.

Exhibit 2: Valuing a European Call Option Using the Arbitrage-Free Binomial Method
Expiration: 2 years; Strike price: 100.25; Current price: 104.643; Volatility assumption: 10%

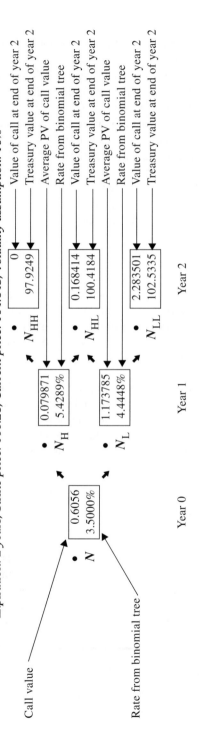

Exhibit 3: Valuing a European Put Option Using the Arbitrage-Free Binomial Method
Expiration: 2 years; Strike price: 100.25; Current price: 104.643; Volatility assumption: 10%

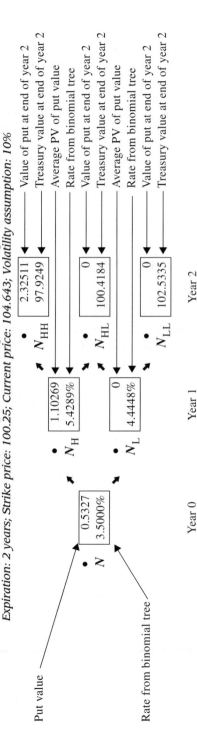

Extension to Futures Options The binomial model can be extended to value futures options. For each node at the expiration date of the futures option, a yield is given. Given the acceptable issues that can be delivered, the conversion factors, and the yield at the expiration date of the futures option, the cheapest-to-deliver Treasury issue can be determined at each node. Therefore at each node at the expiration date of the futures option, there is a cheapest-to-deliver Treasury issue and a value for that issue. From the value of the cheapest-to-deliver Treasury issue and its conversion factor, the value of the underlying Treasury bond futures can be determined.

Based on the strike price, the value of the option at each node at the expiration date of the futures option can be determined. The backward induction method is then used to determine the value of the futures option.

The binomial model allows the consistent valuation of Treasury bonds, Treasury bond futures, and options on Treasury bond futures.

COMPOUND OPTIONS

A *compound* or *split-fee option* is an option to purchase an option. We can explain the elements of a compound option by using a long call option on a long put option. This compound option gives the buyer of the option the right but not the obligation to require the writer of the compound option to sell the buyer a put option. The compound option would specify the following terms:

1. the day on which the buyer of the compound option has the choice of either requiring the writer of the option to sell the buyer a put option or allowing the option to expire. This date is called the *extension date*.
2. the strike price and the expiration date of the put option that the buyer acquires from the writer. The expiration date of the put option is called the *notification date*.

The payment that the buyer makes to acquire the compound option is called the *front fee*. If the buyer exercises the call option in order to acquire the put option, a second payment is made to the writer of the option. That payment is called the *back fee*.

An option that allows the option buyer to purchase a put option is called a *caput*. A *cacall* grants the option buyer the right to purchase a call option.

Compound options are most commonly used by mortgage originators to hedge pipeline risk. They can also be used in any situation when a manager needs additional time to gather information about the need to purchase an option.

CAPS AND FLOORS

An interest cap and floor are agreements between two parties whereby one party, for an upfront premium, agrees to compensate the other if a designated rate, called the reference rate, is different from a predetermined level. The party that benefits if the reference rate differs from a predetermined level is called the buyer and the party that must make the payment is called the seller. The predetermined interest rate level is called the *strike rate*. An interest rate cap specifies that the seller agrees to pay the buyer if the reference rate exceeds the strike rate. An interest rate floor specifies that the seller agrees to pay the buyer if the reference rate is below the strike rate.

The terms of an interest rate agreement include (1) the reference rate; (2) the strike rate that sets the cap or floor; (3) the length of the agreement; (4) the frequency of reset; and, (5) the notional principal amount. If a cap or a floor are in the money at a reset date, the payment by the seller is typically made in arrears.

The payoff for the cap buyer at a reset date if the value of the reference rate exceeds the cap rate on that date is as follows:

Notional principal amount × (Value of reference rate − Cap rate)
× (Number of days in settlement period / Number of days in year)

For the floor buyer, the payoff at a reset date is as follows if the value of the reference rate at the reset date is less than the floor rate:

Notional principal amount × (Floor rate − Value of reference rate)
× (Number of days in settlement period / Number of days in year)

For example, consider the following interest rate cap:

reference rate   = 3-month LIBOR
strike rate   = 8%
term   = 1 year
frequency of reset   = 4 per year (every 3 months)
notional principal amount = $10 million

The payoff for the cap buyer is as follows:

If 3-month LIBOR exceeds 8%, then:[4]
[$10 million × (LIBOR − 8%)] × 91/360

If 3-month LIBOR is less than or equal to 8%, then the payoff is zero.
Assume the following rates for 3-month LIBOR:

	Date	3-month LIBOR
Day of trade	—	8%
1st reset date	Feb. 1	10%
2nd reset date	May 1	7%
3rd reset date	Aug. 1	11%

---

[4] In practice, instead of 91 in the payoff formula, the number of days in the settlement period is used.

On the first reset date, the payoff to the cap buyer is:

$$[\$10 \text{ million} \times (10\% - 8\%)] \times 91/360 = \$50,556$$

The cap buyer receives this payment on May 1. On the second reset date, there is no payment made by the cap seller since 3-month LIBOR is less than 8%. On the third reset date, the payoff to the cap buyer is:

$$[\$10 \text{ million} \times (11\% - 8\%)] \times 91/360 = \$75,833$$

This payment is received on November 1.

Suppose that instead of an interest rate cap, the agreement is an interest rate floor. The payoff for the floor buyer is:

> If 3-month LIBOR is less than 8%, then:
> $$[\$10 \text{ million} \times (8\% - \text{LIBOR})] \times 91/360$$

If 3-month LIBOR is greater than or equal to 8%, then the payoff is zero.

Assuming the scenarios for 3-month LIBOR are the same as above to illustrate the payoff of a cap, then for the first reset and third reset dates, the floor buyer does not receive a payment from the floor seller. On the second reset date, the floor buyer receives the following from the floor seller on August 1:

$$[\$10 \text{ million} \times (8\% - 7\%)] \times 91/360 = \$25,278$$

Interest rate caps and floors can be combined to create an interest rate collar. This is done by buying an interest rate cap and selling an interest rate floor. Some commercial banks and investment banking firms now write options on interest rate caps and floors for customers. Options on caps are called *captions*; options on floors are called *flotions*.

Risk and Return Characteristics

In an interest rate cap and floor, the buyer pays an upfront fee, which represents the maximum amount that the buyer can lose and the maximum amount that the seller of the agreement can gain. The only party that is required to perform is the seller of the interest rate agreement. The buyer of an interest rate cap benefits if the reference rate rises above the strike rate because the seller must compensate the buyer. The buyer of an interest rate floor benefits if the reference rate falls below the strike rate because the seller must compensate the buyer.

How can we better understand interest rate caps and interest rate floors? In essence these contracts are equivalent to a package of interest rate options. As with a swap, a complex contract can be seen to be a package of basic contracts — options in the case of caps and floors.

The question is what type of package of options is a cap and a floor. Recall from Chapter 8 when we discussed the relationship between futures, forward rate agreements, and swaps, that the relationship depends whether the underlying is a rate or a fixed-income instrument. The same applies to call options, put options, caps, and floors.

If the underlying is considered a fixed-income instrument, its value changes inversely with interest rates. Therefore:

for a call option on a fixed-income instrument:
(1) interest rates increase → fixed-income instrument's price decreases
    → call option value decreases
and
(2) interest rates decrease → fixed-income instrument's price increases
    → call option value increases

for a put option on a fixed-income instrument
(1) interest rates increase → fixed-income instrument's price decreases
    → put option value increases
and
(2) interest rates decrease → fixed-income instrument's price increases
    → put option value decreases

To summarize:

	When interest rates	
Value of:	increase	decrease
long call	decrease	increase
short call	increase	decrease
long put	increase	decrease
short put	decrease	increase

For a cap and floor, the situation is as follows

	When interest rates	
Value of:	increase	decrease
short cap	decrease	increase
long cap	increase	decrease
short floor	increase	decrease
long floor	decrease	increase

Therefore, buying a cap (long cap) is equivalent to buying a package of puts on a fixed-income instrument and buying a floor (long floor) is equivalent to buying a package of calls on a fixed-income instrument.

On the other hand, if the underlying is viewed as an option on an interest rate, then buying a cap (long cap) is equivalent to buying a package of calls on interest rates. Buying a floor (long floor) is equivalent to buying a package of puts on interest rates.

Valuing a Cap and Floor

The binomial method can also be used to value a cap and a floor. Remember that a cap and a floor are nothing more than a package of options. More specifically, they are a package of European options on interest rates. Thus, to value a cap, the value of each period's cap is found and all the period caps are then summed. The same can be done for a floor.

To illustrate how this is done, we will once again use the binomial tree given in Exhibit 10 of Chapter 2. Consider first a 5.2% 3-year cap with a notional principal amount of $10 million. The reference rate is the 1-year rate in the binomial tree. The payoff for the cap is annual.

Exhibits 4a, 4b, and 4c show how this cap is valued by valuing the cap for each year individually. The value for the cap for any year, say year X, is found as follows. First, calculate the payoff in year X at each node as either:

(1) zero if the 1-year rate at the node is less than or equal to 5.2%, or
(2) the notional principal amount of $10 million times the difference between the 1-year rate at the node and 5.2% if the 1-year rate at the node is greater than 5.2%.

Mathematically, this is expressed as follows:

$10,000,000 × Maximum [(Rate at node – 5.2%), 0]

Then, the backward induction method is used to determine the value of the year X cap.

For example, consider the year 3 cap. At the top node in year 3 of Exhibit 4(c), the 1-year rate is 9.1990%. Since the 1-year rate at this node exceeds 5.2%, the payoff in year 3 is:

$10,000,000 × (9.1990% – 5.2%) = $399,212

Using the backward induction method, the value of the year 3 cap is $150,211. Following the same procedure, the value of the year 2 cap is $66,009, and the value of the year 1 cap is $11,058. The value of the cap is then the sum of the cap for each of the three years. Thus, the value of the cap is $227,278, found by adding $150,211, $66,009, and $11,058.

An alternative procedure is to calculate the value of the cap as follows:

Step 1: For each year, determine the payoff of the cap at each node based on the reference rate at the node. Mathematically, the payoff is:

Notional principal amount × Maximum [(Rate at node – cap rate), 0]

Step 2: At each node one period prior to the maturity of the cap, the value of the cap at a node is found as follows:

$$\frac{\text{Average of the value at two nodes in next period}}{1 + \text{Rate at node}} + \text{Value found in Step 1}$$

Exhibit 4: Valuation of a 3-Year 5.2% Cap
(10% Volatility Assumed) By Valuing Each Year's Cap
Assumptions
Cap rate: 5.2%
Notional principal amount: $10,000,000
Payment frequency: Annual

Panel A: The Value of the Year 1 Cap

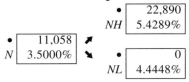

Value of Year 1 cap = $11,058

Panel B: The Value of the Year 2 Cap

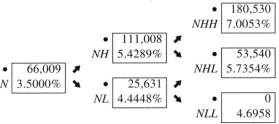

Value of Year 2 cap = $66,009

Panel C: The Value of the Year 3 Cap

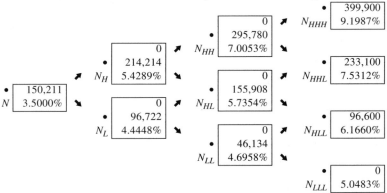

Value of Year 3 cap = $150,211

Summary: Value of 3-Year Cap = $150,211 + $66,009 + $11,058 = $227,278
Note on calculations: Payoff in last box of each exhibit is
$10,000,000 × Maximum[(Rate at node − 5.2%),0]

Exhibit 5: Valuation of a 3-Year 5.2% Cap (10% Volatility Assumed)

Assumptions
Cap rate: 5.2%
Notional principal amount: $10,000,000
Payment frequency: Annual

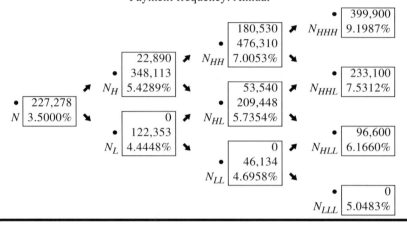

Step 3: Use the backward induction method to determine the value of the cap in year 0.

This is illustrated in Exhibit 5. Notice that the value of the 3-year cap is $227,278, the same value as found earlier.

The value of a floor can be found using the same three-step procedure. However, in Step 1, the payoff is:

Notional principal amount × Maximum [(Floor rate – Rate at node), 0]

Exhibit 6 illustrates the calculation of a 3-year floor with a strike rate of 4.8% and a $10 million notional principal amount. The value of the floor is $19,569.

OPTIONS ON SWAPS

The second generation of products in the interest rate swap market is an option on an interest rate swap, referred to as a *swaption*. The buyer of this option has the right to enter into an interest rate swap agreement on predetermined terms by some specified date in the future. The buyer of a put or call swaption pays the writer a premium.

A *put swaption* is an option allowing the buyer to enter into an interest rate swap in which the buyer pays a fixed rate and receives a floating rate, and the writer receives a fixed rate and pays a floating rate. A *call swaption* is an option that allows the buyer to enter into an interest rate swap where the buyer pays a floating rate and receives a fixed rate, while the writer receives a floating rate and pays a fixed rate. Swaptions may be exercised at any time prior to the expiration date (i.e., American type) or only at the expiration date (i.e., European type).

Exhibit 6: Valuation of a 3-Year 4.8% Floor (10% Volatility Assumed)

Assumptions
Cap rate: 4.8%
Notional principal amount: $10,000,000
Payment frequency: Annual

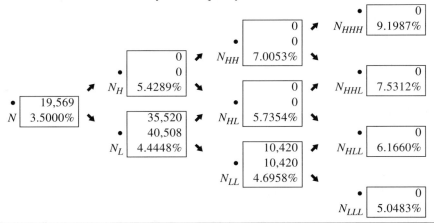

A callable or a putable swap is a swap with an embedded option. A putable swap effectively allows one of the parties to terminate the swap; it is therefore referred to as a *cancelable* or *terminable swap*.

KEY POINTS

1. OTC interest rate options are customized by dealers for their clients in terms of the expiration date, the underlying, and the type of exercise.

2. An OTC option can be created in which the buyer may exercise prior to the expiration date but only on designated dates (so called modified American or Atlantic or Bermuda options).

3. An OTC option can be created whereby the buyer pays the premium at the expiration date.

4. There are OTC options on specific securities.

5. There are OTC options on the spread between two yields.

6. Spread options can be structured with a payoff that is either cash settled or requires an exchange of ownership of the two securities underlying the option.

7. Two common spread options are options on the yield curve and options on the spread between mortgages and Treasuries.

8. The arbitrage-free binomial model is the proper model to value options on fixed-income securities since it takes into account the yield curve.

9. The arbitrage-free binomial model allows for the consistent pricing of Treasury bonds, Treasury bond futures, and options on Treasury bonds.

10. The put-call parity relationship is the pricing relationship between the price of a call option and the price of a put option on the same underlying instrument, with the same strike price and the same expiration date.

11. The put-call parity relationship is satisfied by the binomial model.

12. A compound option (also called a split-fee option) is an option to purchase an option.

13. The front fee for a compound option is the initial payment that the buyer makes.

14. The back fee for a compound option is the fee paid by the buyer if the option is exercised.

15. *An interest rate cap is an agreement whereby the seller agrees to pay the buyer if the reference rate exceeds the strike rate.*

16. *An interest rate floor is an agreement whereby the seller agrees to pay the buyer if the reference rate is below the strike rate.*

17. *The terms of a cap and floor set forth the reference rate, the strike rate, the length of the agreement, the frequency of reset, and the notional principal amount.*

18. *An interest rate collar can be created by buying an interest rate cap and selling an interest rate floor.*

19. *In an interest rate cap and floor, the buyer pays an upfront fee, which represents the maximum amount that the buyer can lose and the maximum amount that the seller of the agreement can gain.*

20. *Buying a cap is equivalent to buying a package of puts on a fixed-income security and buying a floor is equivalent to buying a package of calls on a fixed-income security.*

21. *If an option is viewed as one in which the underlying is an interest rate, then buying a cap is equivalent to buying a package of calls on interest rates and buying a floor is equivalent to buying a package of puts on interest rates.*

22. *The binomial method can be used to value a cap or a floor by valuing the cap or floor for each period and then summing these values.*

23. *A swaption is an option on interest rate swap that gives the buyer the right to enter into an interest rate swap agreement on predetermined terms by some specified date in the future.*

24. *A put swaption gives the buyer the right to enter into an interest rate swap in which the buyer pays a fixed rate and receives a floating rate, and the writer receives a fixed rate and pays a floating rate.*

25. *A call swaption gives the buyer the right to enter into an interest rate swap where the buyer pays a floating rate and receives a fixed rate, while the writer receives a floating rate and pays a fixed rate.*

26. *A callable or a putable swap is a swap with an embedded option.*

Chapter 12
Controlling Interest Rate Risk with Derivatives

In this chapter we look at how to control interest rate risk with derivative instruments. As explained in Chapters 3 and 4, interest rate risk includes level risk and yield curve risk. A risk control strategy can be employed to control the interest rate risk of a portfolio without regard to the price movement of any individual bond comprising the portfolio. This type of risk control strategy is called a *macro strategy*. Alternatively, a risk control strategy can be implemented to control the risk of an individual bond or a group of bonds with similar characteristics. This type of risk control strategy is called a *micro strategy*. With a micro strategy, there may be considerably less exposure to yield curve risk.

In this chapter, our illustration will involve micro strategies using derivative instruments. In the next chapter, we will look at how several derivative instruments can be used in combination to control the level risk and yield curve risk of a complex mortgage-backed securities portfolio.

The objectives of this chapter are to:

1. describe the preliminary steps in any risk control strategy;

2. explain the basic principles of controlling risk with interest rate futures;

3. explain what hedging and cross hedging are;

4. explain the basis risk associated with hedging;

5. demonstrate how interest rate futures can be used to hedge;

6. explain the basic principles of three common hedge strategies employing options — the protective put buying strategy, covered call writing strategy, and collar strategy;

7. illustrate the complexities associated with hedging with futures options;

8. illustrate how an interest rate swap and a swaption can be used to alter the risk exposure of a position; and,

9. explain how caps and floors can be used.

PRELIMINARY STEPS IN
ANY RISK CONTROL STRATEGY

There are four preliminary steps that a risk manager or portfolio manager should take before implementing any strategy to control interest rate risk:

1. Determine which instruments are the most appropriate to employ to control risk.
2. Determine the objectives of the strategy.
3. Determine the position that should be taken in a risk control instrument.
4. Assess the potential outcome of the risk control strategy.

These steps are essential for two reasons. First, by taking these steps, the manager can assess what a risk control strategy can and cannot accomplish. Second, the steps ensure that if the risk control strategy is employed, it is set up in the proper way.

Determining which Instruments
are the Most Appropriate to Employ

To control the interest rate risk of a position or portfolio, a position must be taken in another instrument or instruments. We shall focus on the use of derivative instruments as the risk control instruments. A primary factor in determining which instrument or instruments to use for controlling risk is the degree of correlation between the rate on the derivative instrument and the interest rate that creates the underlying risk that the manager seeks to control. For example, the rate risk associated with a long-term corporate bond portfolio can be better controlled with an instrument that is affected by long-term Treasury rates rather than short-term Treasury bill rates because long-term corporate bond rates are more highly correlated with the former than with the latter.

Correlation is not the only consideration if liquidity is of concern. For a position that requires liquidity, it may not be desirable to control its risk with an illiquid instrument or an instrument in which the value is determined solely by a counterparty. For example, managers who sought to control the risk of mortgage-backed securities found that when their positions were declining in value, the mortgage derivative products they used did not perform as expected because liquidity dried up for these instruments. A manager who uses some of the more complex over-the-counter derivative instruments that are priced by a dealer faces a similar risk. When size is an important consideration, even derivative instruments that are generally viewed as highly liquid may have a liquidity problem. In such cases, it may be necessary for the manager to use several vehicles rather than one.

Determining the Objectives of the Strategy

The measures described earlier in this book provide information about the potential loss from a position. Given the potential loss and the appropriate risk control instruments to employ, the manager should then determine what is expected from the risk control strategy. For example, hedging is a special case of risk control. Suppose that manager wants to hedge the risk associated with a current or anticipated future position of an individual bond (i.e., a micro hedging strategy). The manager should then determine what is expected from the hedge — that is, what rate will, on average, be locked in by the hedge. This is the *target rate* or *target price*. If this target rate is too high (if hedging a sale) or too low (if hedging a purchase), hedging may not be the right strategy for dealing with the unwanted risk.

Determining the Position that Should Be Taken in a Risk Control Instrument

Given the risk control instruments and the objectives of the strategy, the position that should be taken in the risk control instruments must be determined. A position has two dimensions. The first dimension is whether the position should be a long position or a short position. For example, if a manager seeks to reduce the interest rate risk exposure of a long position in a Treasury bond using Treasury bond futures, the appropriate position is a short position in the futures contract. The second dimension is the size of the position in the risk control instrument selected. For example, when using futures and options, it is the number of contracts. In the case of a swap, cap, and floor it is the notional principal amount. The amount of the position will depend on the dollar price volatility of the position whose risk the manager seeks to control relative to the derivative instrument used to control that risk. Later we will explain how this is done.

Assessing the Potential Outcome of the Risk Control Strategy

Given the position in the risk control instrument or instruments, the next step is to determine the potential outcome of the strategy. In many instances, this involves determining the outcome of the strategy under various scenarios that might be expected. That is, scenario analysis is performed. The scenarios analyzed will obviously involve different future interest rate levels.

In addition, because all risk control strategies make certain assumptions, it will be necessary to stress test the outcomes. For example, in the case of Treasury bond futures, a common assumption is that the cheapest-to-deliver issue will not change. In fact, the cheapest-to-deliver will change as interest rates change. The outcome of a risk control strategy can assess the potential impact of a change in the cheapest-to-deliver issue at different interest rate levels. As another example, it is common to make an assumption about the spread between two rates. So, a manager might make an assumption about the spread between single-A corporates and Treasuries when using Treasury bond futures to control the interest rate risk of a single-A corporate bond.

The scenarios analyzed can then be compared to the objectives established for the risk control strategy. It might be found, for example, that under a wide range of scenarios the objectives may be realized. On the other hand, it may turn out that for some scenarios that are reasonably likely to occur, the risk control strategy results in outcomes that are inferior to doing nothing at all.

In complex portfolios, the interaction among the random variables might require that simulation be employed. As explained in Chapter 5, the outcome of a simulation is a probability distribution. Given this distribution, the manager can assess the strategy in light of the objectives.

CONTROLLING INTEREST RATE RISK WITH FUTURES

We begin with the application of interest rate futures to control risk. The price of an interest futures contract moves in the opposite direction from the change in interest rates: when rates rise, the futures price will fall; when rates fall, the futures price will rise. By buying a futures contract, a portfolio's exposure to rate changes is increased. That is, the portfolio's duration increases. By selling a futures contract, a portfolio's exposure to rate changes is decreased. Equivalently, this means that the portfolio's duration is reduced.

The same exposure can be obtained by using cash market instruments. Treasury securities can be used to alter the duration of a position. Specifically, a long bond position's duration can be reduced by shorting an appropriate amount of Treasury securities and a short bond position's duration can be reduced by buying an appropriate amount of Treasury securities.

Using interest rate futures instead of Treasuries has three advantages. First, transactions costs for trading futures are lower than trading in the cash market. Second, margin requirements are lower for futures than for Treasury securities; using futures thus permits greater leverage. Finally, it is easier to sell short in the futures market than in the Treasury market. Consequently, while a manager can alter the duration of a portfolio with cash market instruments, a quick and inexpensive means for doing so (on either a temporary or permanent basis) is to use futures contracts.

General Principle

The general principle in controlling interest rate risk with futures is to combine the dollar value exposure of the current portfolio and that of a futures position so that it is equal to the target dollar exposure. This means that the manager must be able to accurately measure the dollar exposure of both the current portfolio and the futures contract employed to alter the exposure.

Dollar duration can be used to approximate the change in the dollar value of a bond or bond portfolio to changes in interest rates. In the foregoing discussion, when we refer to duration and dollar duration, we mean effective duration and effective dollar duration, respectively.

Suppose that a manager has a $200 million portfolio with a duration of 5 and wants to reduce the duration to 4. Thus, the target duration for the portfolio is 4. Given the target duration, a target dollar duration for a small number of basis point change in interest rates, say 50 basis points, can be obtained. A target duration of 4 means that for a 100 basis point change in rates (assuming a parallel shift in rates of all maturities), the target percentage price change is 4%. For a 50 basis point change, the target percentage price change is 2%. Multiplying the 2% by $250 million gives a target dollar duration of $5 million for a 50 basis point change in rates.

The manager must then determine the dollar duration of the current portfolio for a 50 basis point change in rates. Since the current duration for the portfolio is 5, the current dollar duration for a 50 basis point change in interest rates is $6.25 million. The target dollar duration is then compared to the current dollar duration. The difference between the two dollar durations is the dollar exposure that must be provided by a position in the futures contract. If the target dollar duration exceeds the current dollar duration, a futures position must increase the dollar exposure by the difference. To increase the dollar exposure, an appropriate number of futures contracts must be purchased. If the target dollar duration is less than the current dollar duration, an appropriate number of futures contracts must be sold.

Once a futures position is taken, the portfolio's dollar duration is equal to the current dollar duration without futures and the dollar duration of the futures position. That is,

Portfolio's dollar duration = Current dollar duration without futures
+ Dollar duration of futures position

The objective is to control the portfolio's interest rate risk by establishing a futures position such that the portfolio's dollar duration is equal to the target dollar duration. That is,

Portfolio's dollar duration = Target dollar duration

Or, equivalently,

Target dollar duration = Current dollar duration without futures
+ Dollar duration of futures position   (1)

Over time, the portfolio's dollar duration will move away from the target dollar duration. The manager can alter the futures position to adjust the portfolio's dollar duration to the target dollar duration.

Determining the Number of Contracts

Each futures contract calls for a specified amount of the underlying interest rate instrument. When interest rates change, the value of the underlying interest rate instrument changes, and therefore the value of the futures contract changes. How much the futures dollar value will change when interest rates change must be estimated. This amount is called the *dollar duration per futures contract*. For example, suppose the futures price of an interest rate futures contract is 70 and that the underlying interest rate instrument has a par value of $100,000. Thus, the futures delivery price (i.e., converted price) is $70,000 (0.70 times $100,000). Suppose that a change in interest rates of 50 basis points results in the futures price changing by about 3 points. Then the dollar duration per futures contract is $3,000 (0.03 times $100,000). Or equivalently, it is $3,000 per $100,000 par value of the underlying.

The dollar duration of a futures position is then the number of futures contracts multiplied by the dollar duration per futures contract. That is,

$$\text{Dollar duration of futures position} = \text{Number of futures contracts} \times \text{Dollar duration per futures contract} \tag{2}$$

To determine how many futures contracts are needed to obtain the target dollar duration, we can substitute equation (2) into equation (1). The result is

$$\text{Number of futures contracts} \times \text{Dollar duration per futures contract} = \text{Target dollar duration} - \text{Current dollar duration without futures} \tag{3}$$

Solving for the number of futures contracts we have:

$$\text{Number of futures contracts} = \frac{\text{Target dollar duration} - \text{Current dollar duration without futures}}{\text{Dollar duration per futures contract}} \tag{4}$$

Equation (4) gives the approximate number of futures contracts that are necessary to adjust the portfolio's dollar duration to the target dollar duration. A positive number means that the futures contract must be purchased; a negative number means that the futures contract must be sold. Notice that if the target dollar duration is greater than the current dollar duration without futures, the numerator is positive and therefore futures contracts are purchased. If the target dollar duration is less than the current dollar duration without futures, the numerator is negative and therefore futures contracts are sold.

HEDGING WITH FUTURES

Hedging with futures calls for taking a futures position as a temporary substitute for transactions to be made in the cash market at a later date. If cash and futures prices move together, any loss realized by the hedger from one position (whether cash or futures) will be offset by a profit on the other position. Hedging is a special case of controlling interest rate risk. In a hedge, the manager seeks a target duration or target dollar duration of zero.

Typically the bond or portfolio to be hedged is not identical to the bond underlying the futures contract. This type of hedging is referred to as *cross hedging*. There may be significant risks in cross hedging.

A *short* (or *sell*) *hedge* is used to protect against a decline in the cash price of a bond. To execute a short hedge, futures contracts are sold. By establishing a short hedge, the manager has fixed the future cash price and transferred the price risk of ownership to the buyer of the futures contract. A *long* (or *buy*) *hedge* is undertaken to protect against an increase in the cash price of a bond.

Hedge Effectiveness and Residual Hedging Risk

Earlier we described the four preliminary steps that a manager should undertake prior to the employment of a risk control strategy. In the case of hedging, the manager must try to assess the hedge effectiveness and the residual hedging risk. *Hedge effectiveness* lets the manager know what percent of risk is eliminated by hedging. For example, if the hedge effectiveness is determined to be 85% effective, over the long run a hedged position will have only 15% of the risk (that is, the standard deviation) of an unhedged position.

The *residual hedging risk* is the absolute level of risk in the hedged position. This risk tells the manager how much risk remains after hedging. While it may be comforting to know, for example, that 85% of the risk is eliminated by hedging, without additional statistics the manager still does not know how much risk remains. The residual hedging risk in a hedged position is expressed as a standard deviation. For example, it might be determined that the hedged position has a standard deviation of 10 basis points. Assuming a normal distribution of hedging errors, the manager will then obtain the target rate plus or minus 10 basis points 66% of the time. The probability of obtaining the target rate plus or minus 20 basis points is 95%, and the probability of obtaining the target rate plus or minus 30 basis points is greater than 99%.

The target rate, the hedge effectiveness, and the residual hedging risk determine the basic trade-off between risk and expected return. Consequently, these statistics give the manager the information needed to decide whether to employ a hedge strategy. Using these statistics, the manager can construct confidence intervals for hedged and unhedged positions. Comparing these confidence intervals, the manager can determine whether hedging is the best alternative. Furthermore, if hedging is the right decision, the level of confidence in the hedge is defined in advance.

It is important for a manager to realize that the hedge effectiveness and the residual hedging risk are not necessarily constant from one hedge to the next. Hedges for dates near a futures delivery date will tend to be more effective and have less residual hedging risk than those lifted on other dates. The life of the hedge, that is, the amount of time between when the hedge is set and when it is lifted, also generally has a significant impact on hedge effectiveness and residual hedging risk. For example, a hedge held for six months might be 95% effective, whereas a hedge held for one month might be only 30% effective. This is because the security to be hedged and the hedging instrument might be highly correlated over the long run, but only weakly correlated over the short run. On the other hand, residual hedging risk usually increases as the life of the hedge increases. The residual hedging risk on a 6-month hedge may be 80 basis points while the residual hedging risk for a 1-month hedge may be only 30 basis points. It may seem surprising that hedges for longer periods have more risk if they are also more effective. However, hedge effectiveness is a measure of relative risk, and because longer time periods exhibit greater swings in interest rates, the greater percentage reduction in risk for longer hedges does not mean that there is less risk left over.

The target rate, the residual risk, and the effectiveness of a hedge are relatively simple concepts. However, because these statistics are usually estimated using historical data, the manager who plans to hedge should be sure that these figures are estimated correctly.

Risk and Expected Return in a Hedge

In a micro hedge strategy, when a manager enters into a hedge, the objective is to "lock in" a rate for the sale or purchase of a security. However, there is much disagreement about what rate a manager should expect to lock in when futures are used to hedge. One view is that the manager can, on average, lock in the current spot rate for the security. The opposing view is that the manager will, on average, lock in the rate at which the futures contracts are bought or sold. The truth usually lies somewhere in between these two positions. However, as the following cases illustrate, each view is entirely correct in certain situations.

The Target for Hedges Held to Delivery Minimum variance hedges that are held until the futures delivery date provide an example of a hedge that locks in the futures rate. The complication in the case of using Treasury bond futures and Treasury note futures to hedge the value of intermediate- and long-term bonds, is that because of the delivery options the manager does not know for sure when delivery will take place or which bond will be delivered.

To illustrate how a Treasury bond futures held to the delivery date locks in the futures rate, assume for the sake of simplicity, that the manager knows which Treasury bond will be delivered and that delivery will take place on the last day of the delivery month. Consider the 7⅝s Treasury bonds maturing on February 15, 2007.[1] For delivery on the June 1985 contract, the conversion factor for these bonds was 0.9660, implying that the investor who delivers the 7⅝s would receive from the buyer 0.9660 times the futures settlement price, plus accrued interest. Consequently, at delivery, the (flat) spot price and the futures price times the conversion factor must converge. *Convergence* refers to the fact that at delivery there can be no discrepancy between the spot and futures price for a given security. If convergence does not take place, arbitrageurs would buy at the lower price and sell at the higher price and earn risk-free profits. Accordingly, a manager could lock in a June sale price for the 7⅝s by selling Treasury bond futures contracts equal to 0.9660 times the face value of the bonds. For example, $100 million face value of 7⅝s would be hedged by selling $96.6 million face value of bond futures (rounded to 967 contracts).

---

[1] This example is taken from Chapter 9 in Mark Pitts and Frank J. Fabozzi, *Interest Rate Futures and Options* (Chicago, IL: Probus Publishing, 1989).

Exhibit 1: Treasury Bond Hedge Held to Delivery

Instrument to be hedged: 7⅝s Treasury bonds of 2/15/07
Conversion factor for June 1985 delivery = 0.9660
Price of futures contract when sold = 70
Target price = 0.9660 × 70 = 67.62

Actual sale price for 7⅝s Treasury bond ($)	Final futures price ($)*	Gain or loss on 967 contracts ($; $10/0.01/contract)**	Effective sale price ($)***
62	64.182	5,620,188	67,620,118
63	65.217	4,620,378	67,620,378
64	66.253	3,619,602	67,619,602
65	67.288	2,619,792	67,619,792
66	68.323	1,619,982	67,619,982
67	69.358	620,172	67,620,172
68	70.393	−379,638	67,620,362
69	71.429	−1,380,414	67,619,568
70	72.464	−2,380,224	67,619,776
71	73.499	−3,380,034	67,619,966
72	74.534	−4,379,844	67,620,156
73	75.569	−5,379,654	67,620,346
74	76.605	−6,380,430	67,619,570
75	77.640	−7,380,240	67,619,760

*By convergence, must equal bond price divided by the conversion factor.
**Bond futures trade in even increments of 1⁄32. Accordingly, the futures prices and margin flows are only approximate.
***Transaction costs and the financing of margin flows are ignored.

The sale price that the manager locks in would be 0.9660 times the futures price. Thus, if the futures price is 70 when the hedge is set, the manager locks in a sale price of 67.62 (70 times 0.9660) for June delivery, regardless of where rates are in June. Exhibit 1 shows the cash flows for a number of final prices for the 7⅝s and illustrates how cash flows on the futures contracts offset gains or losses relative to the target price of 67.62. In each case, the effective sale price is very close to the target price (and, in fact, would be exact if enough decimal places were carried through the calculations). However, the target price is determined by the futures price, so the target price may be higher or lower than the cash market price when the hedge is set.

When we admit the possibility that bonds other than the 7⅝s of 2007 can be delivered, and that it might be advantageous to deliver other bonds, the situation becomes somewhat more involved. In this more realistic case, the manager may decide not to deliver the 7⅝s, but if she does decide to deliver them, the manager is still assured of receiving an effective sale price of approximately 67.62. If the manager does not deliver the 7⅝s, it would be because another bond can be delivered more cheaply, and thus the manager does better than the targeted price.

In summary, if a manager sets a risk minimizing futures hedge that is held until delivery, the manager can be assured of receiving an effective price dictated by the futures rate (not the spot rate) on the day the hedge is set.

The Target for Hedges with Short Holding Periods When a manager must lift (remove) a hedge prior to the delivery date, the effective rate that is obtained is much more likely to approximate the current spot rate than the futures rate the shorter the term of the hedge. The critical difference between this hedge and the hedge held to the delivery date is that convergence will generally not take place by the termination date of the hedge. This will be the case regardless of whether the manager is hedging with one of the short-term contracts (such as Eurodollar CD futures or Treasury bill futures) or hedging longer-term instruments with the intermediate- and long-term contracts.

To illustrate why a manager should expect the hedge to lock in the spot rate rather than the futures rate for very short-lived hedges, let's return to the simplified example used earlier to illustrate a hedge to the delivery date. It is assumed that the 7⅝s of 2007 were the only deliverable Treasury bonds for the Treasury bond futures contract. Suppose that the hedge is set three months before the delivery date and the manager plans to lift the hedge after one day. It is much more likely that the spot price of the bond will move parallel to the converted futures price (that is, the futures price times the conversion factor) than that the spot price and the converted futures price will converge by the time the hedge is lifted.

A 1-day hedge is, admittedly, an extreme example. However, it is not uncommon for traders and risk managers to have such a short horizon. Few money managers are interested in such a short horizon. The very short-term hedge does illustrate a very important point: when hedging, a manager should not expect to lock in the futures rate (or price) just because he is hedging with futures contracts. The futures rate is locked in only if the hedge is held until delivery, at which point convergence must take place. If the hedge is held for only one day, the manager should expect to lock in the 1-day forward rate, which will very nearly equal the spot rate. Generally hedges are held for more than one day, but not necessarily to delivery.

How the Basis Affects the Target Rate for a Hedge

The proper target for a hedge that is to be lifted prior to the delivery date depends on the basis. The *basis* is simply the difference between the spot (cash) price of a security and its futures price. That is:

Basis = Spot price − Futures price

In the bond market, a problem arises when trying to make practical use of the concept of the basis. The quoted futures price does not equal the price that one receives at delivery. For the Treasury bond and note futures contracts, the actual futures price equals the quoted futures price times the appropriate conversion factor. Consequently, to be useful the basis in the bond market should be defined using actual futures delivery prices rather than quoted futures prices. Thus, the price basis for bonds should be redefined as:

Price basis = Spot price − Futures delivery price

Unfortunately, problems still arise due to the fact that bonds age over time. Thus, it is not exactly clear what is meant by the "spot price." Does spot price mean the current price of the actual instrument that can be held and delivered in satisfaction of a short position, or does it mean the current price of an instrument that currently has the characteristics called for in the futures contract? For example, when the basis is defined for a 3-month Treasury bill contract maturing in three months, should spot price refer to the current price of a 6-month Treasury bill, which is the instrument that will actually be deliverable on the contract (because in three months it will be a 3-month Treasury bill), or should spot price refer to the price of the current 3-month Treasury bill? In most cases the former definition of the spot price makes the most sense.

For hedging purposes it is also frequently useful to define the basis in terms of interest rates rather than prices. The rate basis is defined as:

Rate basis = Spot rate − Futures rate

where spot rate refers to the current rate on the instrument to be hedged and the futures rate is the interest rate corresponding to the futures delivery price of the deliverable instrument.

The rate basis is helpful in explaining why the two types of hedges explained earlier are expected to lock in such different rates. To see this, we first define the *target rate basis*. This is defined as the expected rate basis on the day the hedge is lifted. A hedge lifted on the delivery date is expected to have, and by convergence will have, a zero rate basis when the hedge is lifted. Thus, the target rate for the hedge should be the rate on the futures contract plus the expected rate basis of zero, or in other words, just the futures rate. When a hedge is lifted prior to the delivery date, one would not expect the basis to change very much in one day, so the target rate basis equals the futures rate plus the current difference between the spot and futures rate, i.e., the current spot rate.

The manager can set the target rate for any hedge equal to the futures rate plus the target rate basis. That is,

Target rate for hedge = Futures rate + Target rate basis

If projecting the basis in terms of price rather than rate is more manageable (as is often the case for intermediate- and long-term futures), it is easier to work with the target price basis instead of the target rate basis. The target price basis is just the projected price basis for the day the hedge is to be lifted. For a deliverable security, the target for the hedge then becomes

Target price for hedge = Futures delivery price + Target price basis

The idea of a target price or rate basis explains why a hedge held until the delivery date locks in a price with certainty, and other hedges do not. As is often said, hedging substitutes basis risk for price risk, and the examples have shown that this is true. For the hedge held to delivery, there is no uncertainty surrounding the target basis; by convergence, the basis on the day the hedge is lifted is certain to be zero. For the short-lived hedge, the basis will probably approximate the current basis when the hedge is lifted, but its actual value is not known. For hedges longer than one day but ending prior to the futures delivery date, there can be considerable risk because the basis on the day the hedge is lifted can end up being anywhere within a wide range. Thus, the uncertainty surrounding the outcome of a hedge is directly related to the uncertainty surrounding the basis on the day the hedge is lifted, that is, the uncertainty surrounding the target basis.

For a given investment horizon hedging substitutes basis risk for price risk. Thus, one trades the uncertainty of the price of the hedged security for the uncertainty of the basis. Consequently, when hedges do not produce the desired results, it is customary to place the blame on "basis risk." However, basis risk is the real culprit only if the target for the hedge is properly defined. Basis risk should refer only to the unexpected or unpredictable part of the relationship between cash and futures. The fact that this relationship changes over time does not in itself imply that there is basis risk.

Basis risk, properly defined, refers only to the uncertainty associated with the target rate basis or target price basis. Accordingly, it is imperative that the target basis be properly defined if one is to correctly assess the risk and expected return in a hedge.

Cross Hedging

Earlier, we defined a cross hedge in the futures market as a hedge in which the security to be hedged is not deliverable into the futures contract used in the hedge. For example, a manager who wants to hedge the sale price of long-term corporate bonds might hedge with the Treasury bond futures contract, but since corporate bonds cannot be delivered in satisfaction of the contract, the hedge would be considered a cross hedge. Similarly, on the short end of the yield curve, a manager might want to hedge a 3-month rate that does not perfectly track the Treasury bill rate or the Eurodollar rate. A manager might also want to hedge a rate that is of the same quality as the rate specified in one of the contracts, but that has a different maturity. For example, it is necessary to cross hedge to hedge a Treasury bond, note, or bill with a maturity that does not qualify for delivery on any futures contract. Thus, when the security to be hedged differs from the futures contract specification in terms of either quality or maturity, one is led to the cross hedge.

Conceptually, cross hedging is somewhat more complicated than hedging deliverable securities, because it involves two relationships. First, there is the relationship between the cheapest-to-deliver (CTD) issue and the futures contract. Second, there is the relationship between the security to be hedged and the CTD. Practical considerations may at times lead a manager to shortcut this two-step relationship and focus directly on the relationship between the security to be hedged and the futures contract, thus ignoring the CTD altogether. However, in so doing, a manager runs the risk of miscalculating the target rate and the risk in the hedge. Furthermore, if the hedge does not perform as expected, the shortcut makes it difficult to tell why the hedge went awry.

The Hedge Ratio

The key to minimize risk in a cross hedge is to choose the right *hedge ratio*. The hedge ratio depends on the relative dollar duration of the bond to be hedged and the futures position. Equation (4) indicates the number of futures contract to achieve a particular target dollar duration. The objective in hedging is make the target dollar duration equal to zero. Substituting zero for target dollar duration in equation (4), we obtain:

$$\text{Number of futures contracts} = -\frac{\text{Current dollar duration without futures}}{\text{Dollar duration per futures contract}} \quad (5)$$

To calculate the dollar duration of a bond, the manager must know the precise point in time that the dollar duration is to be calculated (because volatility generally declines as a bond seasons) as well as the price or yield at which to calculate dollar duration (because higher yields generally reduce dollar duration for a given yield change). The relevant point in the life of the bond for calculating volatility is the point at which the hedge will be lifted. Dollar duration at any other point is essentially irrelevant because the goal is to lock in a price or rate only on that particular day. Similarly, the relevant yield at which to calculate dollar duration initially is the target yield. Consequently, the numerator of equation (5) is the dollar duration on the date the hedge is expected to be delivered. The yield that is to be used on this date in order to determine the dollar duration is the forward rate.

An example for a single bond rather than a portfolio shows why dollar duration weighting leads to the correct hedge ratio.[2] Suppose that on April 19, 1985, a money manager owned $10 million face value of the Southern Bell 11¾% bonds of 2023 and sold June 1985 Treasury bond futures to hedge a future sale of the bonds. This is an example of a cross hedge. Suppose that (1) the Treasury 7⅝s of 2007 were the cheapest-to-deliver issue on the contract and that they were trading at 11.50%, (2) the Southern Bell bonds were at 12.40%, and (3) the Treasury bond futures were at a price of 70. To simplify, assume also that the yield spread between the two bonds remains at 0.90% (i.e., 90 basis points) and that the anticipated sale date was the last business day in June 1985.

Because the conversion factor for the deliverable 7⅝s for the June 1985 contract was 0.9660, the target price for hedging the 7⅝s would be 67.62 (70×0.9660), and the target yield would be 11.789% (the yield at a price of 67.62). The yield on the telephone bonds is assumed to stay at 0.90% above the yield on the 7⅝s, so the target yield for the Southern Bell bonds would be

---

[2] This example is adapted from Pitts and Fabozzi, *Interest Rate Futures and Options*.

12.689%, with a corresponding price of 92.628. At these target levels, the dollar duration for a 50 basis point change in rates for the 7⅝s and telephone bonds per $100 of par value are, respectively, $2.8166 and $3.6282. As indicated earlier, all these calculations are made using a settlement date equal to the anticipated sale date, in this case the end of June 1985. The dollar duration for $10 million par value of the Southern Bell bonds is $362,820 ($10 million/100 times $3.6282). Per $100,000 of par value for the futures contract, the dollar duration per futures contract is $2,817 ($100,000/100 times $2.8166). Therefore:

> Current dollar duration without futures =
> Dollar duration of the Southern Bell bonds = $362,820

and

> Dollar duration of the CTD = $2,817

However, to calculate the hedge ratio, we need the dollar duration not of the CTD, but of the hedging instrument, that is, of the futures contract. Fortunately, knowing the dollar duration of the bond to be hedged relative to the CTD and the dollar duration of the CTD relative to the futures contract, we can easily obtain the hedge ratio:

$$\text{Hedge ratio} = -\frac{\text{Current dollar duration without futures}}{\text{Dollar duration of the CTD}}$$
$$\times \frac{\text{Dollar duration of the CTD}}{\text{Dollar duration per futures contract}} \tag{6}$$

Assuming a fixed yield spread between the bond to be hedged and the CTD, the hedge ratio given by equation (6) can be rewritten as:

$$\text{Hedge ratio} = -\frac{\text{Current dollar duration without futures}}{\text{Dollar duration of the CTD}}$$
$$\times \text{Conversion factor for the CTD} \tag{7}$$

Substituting the values from our example into equation (7):

$$\text{Hedge ratio} = -\frac{\$362,820}{\$2,817} \times 0.9660 = -124 \text{ contracts}$$

Thus, to hedge the Southern Bell position, 124 Treasury bond futures contracts must be shorted.

Scenario analysis can be used to show the potential outcome of this hedge. Exhibit 2 shows that, if the simplifying assumptions hold, a futures hedge using the recommended hedge ratio very nearly locks in the target price for $10 million face value of the telephone bonds.[3]

---

[3] In practice, most of the remaining error could be eliminated by frequent adjustments to the hedge ratio to account for the fact that the dollar duration changes as rates move up or down.

Exhibit 2: Hedging a Nondeliverable Bond to a Delivery Date with Futures: Scenario Analysis

Instrument to be hedged: Southern Bell 11¾s of 4/19/23
Par value = $10 million
Hedge ratio = 124
Price of futures contract when sold = 70
Target price for Southern Bell bonds = 92.628

Actual sale price of telephone bonds ($)	Yield at sale (%)	Yield on Treasury 7⅝s* (%)	Price of Treasury 7⅝s	Futures price**	Gain (loss) on 124 contracts ($10/0.01/contract) ($)	Effective sale price ($)***
7,600,000	15.468	14.568	54.590	56.511	1,672,636	9,272,636
7,800,000	15.072	14.172	56.167	58.144	1,470,144	9,270,144
8,000,000	14.696	13.769	57.741	59.773	1,268,148	9,268,148
8,200,000	14.338	13.438	59.313	61.401	1,066,276	9,266,276
8,400,000	13.996	13.096	60.887	63.030	864,280	9,264,280
8,600,000	13.671	12.771	62.451	64.649	663,524	9,263,524
8,800,000	13.359	12.459	64.018	66.271	462,396	9,262,396
9,000,000	13.061	12.161	65.580	67.888	261,888	9,261,888
9,200,000	12.776	11.876	67.134	69.497	62,372	9,262,372
9,400,000	12.503	11.603	68.683	71.100	(136,400)	9,263,600
9,600,000	12.240	11.340	70.233	72.705	(335,420)	9,264,580
9,800,000	11.988	11.088	71.773	74.299	(533,076)	9,266,924
10,000,000	11.745	10.845	73.312	75.892	(730,608)	9,269,392
10,200,000	11.512	10.612	74.839	77.473	(926,652)	9,273,348
10,400,000	11.287	10.387	76.364	79.052	(1,122,448)	9,277,552
10,600,000	11.070	10.170	77.884	80.625	(1,317,500)	9,282,500
10,800,000	10.861	9.961	79.394	82.188	(1,511,312)	9,288,688
11,000,000	10.659	9.759	80.889	83.746	(1,704,504)	9,295,496
11,200,000	10.463	9.563	82.403	85.303	(1,897,572)	9,302,428

* By assumption, the yield on the 7⅝s of 2007 is 90 basis points lower than the yield on the Southern Bell bond.
** By convergence, the futures price equals the price of the 7⅝s of 2007 divided by 0.9660 (the conversion factor).
*** Transaction costs and the financing of margin flows are ignored.

Another refinement in the hedging strategy is usually necessary for hedging nondeliverable securities. This refinement concerns the assumption about the relative yield spread between the CTD and the bond to be hedged. In the prior discussion, we assumed that the yield spread was constant over time. Yield spreads, however, are not constant over time. They vary with the maturity of the instruments in question and the level of rates, as well as with many unpredictable and nonsystematic factors.

Regression analysis allows the manager to capture the relationship between yield levels and yield spreads and use it to advantage. For hedging purposes, the variables are the yield on the bond to be hedged and the yield on the CTD. The regression equation takes the form:[4]

$$\text{Yield on bond to be hedged } = \alpha + \beta \times \text{Yield on CTD} + \text{error} \qquad (8)$$

The regression procedure provides an estimate of β (the *yield beta*), which is the expected relative yield change in the two bonds. Our example that used a constant spread implicitly assumes that the yield beta, β, equals 1.0 and α equals 90 basis points (the assumed spread).

For the two issues in question, that is, the Southern Bell 11¾s and the Treasury 7⅝s, suppose that the estimated yield beta was 1.05. Thus, yields on the corporate issue are expected to move 5% more than yields on the Treasury issue. To calculate the hedge ratio correctly, this fact must be taken into account; thus, the hedge ratio derived in our earlier example is multiplied by the factor 1.05. Consequently, instead of shorting 124 Treasury bond futures contracts to hedge $10 million of telephone bonds, the investor would short 130 contracts.

The formula for the hedge ratio is revised as follows to incorporate the impact of the yield beta:

$$\text{Hedge ratio } = -\;\frac{\text{Current dollar duration without futures}}{\text{Dollar duration of the CTD}}$$
$$\times \text{Conversion factor for CTD} \times \text{Yield beta} \qquad (9)$$

where the yield beta is derived from the yield of the bond to be hedged regressed on the yield of the CTD [equation (8)].

The effect of a change in the CTD and the yield spread can be assessed a priori. An exhibit similar to that of Exhibit 2 can be constructed under a wide range of assumptions. For example, at different yield levels at the date the hedge is to be lifted (the second column in Exhibit 2), a different yield spread may be appropriate and a different acceptable issue will be the CTD. The manager can determine what this will do to the outcome of the hedge.

Monitoring and Evaluating the Hedge

After a target is determined and a hedge is set, there are two remaining tasks. The hedge must be monitored during its life, and evaluated after it is over. A futures hedge may require very little active monitoring during its life. In fact, overactive manage-

---

[4] For an explanation of regression analysis, see Chapter 7.

ment may pose more of a threat to most hedges than does inactive management. The reason for this is that the manager usually will not receive enough new information during the life of the hedge to justify a change in the hedging strategy. For example, it is not advisable to readjust the hedge ratio every day in response to a new data point and a possible corresponding change in the estimated value of the yield beta.

There are, however, exceptions to this general rule. As rates change, dollar duration changes. Consequently, the hedge ratio may change slightly. In other cases, there may be sound economic reasons to believe that the yield beta has changed. While there are exceptions, the best approach is usually to let a hedge run its course using the original hedge ratio with only slight adjustments.

A hedge can normally be evaluated only after it has been lifted. Evaluation involves, first, an assessment of how closely the hedge locked in the target rate, that is, how much error there was in the hedge. To provide a meaningful interpretation of the error, the manager should calculate how far from the target the sale (or purchase) would have been, had there been no hedge at all.

One good reason for evaluating a completed hedge is to ascertain the sources of error in the hedge in the hope that a manager will gain insights that can be used to advantage in subsequent hedges. A manager will find that there are three major sources of hedging errors:

1. The projected value of the basis at the lift date can be in error.
2. The parameters estimated from the regression (α and β) can be inaccurate.
3. The error term in the regression may not equal zero.

Frequently, at least in the short run, the last two sources of error are indistinguishable. The manager will generally only know that the regression equation did not give an accurate estimate of the rate to be hedged. However, such inaccuracy could have occurred either from poor parameter estimates or from very accurate parameter estimates in conjunction with a large error term.

The first major source of errors in a hedge — an inaccurate projected value of the basis — is the more difficult problem. Unfortunately, there are no satisfactory simple models like the regression that can be applied to the basis. Simple models of the basis violate certain equilibrium relationships for bonds that should not be violated. On the other hand, theoretically rigorous models are very unintuitive and usually soluble only by complex numerical methods. Modeling the basis is undoubtedly one of the most important and difficult problems that managers seeking to hedge face.

HEDGING WITH OPTIONS

There are three popular hedge strategies employing options: (1) a protective put buying strategy, (2) a covered call writing strategy, and (3) a collar strategy. We begin with basic hedging principles for each strategy. Then we illustrate the first two strategies using futures options to hedge the Southern Bell bonds in which a futures hedge was used. Using futures options in our illustration of hedging the Southern Bell bonds is a worthwhile exercise because it shows how complicated hedging with futures options is and the key parameters involved in the process. We also compare the outcome of hedging with futures and hedging with futures options.[5]

Basic Hedging Strategies

Protective Puts Consider first a money manager who has a bond and wants to hedge against rising interest rates. The most obvious options hedging strategy is to buy puts on bonds. These *protective puts* are usually out-of-the-money puts and may be either puts on cash bonds or puts on interest rate futures. If interest rates rise, the puts will increase in value (holding other factors constant), offsetting some or all the loss on the bonds in the portfolio.

This strategy is a simple combination of a long put option with a long position in a cash bond. The result is a payoff pattern that resembles a long position in a call option alone. Such a position has limited downside risk, but large upside potential. However, if rates fall, the price appreciation on the securities in the portfolio will be diminished by the amount paid for the puts. Exhibit 3 compares the protective put strategy to an unhedged position.

The protective put strategy is very often compared to purchasing insurance. Like insurance, the premium paid for the protection is nonrefundable and is paid before the coverage begins. The degree to which a portfolio is protected depends upon the strike price of the options; thus, the strike price is often compared to the deductible on an insurance policy. The lower the deductible (that is, the higher the strike on the put), the greater the level of protection and the more the protection costs. Conversely, the higher the deductible (the lower the strike on the put), the more the portfolio can lose in value; but the cost of the insurance is lower. Exhibit 4 compares an unhedged position with several protective put positions, each with a different strike price, or level of protection. As the exhibit shows, no one strategy dominates any other strategy, in the sense of performing better at all possible rate levels. Consequently, it is impossible to say that one strike price is necessarily the "best" strike price, or even that buying protective puts is necessarily better than doing nothing at all.

Covered Call Writing Another options hedging strategy used by many portfolio managers is to sell calls against the bond portfolio; that is, to do *covered call writing*. The calls that are sold are usually out-of-the-money calls, and can be either calls on cash bonds or calls on interest rate futures. Covered call writing is just an outright long position combined with a short call position. The strategy thus results in a payoff pattern that resembles a short position in a put option alone. Obviously, this strategy entails much more downside risk than buying a put to protect the value of the portfolio. In fact, many portfolio managers do not consider covered call writing a hedge.

---

[5] The illustrations in this section are taken from Chapter 10 of Pitts and Fabozzi, *Interest Rate Futures and Options*.

Exhibit 3: Protective Put

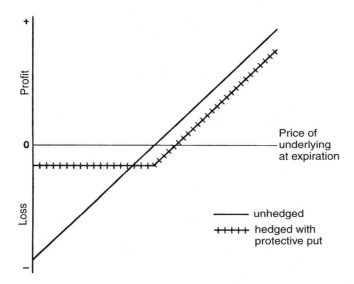

Exhibit 4: Protective Put with Different Strike Prices

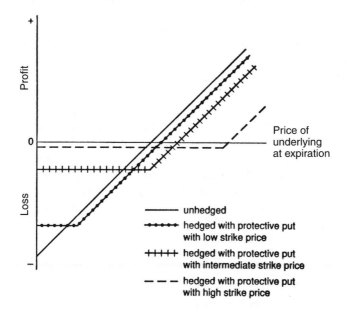

Regardless of how it is classified, it is important to recognize that while covered call writing has substantial downside risk, it has less downside risk than an unhedged long position alone. On the downside, the difference between the long position alone and the covered call writing strategy is the premium received for the calls that are sold. This premium acts as a cushion for downward movements in prices, reducing losses when rates rise. The cost of obtaining this cushion is that the manager gives up some of the potential on the upside. When rates decline, the call options become greater liabilities for the covered call writer. These incremental liabilities decrease the gains the portfolio manager would otherwise have realized on the portfolio in a declining rate environment. Thus, the covered call writer gives up some (or all) of the upside potential of the portfolio in return for a cushion on the downside. The more upside potential that is forfeited (that is, the lower the strike price on the calls), the more cushion there is on the downside. Like the protective put strategy, there is no "right" strike price for the covered call writer.

Comparing the two basic strategies for hedging with options, one cannot say that the protective put strategy or the covered call writing strategy is necessarily the better or more correct options hedge. The best strategy (and the best strike prices) depends upon the manager's view of the market. Purchasing a put and paying the required premium is appropriate if the manager is fundamentally bearish. If, on the other hand, the manager is neutral to mildly bearish, it is better to take in the premium on the covered call writing strategy. If the manager prefers to take no view on the market at all, and as little risk as possible, then a futures hedge is most appropriate. If the manager is fundamentally bullish, then no hedge at all is probably the best strategy.

Collars There are other options hedging strategies frequently used by money managers. For example, many managers combine the protective put strategy and the covered call writing strategy. By combining a long position in an out-of-the-money put and a short position in an out-of-the-money call, the manager creates a long position in a *collar*. The manager who uses the collar eliminates part of the portfolio's downside risk by giving up part of its upside potential.

The collar in some ways resembles the protective put, in some ways resembles covered call writing, in some ways resembles an unhedged position, and in some ways resembles a futures or forward hedge. The collar is like the protective put strategy in that it limits the possible losses on the portfolio if interest rates go up. Like the covered call writing strategy, the portfolio's upside potential is limited. Like an unhedged position, within the range defined by the strike prices the value of the portfolio varies with interest rates. On the other hand, if the put strike price and the call strike price are both equal to the forward price, the collar is just like a forward hedge, and the effective sale price is not dependent upon interest rates.

Options Hedging Preliminaries

As explained earlier, there are certain preliminaries that managers should consider before undertaking a risk control strategy. The best options contract to use depends upon several factors. These include option price, liquidity, and correlation with the bond(s) to be hedged.

In price-inefficient markets, the option price is important because not all options will be priced in the same manner or with the same volatility assumption. Consequently, some options may be overpriced and some underpriced. Obviously, with other factors equal, it is better to use the underpriced options when buying and the overpriced options when selling.

Whenever there is a possibility that the option position may be closed out prior to expiration, liquidity is also an important consideration. If the particular option is illiquid, closing out a position may be prohibitively expensive, and the manager loses the flexibility of closing out positions early, or rolling into other positions that may become more attractive.

Correlation with the underlying bond(s) to be hedged is another factor in selecting the right contract. The higher the correlation, the more precisely the final profit and loss can be defined as a function of the final level of rates. Poor correlation leads to more uncertainty. While most of the uncertainty in an options hedge usually comes from the uncertainty of interest rates themselves, slippage between the bonds to be hedged and the instruments underlying the options contracts add to that risk. Thus, the degree of correlation between the two underlying instruments is one of the determinants of the risk in the hedge.

Hedging Long-Term Bonds with Puts on Futures

As explained above, managers who want to hedge their bond positions against a possible increase in interest rates will find that buying puts on futures is one of the easiest ways to purchase protection against rising rates. To illustrate this strategy, we can use the same utility bond example that we used to demonstrate how to hedge with Treasury bond futures. In that example, a manager held Southern Bell 11¾s of 2023 and used futures to lock in a sale price for those bonds on a futures delivery date. Now we want to show how the manager could have used futures options instead of futures to protect against rising rates.

In the example, rates were already fairly high; the hedged bonds were selling at a yield of 12.40%, the Treasury 7⅝s of 2007 (the cheapest-to-deliver issue at the time) were at 11.50%. For simplicity, it was assumed that this yield spread would remain at 90 basis points.

Selecting the Strike Price The manager must determine the minimum price that he wants to establish for the hedged bonds. In our illustration it is assumed that the minimum price is 87.668. This is equivalent to saying that the manager wants to establish a strike price for a put option on the hedged bonds of 87.668. But, the manager is not buying a put option on the utility bonds. He is buying a put option on a Treasury bond futures contract. Therefore, the manager must determine the strike price for a put option on a Treasury bond futures contract that is equivalent to a strike price of 87.668 for the utility bonds.

Exhibit 5: Calculating Equivalent Prices and Yields For Hedging with Futures Options

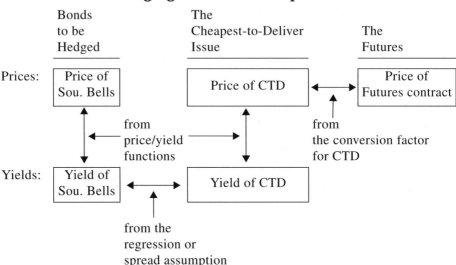

This can be done with the help of Exhibit 5. We begin at the top left hand box of the exhibit. Since the minimum price is 87.668 for the utility bonds, this means that the manager is attempting to establish a maximum yield of 13.41%. This is found from the relationship between price and yield: given a price of 87.668 for the utility bond, this equivalent to a yield of 13.41%. (This gets us to the lower left hand box in Exhibit 5.) From the assumption that the spread between the utility bonds and the cheapest-to-deliver issue is a constant 90 basis points, setting a maximum yield of 13.41% for the utility bond is equivalent to setting a maximum yield of 12.51% for the CTD. (Now we are at the lower box in the middle column of Exhibit 5.) Given the yield of 12.51% for the CTD, the minimum price can be determined (the top box in the middle column of the exhibit). A 12.51% yield for the Treasury 7⅝s of 2007 (the CTD at the time) gives a price of 63.756. The corresponding futures price is found by dividing the price of the CTD by the conversion factor. This gets us to the box in the right hand column of Exhibit 5. Since the conversion factor is 0.9660, the futures price is about 66 (63.7567 divided by 0.9660). This means that a strike price of 66 for a put option on a Treasury bond futures contract is roughly equivalent to a put option on the utility bonds with a strike price of 87.668.

The foregoing steps are always necessary to obtain the appropriate strike price on a put futures option. The process is not complicated. It simply involves (1) the relationship between price and yield, (2) the assumed relationship between the yield spread between the hedged bonds and the CTD, and (3) the conversion factor for the CTD. As with hedging employing futures illustrated earlier in this chapter, the success of the hedging strategy will depend on (1) whether the CTD changes and (2) the yield spread between the hedged bonds and the CTD.

Calculating the Hedge Ratio The hedge ratio is determined using the following equation similar to equation (7) since we will assume a constant yield spread between the security to be hedged and the CTD issue:

$$\text{Hedge ratio} = \frac{\text{Current dollar duration without option}}{\text{Dollar duration of the CTD}}$$
$$\times \text{Conversion factor for CTD}$$

For increased accuracy, we calculate the dollar durations at the option expiration date (assumed to be June 28, 1985 in our illustration) and at the yields corresponding to the futures strike price of 66 (12.51% for the CTD and 13.41% for the hedged bonds). The dollar durations are as follows per 50 basis point change in rates:

Current dollar duration without options = $326,070
Dollar duration of the CTD = $2,548

Notice that the dollar durations are different from those used in calculating the hedge ratio for the futures hedge in the previous chapter. This is because the dollar durations are calculated at prices corresponding to the strike price of the futures option (66), rather than the futures price (70). The hedge ratio is then:

$$\text{Hedge ratio} = \frac{\$326,070}{\$2,548} \times 0.9660 = 124 \text{ put options}$$

Thus, to hedge the Southern Bell position with put options on Treasury bond futures, 124 put options must be purchased.

Outcome of the Hedge To create a table for the protective put hedge, we can use some of the numbers from Exhibit 2. Everything will be the same except the last two columns. For the put option hedge we have to insert the value of the 124 futures put options in place of the 124 futures contracts in the next-to-last column. This is easy because the value of each option at expiration is just the strike price of the futures option (66) minus the futures price (or zero if that difference is negative), all multiplied by $1,000. The effective sale price for the hedged bonds is then just the actual market price for the hedged bonds plus the value of the options at expiration minus the cost of the options.

Suppose that the price of the put futures option with a strike price of 66 is 24. An option price of 24 means $24/64$ of 1% of par value, or $375. With a total of 124 options, the cost of the protection would have been $46,500 (124 × $375, not including financing costs and commissions). This cost, together with the final value of the options, is combined with the actual sale price of the hedged bonds to arrive at the effective sale price for the hedged bonds. These final prices are shown in the last column of Exhibit 6. This effective price is never less than 87.203. This equals the price of the hedged bonds equivalent to the futures strike price of 66 (i.e., 87.668), minus the cost of the puts (that is, $0.4650 = 1.24 \times {}^{24}/_{64}$). This minimum effective price is something that can be calculated before the hedge is ever initiated. As prices decline, the effective sale price actually exceeds the projected effective minimum sale price of 87.203 by a small amount. This is due only to rounding and the fact that the hedge ratio is left unaltered although the relative dollar durations that go into the hedge ratio calculation change as yields change. As prices increase, however, the effective sale price of the hedged bonds increases as well; unlike the futures hedge shown in Exhibit 2, the options hedge protects the investor if rates rise, but allows the investor to profit if rates fall.

Exhibit 6: Hedging a Nondeliverable Bond to a Delivery Date With Puts on Futures: Scenario Analysis

Instrument to be hedged: Southern Bell 11C\vs of 4/19/23
Hedge ratio = 124 puts
Strike price for puts on futures = 66-0
Target minimum price for hedged bonds = 87.203
Option price per contract = $375

Actual sale price of hedged bonds ($)	Yield at sale (%)	Futures price[*]	Value of 124 put options ($)[**]	Cost of 124 put options ($)	Effective sale price ($)[***]
7,600,000	15.468	56.511	1,176,636	46,500	8,730,136
7,800,000	15.072	58.144	974,144	46,500	8,727,644
8,000,000	14.696	59.773	772,148	46,500	8,725,648
8,200,000	14.338	61.401	570,276	46,500	8,723,776
8,400,000	13.996	63.030	368,280	46,500	8,721,780
8,600,000	13.671	64.649	167,524	46,500	8,721,024
8,800,000	13.359	66.271	0	46,500	8,753,500
9,000,000	13.061	67.888	0	46,500	8,953,500
9,200,000	12.776	69.497	0	46,500	9,153,500
9,400,000	12.503	71.100	0	46,500	9,353,500
9,600,000	12.240	72.705	0	46,500	9,553,500
9,800,000	11.988	74.299	0	46,500	9,753,500
10,000,000	11.745	75.892	0	46,500	9,953,500
10,200,000	11.512	77.473	0	46,500	10,153,500
10,400,000	11.287	79.052	0	46,500	10,353,500
10,600,000	11.070	80.625	0	46,500	10,553,500
10,800,000	10.861	82.188	0	46,500	10,753,500
11,000,000	10.659	83.746	0	46,500	10,953,500
11,200,000	10.463	85.303	0	46,500	11,153,500

* These numbers are approximate because futures trade in even 32nds.
** From $124 \times \$1,000 \times \text{Max}\{(66 - \text{Futures Price}), 0\}$.
*** Does not include transaction costs or the financing of the options position.

Covered Call Writing with Futures Options

Unlike the protective put strategy, covered call writing is not entered into with the sole purpose of protecting a portfolio against rising rates. The covered call writer, believing that the market will not trade much higher or much lower than its present level, sells out-of-the-money calls against an existing bond portfolio. The sale of the calls brings in premium income that provides partial protection in case rates increase. The premium received does not, of course, provide the kind of protection that a long put position provides, but it does provide some additional income that can be used to offset declining prices. If, on the other hand, rates fall, portfolio appreciation is limited because the short call position constitutes a liability for the seller, and this liability increases as rates go down. Consequently, there is limited upside potential for the covered call writer. Of course, this is not so bad if prices are essentially going nowhere; the added income from the sale of call options is obtained without sacrificing any gains.

To see how covered call writing with futures options works for the bond used in the protective put example, we construct a table much as we did before. With futures selling around 71-24 on the hedge initiation date, a sale of a 78 call option on futures might be appropriate. As before, it is assumed that the hedged bond will remain at a 90 basis point spread off the CTD (the 7⅝s of 2007). We also assume for simplicity that the price of the 78 calls is 24/64. The number of options contracts sold will be the same, namely 124 contracts for $10 million face value of underlying bonds. Exhibit 7 shows the results of the covered call writing strategy given these assumptions.

To calculate the effective sale price of the bonds in the covered call writing strategy, the premium received from the sale of calls is added to the actual sale price of the bonds, while the liability associated with the short call position is subtracted from the actual sale price. The liability associated with each call is the futures price minus the strike price of 78 (or zero if this difference is negative), all multiplied by $1,000. The middle column in Exhibit 7 is just this value multiplied by 124, the number of options sold.

Just as the minimum effective sale price could be calculated beforehand for the protective put strategy, the maximum effective sale price can be calculated beforehand for the covered call writing strategy. The maximum effective sale price will be the price of the hedged security corresponding to the strike price of the option sold, plus the premium received. In this case, the strike price on the futures call option was 76. A futures price of 76 corresponds to a price of 75.348 (from 76 times the conversion factor), and a corresponding yield of 10.536% for the CTD (the 7⅝s of 2007). The equivalent yield for the hedged bond is 90 basis points higher, or 11.436%, for a corresponding price of 102.666. Adding on the premium received, 0.465 points, the final maximum effective sale price will be about 103.131. As Exhibit 7 shows, if the hedged bond does trade at 90 basis points over the CTD as assumed, the maximum effective sale price for the hedged bond is, in fact, slightly over 103. The discrepancies shown in the exhibit are due to rounding and the fact that the position is not adjusted even though the relative dollar durations change as yields change.

Exhibit 7: Hedging a Nondeliverable Bond to a Delivery Date With Calls on Futures: Scenario Analysis

Instrument to be hedged: Southern Bell 11C\vs of 4/19/23
Hedge ratio = 124 calls
Strike price for calls on futures = 78-0
Expected maximum price for hedged bonds = 103.131
Option price per contract = $375

Actual sale price of hedged bonds ($)	Yield at sale (%)	Futures price[*]	Liability of 124 call options ($)[**]	Premium from 124 call options ($)	Effective sale price ($)[***]
7,600,000	15.468	56.511	0	46,500	7,646,500
7,800,000	15.072	58.144	0	46,500	7,846,500
8,000,000	14.696	59.773	0	46,500	8,046,500
8,200,000	14.338	61.401	0	46,500	8,246,500
8,400,000	13.996	63.030	0	46,500	8,446,500
8,600,000	13.671	64.649	0	46,500	8,646,500
8,800,000	13.359	66.271	0	46,500	8,846,500
9,000,000	13.061	67.888	0	46,500	9,046,500
9,200,000	12.776	69.497	0	46,500	9,246,500
9,400,000	12.503	71.100	0	46,500	9,446,500
9,600,000	12.240	72.705	0	46,500	9,646,500
9,800,000	11.988	74.299	0	46,500	9,846,500
10,000,000	11.745	75.892	0	46,500	10,046,500
10,200,000	11.512	77.473	0	46,500	10,246,500
10,400,000	11.287	79.052	130,448	46,500	10,316,052
10,600,000	11.070	80.625	325,500	46,500	10,321,000
10,800,000	10.861	82.188	519,312	46,500	10,327,188
11,000,000	10.659	83.746	712,504	46,500	10,333,996
11,200,000	10.463	85.303	905,572	46,500	10,340,928

* These numbers are approximate because futures trade in even 32nds.
** From $124 \times \$1,000 \times \text{Max}\{(\text{Futures Price} - 76), 0\}$.
*** Does not include transaction costs.

Comparing Alternative Strategies

We reviewed three basic strategies for hedging a bond position: (1) hedging with futures, (2) hedging with out-of-the-money puts, and (3) covered call writing with out-of-the-money calls. Similar, but opposite, strategies exist for those whose risks are that rates will decrease. As might be expected, there is no "best" strategy. Each strategy has its advantages and its disadvantages, and we never get something for nothing. To get anything of value, something else of value must be forfeited.

To make a choice among strategies, it helps to lay the alternatives side by side. Using the futures and futures options examples from this chapter, Exhibit 8 shows the final values of the portfolio for the various hedging alternatives. It is easy to see from Exhibit 8 that if one alternative is superior to another alternative at one level of rates, it will be inferior at some other level of rates.

Exhibit 8: Alternative Hedging Strategies Compared

Actual sale price of bonds ($)	Yield at sale (%)	Effective sale price with futures hedge ($)	Effective sale price with protective puts ($)	Effective sale price with covered calls ($)
7,600,000	15.468	9,272,636	8,730,136	7,646,500
7,800,000	15.072	9,270,144	8,727,644	7,846,500
8,000,000	14.696	9,268,148	8,725,648	8,046,500
8,200,000	14.338	9,266,276	8,723,776	8,246,500
8,400,000	13.996	9,264,280	8,721,780	8,446,500
8,600,000	13.671	9,263,524	8,721,024	8,646,500
8,800,000	13.359	9,262,396	8,753,500	8,846,500
9,000,000	13.061	9,261,888	8,953,500	9,046,500
9,200,000	12.776	9,262,372	9,153,500	9,246,500
9,400,000	12.503	9,263,600	9,353,500	9,446,500
9,600,000	12.240	9,264,580	9,553,500	9,646,500
9,800,000	11.988	9,266,924	9,753,500	9,846,500
10,000,000	11.745	9,269,392	9,953,500	10,046,500
10,200,000	11.512	9,273,348	10,153,500	10,246,500
10,400,000	11.287	9,277,552	10,353,500	10,316,052
10,600,000	11.070	9,282,500	10,553,500	10,321,000
10,800,000	10.861	9,288,688	10,753,500	10,327,188
11,000,000	10.659	9,295,496	10,953,500	10,333,996
11,200,000	10.463	9,302,428	11,153,500	10,340,928

Consequently, we cannot conclude that one strategy is the best strategy. The manager responsible for selecting the strategy makes a choice among probability distributions, not usually among specific outcomes. Except for the perfect hedge, there is always some range of possible final values of the portfolio. Of course, exactly what that range is, and the probabilities associated with each possible outcome, is a matter of opinion.

Hedging with Options on Cash Instruments

Hedging a position with options on cash bonds is relatively straightforward. Most strategies, including the purchase of protective puts, covered call writing, and creating collars, are essentially the same whether futures options or options on physicals are used. As explained in Chapters 10 and 11, there are some mechanical differences in the way the two types of contracts are traded, and there may be substantial differences in the liquidity of the two types of contracts. Nonetheless, the basic economics of the strategies are virtually identical.

Using options on physicals frequently relieves the manager of much of the basis risk associated with an options hedge. For example, a manager of Treasury bonds or notes can usually buy or sell options on the exact security held in the portfolio. Using options on futures, rather than options on Treasury bonds, is sure to introduce additional elements of uncertainty.

Given the illustration presented above, and given that the economics of options on physicals and options on futures are essentially identical, additional illustrations for options on physicals are unnecessary. The only important difference is the hedge ratio calculation and the calculation of the equivalent strike. To derive the hedge ratio, we always resort to an expression of relative dollar durations. Thus, for options on physicals, assuming a constant spread the hedge ratio is:

$$\text{Hedge ratio} = \frac{\text{Current dollar duration without options}}{\text{Dollar duration of underlying for option}}$$

If a relationship is estimated between the yield on the bonds to be hedged and the instrument underlying the option, the appropriate hedge ratio is:

$$\text{Hedge ratio} = \frac{\text{Current dollar duration without options}}{\text{Dollar duration of underlying for option}} \times \text{Yield beta}$$

Unlike futures options, there is only one deliverable, so there is no conversion factor. When cross hedging with options on physicals, the procedure for finding the equivalent strike price on the bonds to be hedged is very similar. Given the strike price of the option, the strike yield is easily determined using the price/yield relationship for the instrument underlying the option. Then given the projected relationship between the yield on the instrument underlying the option and the yield on the bonds to be hedged, an equivalent strike yield is derived for the bonds to be hedged. Finally, using the yield-to-price formula for the bonds to be hedged, the equivalent strike price for the bonds to be hedged can be found.

CONTROLLING INTEREST RATE RISK WITH SWAPS

As we explained in Chapter 9, an interest rate swap is equivalent to a package of forward/futures contracts. Consequently, swaps can be used in the same way as futures and forwards for controlling interest rate risk. The dollar duration of an interest rate swap was explained in Chapter 3.

The following illustration demonstrates how an interest rate swap can be used to hedge interest rate risk by altering the cash flow characteristics of a portfolio so as to match assets and liabilities. In our illustration we will use two hypothetical financial institutions — a commercial bank and a life insurance company.

Suppose a bank has a portfolio consisting of 4-year term commercial loans with a fixed interest rate. The principal value of the portfolio is $100 million, and the interest rate on all the loans in the portfolio is 11%. The loans are interest-only loans; interest is paid semiannually, and the principal is paid at the end of four years. That is, assuming no default on the loans, the cash flow from the loan portfolio is $5.5 million every six months for the next four years and $100 million at the end of four years. To fund its loan portfolio, assume that the bank can borrow at 6-month LIBOR for the next four years.

The risk that the bank faces is that 6-month LIBOR will be 11% or greater. To understand why, remember that the bank is earning 11% annually on its commercial loan portfolio. If 6-month LIBOR is 11%, there will be no spread income. Worse, if 6-month LIBOR rises above 11%, there will be a loss; that is, the cost of funds will exceed the interest rate earned on the loan portfolio. The bank's objective is to lock in a spread over the cost of its funds.

The other party in the interest rate swap illustration is a life insurance company that has committed itself to pay an 8% rate for the next four years on a guaranteed investment contract (GIC) it has issued. The amount of the GIC is $100 million. Suppose that the life insurance company has the opportunity to invest $100 million in what it considers an attractive 4-year floating-rate instrument in a private placement transaction. The interest rate on this instrument is 6-month LIBOR plus 120 basis points. The coupon rate is set every six months. The risk that the life insurance company faces in this instance is that 6-month LIBOR will fall so that the company will not earn enough to realize a spread over the 8% rate that it has guaranteed to the GIC policyholders. If 6-month LIBOR falls to 6.8% or less, no spread income will be generated. To understand why, suppose that 6-month LIBOR at the date the floating-rate instrument resets its coupon is 6.8%. Then the coupon rate for the next six months will be 8% (6.8% plus 120 basis points). Because the life insurance company has agreed to pay 8% on the GIC policy, there will be no spread income. Should 6-month LIBOR fall below 6.8%, there will be a loss.

We can summarize the asset/liability problems of the bank and the life insurance company as follows.

Bank:
    1. has lent long term and borrowed short term
    2. if 6-month LIBOR rises, spread income declines

Life insurance company:
    1. has lent short term and borrowed long term
    2. if 6-month LIBOR falls, spread income declines

Now let's suppose the market has available a 4-year interest rate swap with a notional principal amount of $100 million. The swap terms available to the bank are as follows:

    1. every six months the bank will pay 9.50% (annual rate)
    2. every six months the bank will receive LIBOR

The swap terms available to the insurance company are as follows:

    1. every six months the life insurance company will pay LIBOR
    2. every six months the life insurance company will receive 9.40%

Now let's look at the position of the bank and the life insurance company after the swap. Exhibit 9 summarizes the position of each institution before and after the swap. Consider first the bank. For every 6-month period for the life of the swap agreement, the interest rate spread will be as follows:

Annual interest rate received:

From commercial loan portfolio	=	11.00%
From interest rate swap	=	6-month LIBOR
Total	=	11.00% + 6-month LIBOR

Annual interest rate paid:

To borrow funds	=	6-month LIBOR
On interest rate swap	=	9.50%
Total	=	9.50% + 6-month LIBOR

Outcome:

To be received	=	11.00% + 6-month LIBOR
To be paid	=	9.50% + 6-month LIBOR
Spread income	=	1.50% or 150 basis points

Thus, whatever happens to 6-month LIBOR, the bank locks in a spread of 150 basis points.

Now let's look at the effect of the interest rate swap on the life insurance company:

Annual interest rate received:

From floating-rate instrument	=	1.20% + 6-month LIBOR
From interest rate swap	=	9.40%
Total	=	10.60% + 6-month LIBOR

Annual interest rate paid:

To GIC policyholders	=	8.00%
On interest rate swap	=	6-month LIBOR
Total	=	8.00% + 6-month LIBOR

Outcome:

To be received	=	10.60% + 6-month LIBOR
To be paid	=	8.00% + 6-month LIBOR
Spread income	=	2.60% or 260 basis points

Regardless of what happens to 6-month LIBOR, the life insurance company locks in a spread of 260 basis points.

Exhibit 9: Position of Bank and Life Insurance Company Before and After Swap

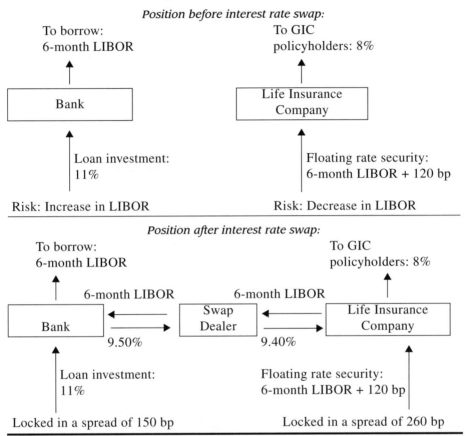

The interest rate swap has allowed each party to accomplish its asset/liability objective of locking in a spread.[6] It permits the two financial institutions to alter the cash flow characteristics of its assets: from fixed to floating in the case of the bank, and from floating to fixed in the case of the life insurance company. This type of transaction is referred to as an *asset swap*. Another way the bank and the life insurance company could use the swap market would be to change the cash flow nature of their liabilities. Such a swap is called a *liability swap*.

Role of Swaptions

Suppose that the commercial loans can be prepaid by the borrowers. Then the strategy using swaps that we have just described exposes the bank to a sharp decline in interest rates. For example, suppose that interest rates decline such that

---

[6] Whether the size of the spread is adequate is not an issue to us in this illustration.

borrowers can obtain a commercial loan at an 8% rate. This is far below the 11% rate on the loans. As a result, suppose that the borrowers take advantage of this situation and prepay their commercial loan. The bank is still obligated under the swap agreement to make payments of 9.5%. Where will the funds to satisfy that obligation going to come from? The bank must reinvest the proceeds from the prepaid commercial loans in some other fixed-rate investment that will generate at least 9.5%. However, by assumption the rates are assumed to have fallen to 8%.

This situation clearly indicates the need for an instrument that allows a party to a swap to exit the swap. As we explained in Chapter 11, this derivative instrument is an option on a swap (swaption).

USING CAPS AND FLOORS TO CONTROL RISK

Interest rate caps can be used by a liability manager to create a cap for funding costs. Combining a cap and a floor creates a collar for funding costs. Floors can be used by buyers of floating-rate instruments to set a floor on the periodic interest earned. To reduce the cost of a floor, a manager can sell a cap. By doing so, the manager limits the upside on the coupon rate of a floating rate instrument should rates rise, thereby creating a collar for the coupon interest on a floating-rate instrument.

To see how interest rate agreements can be used for asset/liability management, consider the problems faced by the commercial bank and the life insurance company we just discussed in demonstrating the use of an interest rate swap. The bank's objective is to lock in a spread over its cost of funds. Yet because it borrows short term, its cost of funds is uncertain. The bank may be able to purchase a cap, however, so that the cap rate plus the cost of purchasing the cap is less than the rate it is earning on its fixed-rate commercial loans. If short-term rates decline, the bank does not benefit from the cap, but its cost of funds declines. The cap therefore allows the bank to impose a ceiling on its cost of funds while retaining the opportunity to benefit from a decline in rates. This is consistent with the view of an interest rate cap as simply a package of options.

The bank can reduce the cost of purchasing the cap by selling a floor. In this case, the bank agrees to pay the buyer of the floor if the reference rate falls below the strike rate. The bank receives a fee for selling the floor, but it has sold off its opportunity to benefit from a decline in rates below the strike rate. By buying a cap and selling a floor, the bank has created a predetermined range for its cost of funds (i.e., a collar).

Recall the problem of the life insurance company that guarantees a 9% rate on a GIC for the next four years and is considering the purchase of an attractive floating-rate instrument in a private placement transaction. The risk that the company faces is that interest rates will fall so that it will not earn enough to realize the 9% guaranteed rate plus a spread. The life insurance company may be able to purchase a floor to set a lower bound on its investment return, yet retain the opportunity to benefit should rates increase. To reduce the cost of purchasing the floor, the life insurance company can sell an interest rate cap. By doing so, however, it gives up the opportunity of benefiting from an increase in the reference rate above the strike rate of the interest rate cap.

KEY POINTS

1. A macro risk control strategy is one used to control the interest rate risk of a portfolio without regard to the price movement of any individual bond comprising the portfolio.

2. A micro risk control strategy can be implemented to control the risk of an individual bond or a group of bonds with similar characteristics.

3. There are four preliminary steps that should be taken before a risk control strategy is initiated so that a manager can assess what a hedge strategy can and cannot accomplish.

4. The key factor to determine which derivative instrument or instruments to use is the degree of correlation between the rate underlying the derivative instrument and the rate that creates the risk that the manager seeks to control.

5. Buying an interest rate futures contract increases a portfolio's duration; selling an interest rate futures contract decreases a portfolio's duration.

6. The advantages of adjusting a portfolio's duration using futures rather than cash market instruments are transactions costs are lower, margin requirements are lower, and it is easier to sell short in the futures market.

7. The general principle in controlling interest rate risk with futures is to combine the dollar exposure of the current portfolio and that of a futures position so that it is equal to the target dollar exposure.

8. The number of futures contracts needed to achieve the target dollar duration depends on the current dollar duration of the portfolio without futures and the dollar duration per futures contract.

9. Hedging with futures calls for taking a futures position as a temporary substitute for transactions to be made in the cash market at a later date, with the expectation that any loss realized by the manager from one position (whether cash or futures) will be offset by a profit on the other position.

10. Hedging is a special case of controlling interest rate risk in which the target duration or target dollar duration is zero.

11. Cross hedging occurs when the bond to be hedged is not identical to the bond underlying the futures contract.

12. *A short or sell hedge is used to protect against a decline in the cash price of a bond; a long or buy hedge is employed to protect against an increase in the cash price of a bond.*

13. *The manager should determine the target rate or target price, which is what is expected from the hedge.*

14. *The manager should estimate the hedge effectiveness, which indicates what percent of risk is eliminated by hedging.*

15. *The manager should estimate the residual hedging risk, which is the absolute level of risk in the hedged position and indicates how much risk remains after hedging.*

16. *The target rate, the hedge effectiveness, and the residual hedging risk determine the basic trade-off between risk and expected return and these statistics give the manager the information needed to decide whether to employ a hedge strategy.*

17. *The hedge ratio is the number of futures contracts needed for the hedge.*

18. *The basis is the difference between the spot price (or rate) and the futures price (or rate).*

19. *In general, when hedging to the delivery date of the futures contract, a manager locks in the futures rate or price.*

20. *Hedging with Treasury bond futures and Treasury note futures is complicated by the delivery options embedded in these contracts.*

21. *When a hedge is lifted prior to the delivery date, the effective rate (or price) that is obtained is much more likely to approximate the current spot rate than the futures rate the shorter the term of the hedge.*

22. *The proper target for a hedge that is to be lifted prior to the delivery date depends on the basis.*

23. *Basis risk refers only to the uncertainty associated with the target rate basis or target price basis.*

24. *Hedging substitutes basis risk for price risk.*

25. *Hedging non-Treasury securities with Treasury bond futures requires that the hedge ratio consider two relationships: (1) the cash price of the non-Treasury security and the cheapest-to-deliver issue and (2) the price of the cheapest-to-deliver issue and the futures price.*

26. *After a target is determined and a hedge is set, the hedge must be monitored during its life and evaluated after it is over and the sources of error in a hedge should be determined in order to gain insights that can be used to advantage in subsequent hedges.*

27. *Three popular hedge strategies are the protective put buying strategy, the covered call writing strategy, and the collar strategy.*

28. *A manager can use a protective put buying strategy — a combination of a long put option with a long position in a cash bond — to hedge against rising interest rates.*

29. *A covered call writing strategy involves selling call options against the bond portfolio.*

30. *A covered call writing strategy entails much more downside risk than buying a put to protect the value of the portfolio and many portfolio managers do not consider covered call writing a hedge.*

31. *It is not possible to say that the protective put strategy or the covered call writing strategy is necessarily the better or more correct options hedge since it depends upon the manager's view of the market.*

32. *A collar strategy is a combination of a protective put strategy and a covered call writing strategy which eliminates part of the portfolio's downside risk by giving up part of its upside potential.*

33. *The best options contract to use depends upon the option price, liquidity, and correlation with the bond(s) to be hedged.*

34. *For a cross hedge, the manager will want to convert the strike price on the options that are actually bought or sold into an equivalent strike price for the actual bonds being hedged.*

35. *When using Treasury bond futures options, the hedge ratio is based on the relative dollar duration of the current portfolio, the cheapest-to-deliver issue, and the futures contract at the option expiration date, as well as the conversion factor for the cheapest-to-deliver issue.*

36. *An interest rate swap can be used to hedge interest rate risk by altering the cash flow characteristics of a portfolio of assets so as to match asset and liability cash flows.*

37. *A position in a swap can expose a position to greater interest rate risk if it is not coupled with a swaption.*

38. *Interest rate caps can be used in liability management to create a cap for funding costs.*

39. *Combining a cap and a floor creates a collar for funding costs.*

40. *Floors can be used by buyers of floating-rate instruments to set a floor on the periodic interest earned and the sale of a cap can reduce the cost of a floor.*

Chapter 13
Controlling Interest Rate Risk of an MBS Derivative Portfolio[1]

Investors in mortgage-backed securities (MBS) are exposed to level risk and yield curve risk. While we have demonstrated the yield curve risk for a bond portfolio, the value of an individual MBS is particularly vulnerable to changes in the shape of the yield curve. In this chapter, we will present a fairly simple approach to systematically measure and control the exposure of an MBS portfolio to changes in the level and slope of the yield curve. More specifically, we look at a portfolio of MBS derivative products. These products include collateralized mortgage obligations and stripped mortgage-backed securities.[2] For simplicity, we shall refer to these derivative products as simply collateralized mortgage obligations (CMOs).

The objectives of this chapter are to:

1. review the slope elasticity measure of yield curve risk;

2. explain what is meant by positive and negative slope elasticity;

3. demonstrate the importance of yield curve risk for an MBS;

4. look at the yield curve risk for different types of collateralized mortgage obligation bonds;

5. look at the yield curve risk for different potential hedging instruments; and,

6. demonstrate the steps that a manager can follow to measure and control level and yield curve risk exposures of an MBS portfolio.

---

[1] This chapter is coauthored with Michael P. Schumacher, Director of Mortgage Research at Smith Barney, and Daniel Dektar, Principal at Smith Breeden Associates. It is adapted from Michael P. Schumacher, Daniel C. Dektar, and Frank J. Fabozzi, "Yield Curve Risk of CMO Bonds," Chapter 15 in Frank J. Fabozzi (ed.), *CMO Portfolio Management* (Summit, NJ: Frank J. Fabozzi Associates, 1994).

[2] It is assumed that the reader is familiar with these products. For a description, see Frank J. Fabozzi, Chuck Ramsey, and Frank Ramirez, *Collateralized Mortgage Obligations: Structures and Analysis* (New Hope, PA: Frank J. Fabozzi Associates, 1995).

SLOPE ELASTICITY MEASURE OF YIELD CURVE RISK: A REVIEW

In Chapters 3, we explained that the effective duration and convexity of a bond or portfolio is a measure of its exposure to changes in the level of interest rates. In Chapter 4, we demonstrated that duration and convexity are inadequate measures of rate changes if the yield curve does not shift in a parallel fashion. We then described several approaches to the measurement of yield curve risk. The simplest approach is the slope elasticity measure which was defined in Chapter 4. We shall review this measure here.

The slope elasticity measure looks at the sensitivity of a position or portfolio to changes in the slope of the yield curve. The yield curve slope can be defined as the spread between a long-term and short-term on-the-run Treasury yield. In this chapter, we will use the 3-month Treasury bill yield and 30-year Treasury yield as the short-term and long-term yields, respectively. This is basically the longest and the shortest points on the Treasury yield curve. While this is not a perfect definition, it captures most of the effect of changes in yield curve slope.

Changes in the yield curve can be defined as follows: half of any basis point change in the yield curve slope results from a change in the 3-month yield and half from a change in the 30-year yield. For example, with a 100 basis point steepening of the yield curve, the assumption is that 50 basis points of that steepening come from a rise in the 30-year yield, and another 50 basis points come from a fall in the 3-month yield.

The slope elasticity is then defined as the approximate negative percentage change in a bond's price resulting from a 100 basis point change in the slope of the curve. Slope elasticity is calculated as follows:

(1) increase and decrease the yield curve slope,
(2) calculate the price change for these two scenarios after adjusting for the price effect of a change in the level of yields, and
(3) compare the prices to the initial or base price.

More specifically, the slope elasticity for each scenario is calculated as follows:

$$\frac{\text{Price effect of a change in slope}/\text{Base price}}{\text{Change in yield curve slope}}$$

The slope elasticity is then the average of the slope elasticity for the two scenarios.

A bond or portfolio that benefits when the yield curve flattens is said to have *positive slope elasticity*; a bond or portfolio that benefits when the yield curve steepens is said to have *negative slope elasticity*.

YIELD CURVE RISK AND ITS IMPORTANCE

The definition of yield curve risk follows naturally from that of slope elasticity. It is defined as the exposure of the bond to changes in the slope of the yield curve.

Exhibit 1: Yield Curve Slope Based on Treasury Rates as of 12/31/92

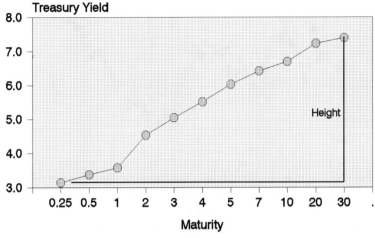

Exhibit 2: Yield Curve Risk for a Principal-Only Strip

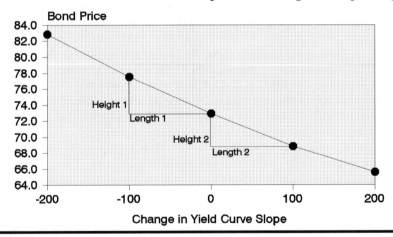

As an illustration, Exhibit 1 shows the yield curve slope based on Treasury rates as of December 31, 1992. Exhibit 2 shows the price behavior of a principal-only (PO) strip, given changes in the yield curve shown in Exhibit 1. As the curve flattens, the price of the PO increases substantially. As the yield curve steepens, the price of the PO declines.

This result is completely independent of changes in the level of interest rates. That is, we assume that the level of rates is fixed and therefore focus only on the effect of changes in the slope of the yield curve. Consequently, a manager who might hedge the effective duration of a PO strip position with interest rate futures will still face extremely significant exposure to changes in the slope of the yield curve.

Exhibit 3: Historical Yield Curve Slope: Dec. 1983-Dec. 1992

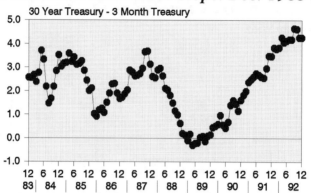

This is important to remember when dealing with CMO bonds because the structures are often complicated, and the cash flows may exhibit very odd patterns. While there is also yield curve risk for a passthrough, it is typically less significant than for CMOs.

Exhibit 3 illustrates the volatility of the yield curve slope from December 1983 to December 1992. In mid-1989 the yield curve was actually inverted. By 1992, the yield curve slope was more than 400 basis points, representing a remarkable steepening of the curve. While managers recognize that the yield curve slope has changed over time, what they may not realize is that this steepening has had an enormous effect on the value of some CMO bonds.

For example, unhedged inverse floater positions typically benefit from both a decline in interest rates and a steepening of the yield curve, but the same position may be adversely affected if the yield curve flattens.

A graphic example of yield curve risk and its importance in the payoff pattern of an interest-only (IO) strip is shown in Exhibit 4. The particular IO shown in the exhibit is Trust 2, backed by FNMA 10% fixed-rate passthroughs. As the yield curve steepens, the IO appreciates significantly. If the yield curve flattens, the IO declines significantly. Basically, this pattern is the opposite of what we saw for the PO in Exhibit 2. This should not be surprising, as IOs and POs typically move in opposite directions with regard to parallel shifts in the yield curve; the same thing is true with regard to changes in the slope of the yield curve.

YIELD CURVE RISK FOR DIFFERENT CMO BONDS

Now that we have demonstrated the importance of yield curve risk, we examine the actual slope exposure for a variety of CMO bonds. The analysis is based on projected prices under different yield curve scenarios using a valuation model. In this chapter, the analysis is performed using the Smith Breeden pricing model. It should be noted that yield curve slope exposure is very structure-specific. Consequently, it is difficult to generalize about the slope exposure of CMO bonds.

Exhibit 4: Yield Curve Risk of Interest-Only Strip

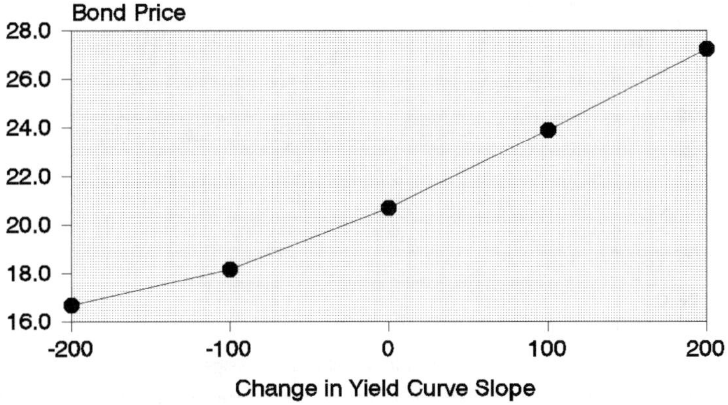

The approach we will use to determine the slope exposure of a particular CMO bond is to assess the impact of changes in yield curve slope on three factors affecting the value of the bond: discount rates, projected prepayment rates (cash flows), and embedded caps and floors. The net slope exposure of the bond is essentially the sum of these three slope components.

The impact of a change in yield curve slope on the appropriate series of discount rates for a CMO bond is usually clear-cut. For instance, a flattening yield curve implies discount rates on distant cash flows decrease, while discount rates on near cash flows increase. A security with a long average life benefits from this change in discount rates because its cash flows are weighted toward the long end of the yield curve. Conversely, a security with a relatively short average life suffers from the change in discount rates resulting from a flattening yield curve because its cash flows are weighted toward the short end of the yield curve.

The second factor affecting a CMO bond's yield curve exposure is the impact of a change in yield curve slope on the bond's projected cash flows. As the yield curve flattens, forward rates decrease; consequently, anticipated prepayment rates increase, and the CMO bond's expected life typically shortens. Not surprisingly, CMO bonds priced below par usually benefit from an increase in projected prepayment rates, while bonds priced at a premium generally suffer when projected prepayment rates increase. The impact of a change in yield curve slope on future cash flows (via changing prepayment rates) can be very powerful, and this component of slope exposure often dominates the other two components.

Finally, the third factor we consider is the effect of a change in yield curve slope on the value of embedded options. Many CMO bonds contain either explicit or implicit embedded options. For instance, most CMO floaters are capped; hence, a manager who owns a CMO floater is short an interest rate cap. The value of this cap varies with changes in yield curve slope and can have a significant influence on the overall yield curve exposure of the bond.

Exhibit 5: Yield Curve Risk of a Fixed-Rate Sequential

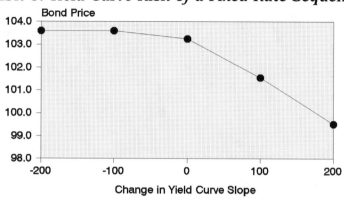

To analyze the change in value of an option embedded in a CMO bond, we consider the behavior of a standard over-the-counter cap or floor, given the same change in the yield curve. We know that a flattening yield curve causes long-term forward rates to decrease. The value of a long-term cap will fall under this scenario because the decrease in long-term forward rates results in the cap being farther out of the money. Conversely, the value of a long-term interest rate floor increases as the yield curve flattens because the drop in forward rates makes the floor more in the money. The values of caps and floors change in opposite directions when the yield curve steepens: long-term caps increase in value, while long-term floors fall in value.

By analyzing these three components of slope sensitivity, we can determine the net slope exposure of a CMO bond. A manager could gain additional insight by quantifying the effect of each of these factors independently, although that evaluation could prove quite complicated and is not necessary. This framework allows us to develop intuition for the likely impact of a change in yield curve slope on the value of a given CMO bond.

Sequential-Pay Bonds

The first CMO bond to be analyzed for yield curve slope risk is a fixed-rate sequential pay bond — basically a plain vanilla CMO bond. The profile is shown in Exhibit 5. A short maturity sequential typically has very little slope risk. Most of these bonds are priced near par, so changes in projected prepayment rates have minimal impact on their value. These bonds are not explicitly capped, and do not have significant embedded options. Therefore, the factor that generally determines the bond's slope exposure is the impact of a change in yield curve slope on the bond's discount rates. As the yield curve flattens, short-term interest rates rise. Since the short sequential bond's cash flows are weighted toward the short end of the yield curve, the change in discount rates will reduce the value of the bond and can result in a small negative slope elasticity.

Changes in projected prepayment rates, however, will dominate the effect of changing discount rates and result in a positive (negative) slope elasticity if the sequential is priced significantly below (above) par. A long sequential bond is more likely than a short sequential to be priced significantly above or below par. If the bond is priced fairly close to par, it will benefit if the yield curve flattens. Again, the flattening yield curve causes long-term discount rates to fall, and short-term discount rates to rise, thereby benefiting the long sequential, which by definition has cash flows weighted toward the long end of the yield curve.

An interesting feature of many CMO bonds is that slope exposure tends to be asymmetric. The short sequential bond is a good example of this effect. Exhibit 5 shows that the sequential bond benefits somewhat when the yield curve flattens 100 basis points. Yet an additional 100 basis points of flattening has little effect on the bond's value. The pattern for a steepening yield curve is quite different. As the yield curve steepens, the sequential bond extends, and it continues to extend over a relatively large range of yield curve slopes. Therefore, the bond loses substantially if the yield curve steepens, but benefits very little if the curve flattens.

PAC Bonds

Exhibit 6 shows the second type of CMO bond, a PAC bond. The PAC bond is very similar to a long sequential bond in terms of its yield curve slope risk. Both a long PAC bond and a long sequential bond benefit from relatively lower discount rates if the yield curve flattens. The major difference between the two bonds is that the PAC bond's cash flows are much more stable than the cash flows from the sequential bond because the bond is protected within a prepayment band. The PAC bond's cash flows are usually therefore much less sensitive than the sequential's cash flows to changes in projected prepayment rates. Consequently, the second component of yield curve slope exposure, the effect of changing prepayment rates, generally has little effect on a PAC bond.

One caveat is that it is impossible to generalize accurately about the exposure of PAC bonds to large changes in slope since the value of a PAC bond is very dependent on its structure. For instance, the huge increase in prepayment rates in 1992 and early 1993 has resulted in prepayment rates on many PAC bonds breaking the PAC band, thereby causing these bonds to behave as sequential bonds.

The example PAC bond in Exhibit 6 has fairly symmetric slope exposure. The slope elasticity is 0.6%. The bond's effective duration is approximately 4 which means this PAC bond's price will change by approximately 4% for a 100 basis point change in rates. Thus, in this case the slope elasticity is 15% of the effective duration. Although yield curve slope risk has a much smaller effect than changes in the actual level of rates, it can have an enormous impact on the value of a CMO portfolio.

VADM Bonds

The next CMO bond we examine is a very accurately defined maturity bond (VADM). The profile with respect to yield curve slope changes is shown in

Exhibit 7. As the exhibit shows, the slope elasticity is very similar to that of a PAC (this is a 10-year VADM as opposed to the 7-year PAC in Exhibit 6). As with a PAC, a short average life VADM has very low slope risk, while a longer VADM generally benefits if the yield curve flattens.

The main difference between a VADM and a PAC bond is that the VADM's cash flows are even better protected from changing prepayment rates than are the PAC bond's cash flows. The VADM receives its paydown from the interest accrual on a Z bond (zero coupon). On a continuum of prepayment sensitivity, sequential bonds are the most sensitive to prepayments, PACs are in the middle, and VADMs have the lowest prepayment sensitivity. The impact of low prepayment sensitivity on slope exposure is that the second component of slope risk, the effect of changing prepayment rates on the value of the bond, is usually quite small for a VADM.

Exhibit 6: Yield Curve Risk of a Planned Amortization Class

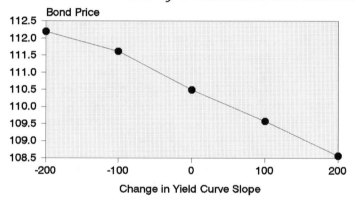

Exhibit 7: Yield Curve Risk of a VADM Bond

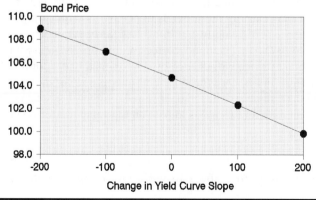

Exhibit 8: Yield Curve Risk of a Pro Rata LIBOR Floater

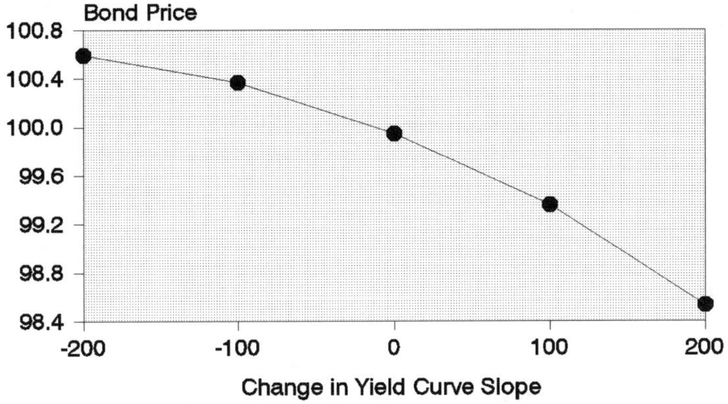

The exception to this rule occurs if prepayment rates have increased or decreased markedly since the VADM was issued. The VADM is not perfectly protected from changing prepayment rates, and a large change in prepayments will affect the value of the bond. Consequently, a VADM's slope sensitivity is usually symmetric for small changes in yield curve slope, but becomes asymmetric for large changes in yield curve slope.

Pro Rata LIBOR Floater

A pro rata floater is a floating-rate class that pays down with the collateral. The coupon on a floater is usually capped; therefore, the investor is short a LIBOR cap. In essence, then, a LIBOR floater can be viewed as a pure floating-rate bond minus a LIBOR cap. Exhibit 8 shows the yield curve risk of a pro rata floater backed by fixed-rate collateral.

Only two of the three components determining net slope exposure are relevant for a pro rata LIBOR floater. The value of a floater is relatively unaffected by the impact on discount rates resulting from a change in yield curve slope, but changes in yield curve slope do affect prepayment rates and the value of embedded options.

The primary effect of a change in yield curve slope on a floater is through the value of embedded options. For example, as the yield curve flattens, forward Treasury and LIBOR rates decrease. A cap is simply a series of put options on forward LIBOR bond prices (or call options on forward LIBOR rates), so falling LIBOR rates reduce the value of the cap. The floater is short a LIBOR cap, so a flattening yield curve increases the value of the floater. Hence, the floater has positive slope elasticity.

The magnitude of the floater's slope elasticity is a function of the strike price of the embedded cap. The floater in Exhibit 8 has a high cap; consequently, its slope elasticity is not large, 0.4%. A floater with an at-the-money LIBOR cap would have a much larger slope elasticity than 0.4%. This pattern can be seen in Exhibit 8 for a 100-basis point flattening and a 100-basis point steepening.

Exhibit 9: Yield Curve Risk of a Discount Inverse Floater

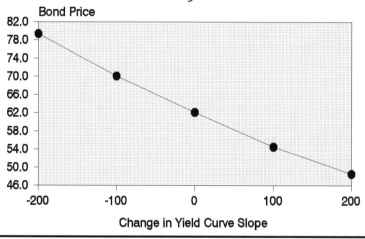

The changes in the price of the floater for small changes in yield curve slope are fairly symmetric, but the floater does not benefit significantly for incremental yield curve flattening in excess of 100 basis points. If the curve steepens, however, the floater will lose considerably. When the yield curve steepens, the cap is coming closer to being in the money; in the parlance of option pricing theory, its delta is becoming more negative. Therefore, the floater's slope elasticity will become more positive, and its price decline as the yield curve steepens will accelerate.

This graph looks quite similar to the profile of the price of a typical fixed-rate mortgage versus changes in the level of rates. So there is negative convexity in slope exposure, just as there is with respect to changes in the level of interest rates.

Inverse Floaters

Inverse floaters come in all shapes and sizes. An inverse floater and a floater can be combined to produce a fixed-rate tranche; so as the floater is short a cap, the inverse floater is long a cap. The long cap and the price at which an inverse floater trades effectively determine the bond's slope elasticity. At the time of this analysis, the inverse floater shown in Exhibit 9 was at a discount. As we go through this example, we explain how the slope elasticity would differ for a portfolio of premium inverse floaters.

The two most important factors to consider in evaluating the slope exposure of an inverse floater are its price (i.e., its tendency to benefit/suffer if prepayment rates increase) and the "delta" of its embedded long LIBOR cap. As is the case with the capped pro rata floater, the cap embedded in the inverse floater decreases in value as the yield curve flattens.

The decline in the value of the cap benefits a floater, since it is short the cap, but reduces the price of the inverse floater since it is long the cap. The decline in the value of the cap would produce negative slope elasticity if no other effects were present. The inverse floater in Exhibit 9, however, has positive slope elasticity and actually benefits substantially as the yield curve flattens. This inverse floater's slope elasticity is positive rather than negative because it gains considerably from increasing prepayment rates. The price of this inverse floater is 62.13, so it is a deep discount bond.

An increase in prepayment rates will clearly benefit the holder of this bond, who will be repaid at par while the bond's price is far below par. A flattening yield curve causes projected prepayment rates to increase, thereby benefiting the inverse floater and overwhelming the impact of the change in value of the embedded long cap.

While the deep discount inverse floater in Exhibit 9 has positive slope elasticity, a premium inverse floater would almost certainly have negative slope elasticity. Suppose we are dealing with a premium inverse floater priced at 105. The investor who purchased this inverse floater would clearly be at a disadvantage if prepayment speeds increase. In this case, a flattening yield curve would hurt the investor, because the long cap position would become less valuable and also because a loss is incurred as the principal is prepaid more quickly.

As a result, a premium inverse floater has a negative slope elasticity, while a discount inverse floater has a positive slope elasticity — +9.6% for the discount inverse floater in Exhibit 9. Thus, it is important to analyze the yield curve risk exposure of each inverse floater.

Interest-Only Strip

Exhibit 10 shows the yield curve risk of a 10% IO strip. This instrument exhibits negative slope elasticity. Investors in IO strips suffer as prepayment rates increase because they do not receive any principal, and the stream of interest payments is shortened. We have seen that a flattening yield curve causes prepayment speeds to increase, while a steepening yield curve produces slower prepayment speeds. In this case, it is very clear why an IO strip has negative slope elasticity, unless it is backed by extremely high-premium collateral that is burned out. Consequently, IOs are a good hedge for a portfolio that has considerable positive slope elasticity (i.e., a portfolio that benefits if the curve flattens and loses if it steepens). IOs are one of the few CMO bonds that a manager can use to counteract positive slope elasticity.

Principal-Only Strip

The PO strip is nearly the opposite of the IO strip. PO holders benefit as prepayment rates increase because they receive their principal more quickly. Consequently, a PO strip increases in value if the yield curve flattens, and decreases in value if the yield curve steepens. The yield curve risk profile shown in Exhibit 11 is for an 8% PO strip that has substantial positive slope elasticity.

Exhibit 10: Yield Curve Risk of a 10% Interest-Only Strip

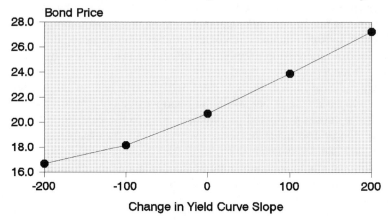

Exhibit 11: Yield Curve Risk of an 8% Principal-Only Strip

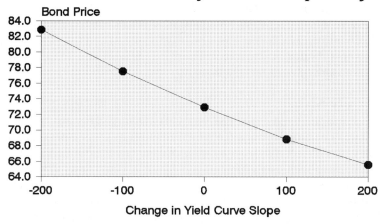

Whether the curve in Exhibit 11 is shaped like this (positively convex) or is in fact bowed down (negatively convex) depends on the spread between the coupon of the collateral backing the PO and the current coupon mortgage rate. At the time of this analysis, the PO in the exhibit is backed by 8s selling at a discount. Had the PO used in the illustration been a PO backed by 11s (a premium), the curve would be negatively convex. Thus, the benefit of a flattening yield curve for a PO backed by high-coupon mortgages would be much less than it would be for a PO backed by low-coupon mortgages. Once again, yield curve risk is specific to the actual deal or structure from which the PO was created.

Exhibit 12 summarizes for various CMO bonds the effective duration and the slope elasticity of the yield curve as of July 31, 1992.

Exhibit 12: Effective Duration and Slope Elasticities for a Variety of CMO Bonds

Type of CMO Bond	Effective duration	Elasticity for Slope of Yield Curve (%)
Sequential	3.3	0.7
LIBOR Floater	0.9	0.4
Inverse Floater	30.7	9.6
PAC	3.6	0.6
VADM	5.7	1.7
IO Strip	−23.9	−11.5
PO Strip	13.1	4.7

MANAGING LEVEL AND SLOPE RISK INDEPENDENTLY

Given the exposure of each CMO bond in a portfolio, a manager should be able to make an informed decision about what kind of hedge to put on or how to manage that risk. For example, a portfolio with a substantial amount of POs benefits significantly if the yield curve flattens, but suffers if the yield curve steepens. It would make sense to restructure the assets or implement hedges to reduce the portfolio's yield curve risk.

The key point is that yield curve slope risk and duration risk (i.e., exposure to parallel shifts in the yield curve) can, for the most part, be managed independently. The reason for this is that the correlation of changes in the level of rates and yield curve slope is very low. What if it were the case that whenever rates rose the yield curve got steeper, or when rates fell the yield curve flattened? In that case, changes in yield curve slope and changes in the level of rates would be highly correlated, and a manager would have to consider the effect or exposure of a portfolio to changes both in the level of rates and in slope simultaneously. A manager could not effectively separate the two effects.

The relationship of changes in the level of rates to changes in yield curve slope is an empirical question. To investigate this question, we calculated the historical correlation between changes in the slope of the curve and changes in the level of rates, as well as changes in the curvature of the yield curve. In this analysis the level of rates is defined as the average of the 6-month, 5-year, and 30-year Treasury yields, while the curvature of the yield curve is defined as the 5-year Treasury rate minus the average of the 6-month and 30-year Treasury yields.

The correlation results, shown in Exhibit 13, are based on monthly data; they would probably be somewhat higher if a longer differencing interval were used. The correlation of 0.12 between changes in the level of rates and changes in the slope of the curve is quite low. While it is not zero, it is low enough to give a manager comfort that yield curve slope exposure can be calculated and managed independently of parallel interest rate shifts. This is an important property because if this were not the case, a manager would have to implement an elaborate Monte Carlo model to assess the joint effect of level and slope exposures based on a correlation between the two factors. This would be a difficult and costly exercise.

Exhibit 13: Correlation Matrix for Changes in Level of Interest Rates, Yield Curve Slope, and Curvature: Monthly Rates from 12/82 through 12/92

Parameter	Level	Slope	Curvature
Level	1.0000		
Slope	0.1152	1.0000	
Curvature	0.4974	0.5540	1.0000

MANAGING YIELD CURVE SLOPE RISK

We know how slope risk affects particular types of CMO bonds. Now let's look at the problem of slope risk in the context of a CMO bond portfolio. We also present an approach for measuring slope risk and how to hedge or manage this risk.

Determining the Slope Elasticity of Potential Risk Control Instruments

The first step is to determine the slope elasticity of the candidates for hedging yield curve risk exposure. The instruments most commonly used to hedge slope exposure are interest rate futures (Treasury bonds, 10-year Treasury notes, 5-year Treasury notes, and Eurodollar CDs), interest rate swaps, yield curve options, and caps and floors. A customized risk control vehicle can be created by a commercial bank or an investment bank, but interest rate futures typically do a very good job of controlling slope exposure.

Slope Exposure of Interest Rate Futures Interest rate futures contracts have different types of yield curve risk, but their yield curve exposures are intuitively obvious. Treasury bond futures are on the long end of the yield curve, so they benefit when the yield curve flattens (long rates decline relative to short rates). Treasury bond futures therefore have large positive slope elasticity.

Ten-year Treasury note futures also benefit when the yield curve flattens. They have positive slope elasticity, but it's less than the slope elasticity for Treasury bonds. Five-year Treasury note futures are largely unaffected by changes in yield curve slope since five years is approximately the center of the yield curve. Given the way slope is defined in this chapter (the 30-year Treasury rate minus the 3-month Treasury bill rate), 5-year Treasury note futures have a very small, positive slope elasticity.

Eurodollar futures are on the short end of the yield curve, so a long position in Eurodollar futures benefits when short rates decline. A decline in short rates corresponds to a steepening yield curve; hence, Eurodollar futures have a negative slope elasticity. Treasury bill futures are also on the short end of the yield curve and have negative slope elasticity.

Exhibit 14: Yield Curve Exposure of Interest Rate Futures

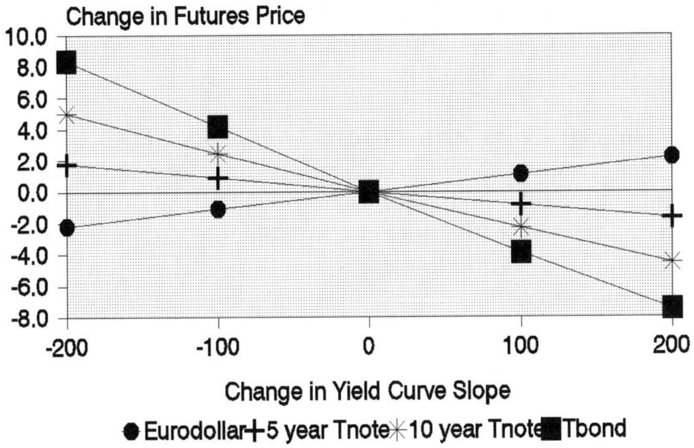

Change in Futures Price

Change in Yield Curve Slope

● Eurodollar ＋ 5 year Tnote ✳ 10 year Tnote ■ Tbond

Exhibit 15: Sample Effective Duration and Slope Elasticities For Interest Rate Futures

Futures Contract	Effective Duration	Elasticity for Slope of Yield Curve (%)
Treasury Bond	9.7	3.6
10-year T Note	6.3	2.1
5-year T Note	3.8	0.8
Eurodollar	0.3	−0.2
Treasury Bill	0.3	−0.2

Exhibit 14 shows the yield curve slope exposure for all but the Treasury bill futures contract. The steepness (or slope) of the line corresponds to the slope elasticity. The line corresponding to the Treasury bond futures contract is the steepest, which means it has the highest slope elasticity.

Thus, a manager who owns a long CMO bond with positive slope elasticity could establish a position that would gain if the curve flattens, simply by shorting bonds. As can be seen from Exhibit 14, as well as Exhibit 15, which shows both the yield curve slope elasticity and effective duration, futures contracts have slope sensitivities that differ in magnitude as well as direction. This means that a manager should be able to manage the risk of a CMO portfolio with these contracts.

Slope Exposure of Interest Rate Swaps An interest rate swap can have either positive or negative slope elasticity, depending on the maturity of the swap. A swap in which the investor receives a fixed rate and makes floating-rate payments is called a "long" swap. A long swap is very similar to a long position in a Treasury note or bond coupled with a short position in Eurodollar futures. A long swap generally has positive slope elasticity if the maturity of the swap is greater than five years; otherwise it has negative slope elasticity.

Slope Exposure of Yield Curve Options Yield curve options can be structured in numerous ways. This flexibility provides a manager with many ways in which to control slope risk, but also makes it difficult to generalize in describing the slope elasticity of these options.

Slope Exposure of Caps and Floors As explained in Chapter 11, an interest rate cap is an agreement in which one party receives payments from a counterparty if the underlying reference rate, usually 3-month LIBOR, exceeds the cap. We have discussed caps in the context of CMO floaters and inverse floaters. A cap is a series of call options on the reference rate. Equivalently, a 3-month LIBOR cap is a series of put options on a strip of Eurodollar futures contracts. If the yield curve flattens, forward rates decrease, and Eurodollar futures prices increase. The put options are then farther out of the money and decrease in value. Therefore, a flattening yield curve reduces the value of the cap, and interest rate caps have negative slope elasticity. Conversely, interest rate floors benefit if the yield curve flattens; floors have positive slope elasticity.

Sample Analysis

Given the elasticity of each of the various risk control instruments, we can now demonstrate the steps that a manager can follow to measure and control yield curve risk exposure. The first step involves defining a set of yield curves that the manager is going to use to analyze the slope exposure of the portfolio. A Monte Carlo model could generate thousands of interest rate paths, each of which would be a yield curve to be used in the analysis.

The second step is to determine the value of every CMO bond and risk control instrument using every yield curve. The third step is to calculate the effective duration and slope elasticity of the yield curve for each bond.

The fourth step is to compute the value of the portfolio for each yield curve. This is done by multiplying the face amount of each bond in the portfolio by its price for each yield curve scenario. The sum of all the market values gives the market value of the portfolio.

The fifth step is to calculate the slope exposure of the portfolio. Basically, this is done by examining the market value of the portfolio for each yield curve and determining how much of the change in the market value is due to a change in the yield curve slope. Given this slope exposure, the sixth step involves determining what kind of hedge should be employed in order to achieve the desired level of exposure. The last step is checking to see that the proposed hedge would actually achieve the goal established.

Below we illustrate these seven steps.

Step 1: The first step is to define the set of yield curves to be used. While Monte Carlo analysis is the preferred way to define the set of yield curves, it is more difficult to implement than simply specifying a set. We use the following five yield curves in our analysis: (1) today's yield curve; (2) a 200-basis point steepening;

(3) a 100-basis point steepening; (4) a 100-basis point flattening; and (5) a 200-basis point flattening.

There is nothing difficult about constructing these yield curves. As we indicate at the outset of the chapter, we assume half the change in the yield curve slope comes from a change in the 3-month rate and half from a change in the 30-year rate. Thus, for a 200-basis point steepening of the curve, the assumption is that 100 basis points of that steepening come from the 30-year rate (i.e., the 30-year rate goes up 100 basis points), and the second 100 basis points come from the 3-month rate (i.e, the 3-month rate goes down 100 basis points).

For changes at other points on the yield curve, however, a methodology must be employed to determine how the rate changes. The procedure we use to construct the full yield curve is based on regressions of long-term changes in rates.[3] For example, suppose that the prevailing yield (i.e., the yield based on today's yield curve) is 3.27% for the 3-month rate, 5.82% for the 5-year rate, and 7.46% for the 30-year rate. A yield curve steepening of 200 basis points means that the 30-year rate goes up 100 basis points to 8.46% and the 3-month rate goes down 100 basis points to 2.27%.

Suppose further that using multiple regression analysis it is found that the coefficient between changes in the 5-year rate and changes in the 3-month rate is 0.21 and between the 5-year rate and the 30-year rate is 0.79. The change in the 5-year rate is determined as follows:

$$0.21(\text{Change in 3-month rate in bp}) + 0.79(\text{Change in 30-year rate in bp})$$

In our illustration, the change in the 5-year rate for a 200-basis point steepening of the yield curve would be:

$$0.21(-100) + 0.79(+100) = 58 \text{ basis points}$$

Since the prevailing 5-year rate is 5.82%, the 5-year rate after the yield curve steepening of 200 basis points is 6.40%.

A general formula can be used to determine the change in basis points for any intermediate maturity on the yield curve for any slope change:

$$b_{3\text{-month}} \times \text{Change}_{3\text{-month}} + b_{30\text{-year}} \times \text{Change}_{30\text{-year}}$$

where

$b_{3\text{-month}}$ = regression coefficient for the 3-month rate
$b_{30\text{-year}}$ = regression coefficient for the 30-year rate
$\text{Change}_{3\text{-month}}$ = change (in basis points) of the 3-month rate
$\text{Change}_{30\text{-year}}$ = change (in basis points) of the 30-year rate

---

[3] Regression analysis is explained in Chapter 7.

Exhibit 16: Determining the Yield Curve

Type	Assumed yield curves:			
	Steepen	Steepen	Flatten	Flatten
Net change (in bp)	200	100	−100	−200
3-month (in bp)	−100	−50	50	100
30-year (in bp)	100	50	50	−100

Regression	Current	Coefficient		Yield curve slope changes			
				Steepen	Steepen	Flatten	Steepen
Maturity	Yield	3 mo	30 yr	200 bp	100 bp	100 bp	200 bp
0.25	3.27	1.00	0.00	2.27	2.77	3.77	4.27
0.50	3.37	0.87	0.13	2.63	3.00	3.74	4.11
1	3.61	0.70	0.30	3.21	3.41	3.81	4.01
2	4.38	0.46	0.54	4.46	4.42	4.34	4.30
3	4.85	0.38	0.62	5.09	4.97	4.73	4.61
4	5.32	0.29	0.71	5.74	5.53	5.11	4.90
5	5.82	0.21	0.79	6.40	6.11	5.53	5.24
7	6.26	0.11	0.89	7.04	6.65	5.87	5.48
10	6.71	0.08	0.92	7.55	7.13	6.29	5.87
20	7.36	0.00	1.00	8.36	7.86	6.86	6.36
30	7.46	0.00	1.00	8.46	7.96	6.96	6.46

The yield for the intermediate maturity is then the prevailing yield plus the change computed using the formula. Exhibit 16 illustrates this approach for the yield curves assumed in our analysis.

Step 2: The second step is to value the CMO bonds in the portfolio and the risk control instruments for every yield curve. Derivation of the market prices for each yield curve must be obtained from a good valuation model. Exhibit 17 shows the estimated market prices for seven CMO bonds and four interest rate futures contracts for each yield curve. The estimated market prices are based on the Smith Breeden pricing model.

Step 3: The third step is to calculate the slope elasticity of each bond. To illustrate this procedure, we use the inverse floater shown in Exhibit 17. The base value, that is, the market price at today's yield curve, is 62.13. The effective duration is 30.7% (see Exhibit 12).

The procedure we use to construct these yield curves produces slight changes in the level of rates as we vary the yield curve slope. For example, in the case where the yield curve steepened 100 basis points, there was also a 10-basis point increase in the level of rates; there was a 9-basis point decrease in the level of rates when the yield curve flattened 100 basis points.

Exhibit 17: Determining the Value of the CMO Bonds and Risk Control Instruments for Every Assumed Yield Curve

CMO bond prices

CMO bond	Current	Steepen 200	Steepen 100	Flatten 100	Flatten 200
Sequential	103.24	99.51	101.55	103.59	103.60
Floater	99.95	98.53	99.36	100.37	100.59
Inverse floater	62.13	48.57	54.51	70.12	79.40
PAC	110.50	108.57	109.58	111.61	112.19
VADM	104.69	99.84	102.31	106.95	108.93
IO	20.70	27.24	23.89	18.17	16.69
PO	72.93	65.60	68.83	77.54	82.85

Futures prices

Futures contract	Current	Steepen 200	Steepen 100	Flatten 100	Flatten 200
Eurodollar	96.48	97.48	96.98	95.98	95.48
5-year T note	108.30	105.81	107.05	109.57	110.86
10-year T note	107.75	101.91	104.78	110.84	114.04
T bond	104.84	95.41	99.95	110.01	115.14

The main virtue of our methodology for measuring and controlling yield curve slope exposure is its simplicity, for which we have sacrificed some precision. The procedure we use to construct the "twisted" yield curves is an instance in which the simple approach is imprecise — it tends to produce slight changes in the level of interest rates when we change the yield curve slope to achieve a desired yield curve slope. A more complicated, iterative procedure could produce the desired change in yield curve slope without affecting the level of rates, but it would be cumbersome to implement.

In any case, when we compare the market value of a CMO bond using twisted yield curves to the market value of that bond using the current yield curve, we need to recognize that some portion of the change in price is due to a small change in the level of interest rates. We need to subtract the portion of the price change in the level of rates from the overall price change to isolate the price impact of the change in yield curve slope.

The deep discount inverse floater illustrates this procedure. The base price of the inverse floater is 62.13. The price decreases to 54.51 if the yield curve slope increases by 100 basis points (and the level of rates increases by ten basis points). Conversely, the price rises to 70.12 if the yield curve slope declines by 100 basis points (and the level of rates drops by 9 basis points).

To isolate the price effect of a change in the level and a change in the slope, we first determine the price effect of a change in the level, which can be found as follows:

$$-\text{Base price} \times \text{Change in yield level} \times \text{Effective duration}/100$$

For example, for the inverse floater, the effect of an increase in the level of 10 basis points is:

$$-62.13 \times 0.10 \times 30.7/100 = -1.91$$

and, for a decrease in the level of 9 basis points is:

$$-62.13 \times (-0.09) \times 30.7/100 = 1.72$$

Given the new price and the price effect due to a change in the level, the effect due to a change in slope can be calculated as follows:

$$\text{New price} - \text{Price effect of a change in level} - \text{Base price}$$

If the change in the level is 10 basis points and the slope change is 100 basis points, the resulting price is 54.51. The price effect of the change in slope is:

$$54.51 - (-1.91) - 62.13 = -5.71$$

A 100 basis point yield curve flattening combined with a 9 point basis point reduction in the level of rates results in a price of 70.12. The price effect of the change in slope is:

$$70.12 - 1.72 - 62.13 = 6.27$$

The slope elasticity for a scenario is:

$$\text{Slope elasticity} = \frac{(\text{Price effect of a change in slope}/\text{Base price})}{\text{Change in yield curve slope}}$$

The slope elasticity for the two scenarios is then:

$$\frac{(5.71/62.13)}{1.00} = 0.092 = 9.2\%$$

$$\frac{(-6.27/62.13)}{-1.00} = 0.101 = 10.1\%$$

The average slope elasticity is then 9.6%.

The general procedure is presented in Exhibit 18.

Exhibit 18: Calculating the Average Slope Elasticity

Scenario 1: +100bp change in slope of curve

New price (estimated based on +100 basis point change in slope and corresponding level)

Price effect due to change in:

Level = −Base price × Change in yield level × Effective duration / 100

Slope = New price − Price effect of change in level − Base price

Slope elasticity in Scenario 1:

$$\text{Slope elasticity} = \frac{(\text{Price effect of a change in slope}/\text{Base price})}{\text{Change in yield curve slope}}$$

Scenario 2: −100bp change in slope of curve

New price (estimated based on −100 basis point change in slope and corresponding level)

Price effect due to change in:

Level = −Base price × Change in yield level × Effective duration / 100

Slope = New price − Price effect of change in level − Base price

Slope elasticity in Scenario 2:

$$\text{Slope elasticity} = \frac{(\text{Price effect of a change in slope}/\text{Base price})}{\text{Change in yield curve slope}}$$

Average slope elasticity

$$\frac{\text{Slope elasticity in Scenario 1} + \text{Slope elasticity in Scenario 2}}{2}$$

Step 4: The fourth step is to compute the value of the portfolio for each yield curve. Exhibit 19 illustrates this step using two hypothetical CMO portfolios. The total market value for each portfolio is $100 million. Notice that Portfolio #1 has only inverse floaters and IO strips. As can be seen from column 3, the effective duration for this portfolio is zero: the effective duration of the inverse floaters offsets the negative effective duration of the IO strips.

Step 5: Calculate the dollar slope exposure of the portfolio. The dollar slope exposure is the sum of the dollar slope exposures of the individual CMO bonds. The dollar slope exposure for a given CMO bond is defined as the market value invested in that bond multiplied by the bond's slope elasticity.

In this example, the slope exposure for any individual bond is less than the level exposure for that bond. Notice that Portfolio #1, which has an effective duration of zero, is hedged with respect to the level of rates but not changes in the slope of the yield curve. The dollar slope exposure for this portfolio is such that the inverse floater gains $4.2 million if the yield curve flattens 100 basis points, but the IO strip loses $6.5 million — a net loss of $2.3 million.

Exhibit 19: Calculating the Value for Two Hypothetical Portfolios and the Slope Exposure of the Portfolio

	Portfolio #1 (in millions of $)			Portfolio #2 (in millions of $)		
	Market	Level $ move	Slope $ move	Market	Level $ move	Slope $ move
Sequential	0	0	0	5,000	164	33
Floater	0	0	0	0	0	0
Inverse Floater	43,789	13,428	4,201	17,662	5,416	1,695
PAC	0	0	0	20,000	711	115
VADM	0	0	0	25,000	1,435	415
IO	56,211	−13,428	−6,468	32,338	−7,725	−3,721
PO	0	0	0	0	0	0
Total	100,000	0	−2,267	100,000	0	−1,462

Step 6: In this step, the hedge position is determined based on the desired exposure to level and slope risks. Focusing on Portfolio #1, the effective duration is zero, but there is slope exposure of $2.3 million if the yield curve flattens by 100 basis points. This means that if the manager wants to eliminate this exposure, it will be necessary to find a risk control instrument or combination of instruments that will gain $2.3 million if the yield curve flattens.

One possibility is to use interest rate futures. Recall from our earlier discussion of interest rate futures that Treasury bond futures and 10-year Treasury note futures benefit if the yield curve flattens. The 5-year note is not affected significantly, but shorter contracts benefit if the yield curve steepens.

Consider this hedge strategy: go long Treasury bond futures and short an appropriate number of Eurodollar futures so that the dollar duration of the combination of long bonds and short Eurodollar futures is zero. This can be done by first calculating the dollar move of both the Treasury bond futures contract and the Eurodollar futures contract, and then finding the hedge ratio that produces a zero duration position in futures.

While the effective duration of this futures position is zero, the slope elasticity is positive. If the yield curve flattens, the long Treasury bond futures position would gain, and the short Eurodollar futures position would also gain. Since both legs of the futures trade gain if the yield curve flattens, the aggregate position clearly benefits from a flattening of the yield curve. We refer to this position as a "T-bond/Eurodollar futures unit."

The number of T-bond/Eurodollar futures units is found by determining the slope exposure for each contract. The following procedure is used to determine the number of futures contracts in the unit given the slope exposure:

1. Construct a zero effective duration T-bond/Eurodollar futures position by determining the hedge ratio, indicating the number of Eurodollar futures contracts for each Treasury bond futures contract as follows:

$$\text{Hedge ratio} = -\frac{\text{Dollar duration of Treasury bond futures}}{\text{Dollar duration of Eurodollar futures}}$$

In our illustration, the dollar duration is $10,180 for the Treasury bond futures and $2,500 for the Eurodollar futures. Therefore, the hedge ratio is −4.072 (−$10,180/$2,500). Thus, for each Treasury bond futures contract purchased, 4.072 Eurodollar futures contracts will be sold.

2. Calculate the slope exposure (in dollars) of one unit of the zero effective duration position as follows:

Dollar slope elasticity of Treasury bond futures position
+ Dollar slope elasticity of Eurodollar futures position × Hedge ratio

In our illustration, the dollar slope elasticity is $3,719 for a long Treasury bond futures contract and −$1,492 for a short Eurodollar futures position. Therefore,

$$\$3,719 + (-4.072) \times (-\$1,492) = \$9,794$$

3. Determine the number of zero effective duration T-Bond/Eurodollar futures units needed as follows:

$$- \frac{\text{Slope exposure of portfolio}}{\text{Slope exposure of 1 unit of zero effective duration position}}$$

In our illustration, since the slope exposure of Portfolio #1 is $2,266,784, then

$$- \frac{\$2,266,784}{\$9,794} = 231.45$$

4. Determine the number of Eurodollar futures contracts to short for each Treasury bond futures contract bought. This is found by multiplying the number of units found in the previous calculation by the hedge ratio. In our illustration, since 231 T-bond/Eurodollar futures units are needed, 231 Treasury bond futures will be purchased and 943 (231 times 4.072) Eurodollar futures will be sold. Rounding these values, the hedge position will include a long position in 231 Treasury bond futures and a short position in 943 Eurodollar futures.

For Portfolio #2 in Exhibit 19, the number of T-bond/Eurodollar futures units needed is 149, consisting of a long position in 149 Treasury bond futures and a short position in 608 Eurodollar futures.

5. Check that the level exposure of the hedge position is zero.

In our illustration, since the dollar duration is $10,180 per Treasury bond futures contract and the dollar duration of the Eurodollar futures contract is $2,500, the dollar duration of the hedged position is

$$231 \times \$10,180 + 943 \times (-\$2,500) = \$5,920$$

The difference is approximately zero, the difference resulting from the rounding of the number of futures contracts.

Exhibit 20: Verification that Hedged Portfolio #1 Has the Expected Sensitivity

	Change in Yield Curve Parameters (in bp)				
Level	−19	−9	0	10	20
Slope	−200	−100	0	100	200

	Market Value of Assets (in $ 000)				
Sequential	0	0	0	0	0
Floater	0	0	0	0	0
Inverse floater	55,961	49,417	43,789	38,418	34,230
PAC	0	0	0	0	0
VADM	0	0	0	0	0
IO	45,321	49,340	56,211	64,873	73,970
PO	0	0	0	0	0
Total: Unhedged	101,283	98,757	100,000	103,290	108,200

	Impact of Hedges (in $ 000)				
T-bond futures	2,383	1,197	0	−1,132	−2,184
Eurodollar futures	2,357	1,178	0	−1,178	−2,357
Total: Hedges	4,739	2,375	0	−2,310	−4,540

Total: Hedged	106,022	101,132	100,000	100,980	103,660

6. Check that the slope exposure of the initial portfolio hedged with the T-bond/ Eurodollar units is zero.

In our illustration, the dollar slope exposure for Portfolio #1 is $2,266,784. The dollar slope exposure for the hedged position is:

$$231 \times \$3,719 + 943 \times \$1,492 = \$2,266,045$$

Therefore, the dollar slope exposure of the hedged portfolio is essentially zero.

7. Check to make sure the hedged portfolio has the target slope exposure. Exhibit 20 demonstrates this for Portfolio #1 and Exhibit 21 for Portfolio #2.

A natural question is whether the hedged portfolio works better than the unhedged portfolio in terms of the target slope exposure. Looking at Exhibit 20, this can be seen for Portfolio #1 by comparing the row showing the unhedged portfolio results with the last line in the exhibit showing the hedged portfolio results. The portfolio begins with a market value of $100 million. If the yield curve flattens by 100 basis points, there is a loss of approximately $1.2 million if it is unhedged but a gain of about $1.1 million if hedged. If the yield curve steepens 100 basis points, there would be a gain of about $3.3 million if unhedged but a gain of just under $1 million if hedged. Thus, the hedged portfolio is relatively insulated for changes in yield curve slope.

Exhibit 21: Verification that Hedged Portfolio #2 Has the Expected Sensitivity

	Change in Yield Curve Parameters (in bp)				
Level	−19	−9	0	10	20
Slope	−200	−100	0	100	200
	Market Value of Assets (in $ 000)				
Sequential	5,017	5,017	5,000	4,918	4,819
Floater	0	0	0	0	0
Inverse floater	22,571	19,932	17,662	15,495	13,806
PAC	20,307	20,202	20,000	19,834	19,651
VADM	26,012	25,541	25,000	24,432	23,845
IO	26,073	28,386	32,338	37,321	42,555
PO	0	0	0	0	0
Total: Unhedged	99,982	99,077	100,000	102,001	104,674
	Impact of Hedges (in $ 000)				
T bond futures	1,537	772	0	−730	−1,409
Eurodollar futures	1,520	760	0	−760	−1,520
Total: Hedges	3,057	1,532	0	−1,490	−2,929
Total: Hedged	103,039	100,609	100,000	105,511	101,745

Notice, however, that for a larger change in yield curve slope, such as 200 basis points, the exposure becomes a little stranger. The reason for this behavior is that Portfolio #1 contains inverse floaters matched with interest-only strips, and the slope exposure of these instruments tends to change substantially as the yield curve slope changes. In other words, there is considerable convexity in the slope exposure. A manager must be aware of this, and must rebalance the portfolio as market conditions change, so as to maintain the desired slope exposure. This is no different from the rebalancing required to maintain a target level exposure (effective duration).

While our focus in this illustration has been on completely hedging yield curve slope exposure, the same approach can be used to position a portfolio to benefit from an anticipated change in the yield curve slope.

KEY POINTS

1. *Duration and convexity can be used to measure the level risk exposure of an MBS portfolio.*

2. *A simple approach to quantify the yield curve risk of an MBS portfolio is the slope elasticity measure.*

3. *The yield curve slope can be defined as the spread between the long-term Treasury (i.e., the 30-year on-the-run issue) and the short-term Treasury (i.e., the 3-month on-the-run issue).*

4. *Changes in the yield curve can be defined as follows: half of any basis point change in the yield curve slope results from a change in the 3-month yield and half from a change in the 30-year yield.*

5. *The slope elasticity is defined as the approximate negative percentage change in a bond's price resulting from a 100 basis point change in the slope of the curve.*

6. *A bond or portfolio that benefits when the yield curve flattens is said to have positive slope elasticity; a bond or a portfolio that benefits when the yield curve steepens is said to have negative slope elasticity.*

7. *Yield curve risk is defined as the exposure of the bond to changes in the slope of the yield curve.*

8. *CMO and stripped MBS (IOs and POs) are particularly sensitive to changes in the yield curve.*

9. *It is difficult to generalize about the slope exposure of individual CMO bonds because the exposure is specific to the actual deal or structure from which the bond was created.*

10. *To examine the slope exposure of a particular CMO bond, the impact of changes in discount rates, projected prepayment rates (cash flows), and embedded caps and floors on the bond's value must be assessed.*

11. *The net slope exposure of a CMO bond is the sum of the three slope components.*

12. *An interesting feature of many CMO bonds is that slope exposure tends to be asymmetric.*

13. *Only two of the three components determining net slope exposure are relevant for a pro rata LIBOR floater since the value of a floater is relatively unaffected by the impact on discount rates resulting from a change in yield curve slope, but changes in yield curve slope do affect prepayment rates and the value of embedded options.*

14. *The primary effect of a change in yield curve slope on a floater is through the value of embedded options.*

15. *The two most important factors to consider in evaluating the slope exposure of an inverse floater are its price (i.e., its tendency to benefit/suffer if prepayment rates increase) and the "delta" of its embedded long LIBOR cap.*

16. *IOs are a good hedge for a portfolio that has considerable positive slope elasticity (i.e., a portfolio that benefits if the curve flattens and loses if it steepens).*

17. *An IO strip is one of the few bonds that a portfolio manager can use to counteract positive slope elasticity.*

18. *A PO strip increases in value if the yield curve flattens, and decreases in value if the yield curve steepens.*

18. *Given the exposure of each CMO bond in a portfolio, a manager should be able to make an informed decision about what kind of hedge to put on or how to manage that risk.*

19. *Yield curve slope risk and duration risk can, for the most part, be managed independently because the correlation of changes in the level of rates and yield curve slope is very low.*

20. *The slope exposure of potential hedging instruments must be estimated in order to control yield curve risk.*

21. *A manager who owns a long CMO bond with positive slope elasticity could establish a position that would gain if the curve flattens, simply by shorting bonds.*

22. *Both the yield curve slope elasticity and effective duration of futures contracts have slope sensitivities that differ in magnitude as well as direction and therefore a manager should be able to manage the risk of a CMO portfolio with these contracts.*

23. *An interest rate swap can have either positive or negative slope elasticity, depending on the maturity of the swap.*

24. *Since yield curve options can be structured in numerous ways, a manager has flexibility in controlling slope risk.*

25. *A flattening yield curve reduces the value of an interest rate cap, and therefore a cap has negative slope elasticity; an interest rate floor benefits if the yield curve flattens and therefore has positive slope elasticity.*

Index

A

Accreting swap, 171
Accrued interest, 154, 155
Active bond portfolio strategies, interest rate
 risk control, 56-59
Adesi-Barone model, 201
Adjustable-rate mortgages (ARMs), 32
American option, 182, 192, 195.
 See also Modified American option
Amortizing swap, 171
Arbitrage, 155
Arbitrage model base.
 See Theoretical futures price
Arbitrage profit, 11, 16, 154
ARCH.
 See Autoregressive conditional heterosce-
 dasticity
ARMs.
 See Adjustable-rate mortgages
Asset swap, 251
Asset/liability management, 252
Asset/liability problems, 249
Asset/liability strategy, 183
Asymmetric risk, 183
Atlantic option, 203-204
Autocorrelation, 97
Autoregressive conditional heteroscedastic-
 ity (ARCH).
 See Generalized autoregressive condi-
 tional heteroscedasticity
 method, 113-117
 variants, 113-117

B

Back fee, 210, 218
Backward induction method, 214, 216
Backward induction process, 207
Bank for International Settlements, 112
Bankers Trust, 4

Barbell portfolio, 72
Barone-Adesi, Giovanni, 195.
 See also Adesi-Barone model
Basel Committee on Banking Supervision,
 100, 112, 113, 118
Basis.
 See Hedges
Basis rate swap, 172
Basis risk, 232, 247
BBI.
 See Bond Buyer Index
Beder, Tanya Styblo, 100
Benchmark spot rate curve, 18
Benchmark zero-coupon rate curve, 18
Bermuda option, 203-204
Bid-offer spread, 171
Bill futures.
 See U.S. Treasury bill futures
Binomial interest rate tree, 19-22, 31, 206,
 207
 construction, 24-27
 usage. *See* Option-free bonds
Binomial method, 19-32, 203, 219, 210
Binomial tree, 214
Black, Fischer, 194, 195, 206
Black-Scholes option pricing model, 181,
 194, 195, 200, 201
Bond Buyer Index (BBI), 149-150
Bond futures.
 See U.S. Treasury bond futures
Bond portfolio, 5
Bond selection strategies, 56
Bonds.
 See Callable corporate bond; CMO
 bonds; Default-free bond; General obli-
 gation bonds; Intermediate-term bonds;
 Junk bonds; Long-term bonds; Noncall-
 able corporate bonds; Option-free bond;
 PAC bonds; Revenue bonds; Sequential-
 pay bonds; Short-term bonds; Underly-
 ing bond; VADM bonds; Zero-coupon
 bond

Fixed Income Books Published By Frank J. Fabozzi

Bond Portfoilo Management, Frank J. Fabozzi, 1996, $65
TOC: Introduction; Investment Objectives of Institutional Investors; Bonds; Mortgage-Backed Securities and Asset-Backed Securities; Interest Rate Derivative Instruments; General Principles of Fixed Income Valuation; Valuation Methodologies; Valuation of Derivative Instruments; Tax Considerations; Total Return Framework; Measuring Interest Rate Risk; Historical Return Performance and Bond Indexes; Active Strategies; Structured Portfolio Strategies; Use of Derivatives in Portfolio Strategies; International Bond Portfolio Strategies; Measuring and Evaluating Performance

Valuation of Fixed Income Securities and Derivatives, Frank J. Fabozzi, 1995, $50
TOC: Fundamental Valuation Principles; Spot Rates and Their Role In Valuation; Forward Rates and Term Structure Theories; Measuring Price Sensitivity to Interest Rate Changes; Overview of the Valuation of Bonds With Embedded Options; Binomial Method; Monte Carlo Method; Valuation of Inverse Floaters; Valuation of Convertible Securities; Valuation of Interest Rate Future Contracts; Valuation of Interest Rate Options; Valuation of Interest Rate Swaps.

Measuring and Controlling Interest Rate Risk, Frank J. Fabozzi, 1996, $55
TOC:Overview of Measurement and Control of Interest Rate Risk; Valuation; Measuring Level Risk: Duration and Convexity; Measuring Yield Curve Risk; Probability Distributions and Their Properties; Measuring and Forecasting Yield Volatility from Historical Data; Correlation Analysis and Regression Analysis; Futures; Swaps; Exchange-Traded Options; OTC Options and Related Products; Controlling Interest Rate Risk with Derivatives; Controlling Interest Rate Risk in an MBS Derivative Portfolio.

Corporate Bonds: Structures & Analysis, Richard S. Wilson and Frank J. Fabozzi, 1996, $65
TOC: Overview of U.S. Corporate Bonds; Bond Indentures; Maturity; Interest Payments; Debt Retirement; Convertible Bonds; Speculative-Grade Bonds; Corporate Debt Ratings; Bond Pricing and Yield Measures; Principles of Valuing Corporate Bonds; Valuing Callable Corporate Bonds; Valuation of Putable Bonds, Structured Notes, Floaters, and Convertibles; and Managing Corporate Bond Portfolios.

Collateralized Mortgage Obligations: Structures & Analysis (2nd Ed), Frank J. Fabozzi, Chuck Ramsey, and Frank R. Ramirez, 1994, $50TOC: Introduction; Collateral for CMOs; Prepayment Conventions and Factors Affecting Prepayments; Sequential-Pay CMOs; Floater, Inverse Floater, PO, and IO Bond Classes; Planned Amortization Class Bonds; TAC Bonds, VADM Bonds, and Support Bonds; Whole-Loan CMOs; Static Cash Flow Yield Analysis; Total Return Framework; Analysis of Inverse Floaters; Accounting for CMO Investments; and Regulatory Considerations.

Asset-Backed Securities, Anand K. Bhattacharya and Frank J. Fabozzi (Eds.), 1996, $65
TOC: The Expanding Frontiers of Asset Securitization; Securitization in Europe; Credit-Card Receivables; Collateralized Automobile Loans; Manufactured Housing Securities; Analysis of Manufactured Housing-Backed Securities; Introduction to the B&C Home-Equity Loan Market; Evolution of the B&C Home-Equity Loan Securities Market; Equipment-Lease Backed Securities; SBA Loan-Backed Securities; The Securitization of Health-Care Receivables; The Commercial Property Market and Underwriting Criteria for Commercial Mortgages; CMBS Structures and Relative Value Analysis; Investing in Interest-Only Commercial Mortgage Backed Securities; Credit Enhancement in ABS Structures; Early Amortization Triggers; Home-Equity Loan Floaters; Dynamics of Cleanup Calls in ABS; ABS B-Pieces; Prepayment Nomenclature in the ABS Market; Prepayments on ABSs; Z-Spreads; Introduction to ABS Accounting

CMO Portfolio Management, Fabozzi (Ed.), 1994, $50
TOC: Overview; The Challenges of CMO Portfolio Management; CMO Collateral Analysis; CMO Structure Analysis; New Challenges in MBS Prepayment Simulation: Issues and Methods; Valuation of CMOs; Advanced Techniques for the Valuation of CMOs; Forward Rates and CMO Portfolio Management; Valuation of PAC Bonds without Complex Models; A Portfolio Manager's Perspective of Inverse and Inverse IOs; Investment Opportunities in Mortgage Residuals; Total Return Analysis in CMO Portfolio Management; Market Neutral trading Strategies; Rule-Based Analysis of CMO Securities and Its Application; and Yield Curve Risk of CMO Bonds.

Commercial Mortgage-Backed Securities, Frank J. Fabozzi and David P. Jacob (Eds.), 1996, $95
TOC: A Property Market Framework for Bond Investors; The Commercial Mortgage Market; Commercial Mortgage Prepayments; The Commercial Mortgage-Backed Securities Market; The Role of the Servicer; Structural Considerations Impacting CMBS; The Effects of Prepayment Restrictions on the Bond Structures of CMBS; An Investor's Perspective on Commercial Mortgage-Backed Coupon Strips; How CMBS Structuring Impacts the Performance of the Bond Classes; Rating of Commercial Mortgage-Backed Securities; Defaults on Commercial Mortgages; Assessing Credit Risk of CMBS; A Framework for Risk and Relative Value Analysis of CMBS: Theory; A Framework for Risk and Relative Value Analysis of CMBS: Practice; Investing in Subordinate CMBS Bonds; High Yield CMBS Bonds; An Option-Based Approach to Valuing Default and Prepayment Risk in CMBS; Performing Financial Due Diligence Associated with Commercial Mortgage Securitizations; Legal Perspectives on Disclosure Issues for CMBS Investors; Evolving Generally Accepted Accounting Principles for Issuers of and Investors in CMBS; Federal Income Taxation of REMICs and CMBS

Valuation of Interest-Sensitive Financial Instruments, David F. Babbel and Craig B. Merrill, 1996, $55 TOC: Spot Interest Rates, Forward Interest Rates, Short Rates, and Yield-to-Maturity; An Introduction to Valuation of Fixed-Interest-Sensitive Cash Flows; Discrete-Time One-Factor Models; Continuous-Time One-Factor Models; Solution Approaches to Single-Factor Models; Multi-Factor Continuous-Time Models; Multi-Factor Discrete-Time Models; Simulation Approaches.

Dictionary of Financial Risk Management, Gary L. Gastineau and Mark P. Kritzman, 1996, $45 Risk management terminology comes by many markets – cash, forwards/futures, swaps, options – and from many disciplines – economics, probability and statistics, tax and financial accounting, and the law. The vocabulary of the risk manager continues to expand with the creation of new products and new concepts. All these words and phrases are carefully defined and illustrated in this comprehensive dictionary.

BOOK ORDER FORM

Name: _____

Company: _____

Address: _____

City: _____ State: _____ Zip: _____

Phone: _____ FAX: _____

Books Published by Frank J. Fabozzi:

Book	Price:	Quantity:	Sub-Total:
Bond Portfolio Management Fabozzi, 1996	$65		
Valuation of Fixed Income Securities and Derivatives Fabozzi, 1995	$50		
Measuring and Controlling Interest Rate Risk Fabozzi, 1996	$55		
Corporate Bonds: Structures & Analysis Wilson and Fabozzi, 1996	$65		
Collateralized Mortgage Obligations: Structures & Analysis Fabozzi, Ramsey, and Ramirez, 1994 2nd Ed.	$50		
Asset-Backed Securities Bhattacharya and Fabozzi (Eds.), 1996	$65		
Commercial Mortgage-Backed Securities Fabozzi and Jacob (Eds), 1996	$95		
Valuation of Interest-Sensitive Financial Instruments Babbel and Merrill, 1996	$55		
Dictionary of Financial Risk Management Gastineau and Kritzman, 1996	$45		
CMO Portfolio Management Fabozzi (Ed.), 1994	$50		

Books Distributed by Frank J. Fabozzi:

Book	Price:	Quantity:	Sub-Total:
Fixed Income Mathematics Fabozzi, (Irwin, 1996) 3rd Ed.	Call for price		
The Handbook of Mortgage-Backed Securities Fabozzi (Ed.), (Irwin, 1995) 4th Ed.	$85		
The Handbook of Fixed Income Securities Fabozzi and Fabozzi (Eds.), (Irwin, 1994) 4th Ed.	$90		
Advanced Fixed Income Portfolio Management Fabozzi and Fong, (Probus, 1994)	$65		
Active Total Return Management of Fixed Income Portfolios Dattatreya and Fabozzi, (Irwin, 1995)	$65		
Municipal Bond Portfolio Management Fabozzi, Fabozzi, and Feldstein, (Irwin, 1994)	$80		
Handbook of Fixed Income Options Fabozzi, (Probus, 1995) Rev. Ed.	$65		
Handbook of Asset/Liability Management Fabozzi and Konishi (Eds.), (Irwin, 1996) Rev. Ed	$75		

SHIPPING: ($4.00 for first book, $1.00 each additional)*

*International or bulk orders please call for shipping estimate (215) 598-8930

TOTAL: _____

Make check payable to Frank J. Fabozzi

Mail order form along with check to:
Frank J. Fabozzi
858 Tower View Circle
New Hope, PA 18938

Forthcoming Books From Frank J. Fabozzi Associates:
Call for information

Fabozzi, *Fixed Income Securities*
Fabozzi (Ed.), *Securities Lending and Repurchase Agreements*
Fabozzi/Ramsey/Ramirez/Marz (Eds.), *Investing In Nonagency Mortgage-Backed Securities*
Fabozzi, *Advances in Fixed Income Valuation Modeling and Risk Control*
Fabozzi/Wickard, *Credit Union Investment Management*

TREPP RISK MANAGEMENT, INC.

a Member of The Trepp Group

DERIVATIVE VALUATION AND MODEL VALIDATION

TREPP PROVIDES AN INDEPENDENT SOURCE OF FAIR VALUE ESTIMATES
FOR A WIDE RANGE OF COMPLEX INVESTMENTS AND OFF-BALANCE
SHEET DERIVATIVES. OUR ANALYSIS SUPPORTS INTERNAL RISK
MANAGEMENT EVALUATIONS, PUBLISHED FINANCIAL STATEMENTS,
OR INTERNAL AUDIT REVIEW OF VALUATIONS.

UNPARALLELED EXPERTISE. We are a long standing national expert with years of experience in structured finance and derivative contracts.

STRESS TEST EVALUATIONS. Valuations can be provided for various stress test conditions as specified by each client.

RISK PARAMETERS. Trepp provides clients with risk parameters (e.g., duration, convexity, etc.) on a customized basis as selected by each organization to support its risk management activities.

CUSTOMIZED VALUATIONS. Every assignment is tailored to the specific requirements of each client, and is based on detailed instrument by instrument analysis.

COMPREHENSIVE REPORTS. Comprehensive, customized reports are provided showing fair value estimates, stress test results, and risk parameters requested by clients.

COUNTERPARTY CREDIT EXPOSURE. Reports can be prepared to your specifications that present counterparty credit exposure.

NEW YORK • BOSTON • DENVER

477 MADISON AVE. - NEW YORK, NY   212.754.1010
22 PITTSBURGH ST. - BOSTON, MA   617.856.1206

TREPP RISK MANAGEMENT, INC.
a Member of The Trepp Group

ASSET/LIABILITY MANAGEMENT SERVICES

TREPP CAN HELP YOU FINE TUNE YOUR ALM PRACTICES
WITH COMPREHENSIVE OR NARROWLY FOCUSED ENGAGEMENTS
THAT ADDRESS A WIDE RANGE OF IMPORTANT ISSUES.

SOFTWARE SELECTION. Select and implement ALM, transfer pricing, profitability reporting, data warehouse investment and derivatives software systems.

DATA EXTRACTION. Extract data from legacy systems and populate data warehouses or ALM systems.

INTEREST RATE RISK MEASUREMENT. Assess the exposure of earnings and market values to changes in economic and interest rate environments.

PERFORMANCE IMPROVEMENT STRATEGIES. Develop balance sheet strategies to increase earnings and more effectively manage risk. Strategies may include investments, loans, deposits, non-deposit funding, and derivatives.

INVESTMENT PORTFOLIO STRATEGIES. Assist in the development of investment strategies (including CMOs, MBS and structured notes) to optimize total balance sheet performance.

PREPAYMENT MODELING. Assist in measuring your historic prepayment experience and developing models to project future activity.

NON-MATURITY DEPOSIT STUDIES. Estimate the interest rate risk characteristics of savings, NOW and demand deposit accounts.

ALM AND INVESTMENT COMPLIANCE. Conduct comprehensive reviews of ALM practices for compliance with current and prospective regulatory requirements.

NEW YORK • BOSTON • DENVER

477 MADISON AVE. - NEW YORK, NY   212.754.1010
22 PITTSBURGH ST. - BOSTON, MA   617.856.1206

Trepp Risk Management, Inc.
a Member of The Trepp Group

Internal Audit Assistance

IN RECENT YEARS, MANY COMPANIES HAVE INCREASED THE EMPHASIS ON THE REVIEW OF ASSET/LIABILITY MANAGEMENT, DERIVATIVE AND TRADING RISKS. TREPP'S BROAD EXPERIENCE WITH CAPITAL MARKETS AND SECURITIES ACTIVITY CAN ASSIST YOUR RISK MANAGEMENT OR INTERNAL AUDIT DEPARTMENT WITH THESE REVIEWS.

Asset/Liability Management

MODEL VALIDATION. Review the reliability of model input, assumptions, structure and model validation.

RISK MEASUREMENT. Review risk measurement methodologies (such as simulation, duration, Monte Carlo, OAS) and compare to industry standards.

SCENARIOS. Review scenarios (e.g., shocks, ramps, best/worst case) and compare them to industry practices.

REPORTING. Review management and Board reports for coverage, accuracy, clarity and disclosure of risk and return.

STRATEGY EFFECTIVENESS. Assess the effectiveness of strategies to achieve objectives and consistency with policy.

POLICIES AND PROCEDURES. Compare your practices to industry standards.

REGULATORY COMPLIANCE. Evaluate compliance with regulatory policies.

Derivatives and Trading Activity

FAIR VALUE ESTIMATES. Validation and confirmation of fair value estimates.

MODEL VALIDATION. Validation of value derivative valuation models.

RISK MEASUREMENT. Reliability of risk measurement practices such as VAR and other risk measures.

CREDIT RISK. Measuring and monitoring counterparty credit exposure.

POLICIES AND PROCEDURES. Review of policies and procedures including limits.

COMPLIANCE. Review of compliance with regulations and industry practices.

NEW YORK • BOSTON • DENVER

477 MADISON AVE. - NEW YORK, NY   212.754.1010
22 PITTSBURGH ST. - BOSTON, MA   617.856.1206

TREPP RISK MANAGEMENT, INC.
a Member of The Trepp Group

NON-MATURITY DEPOSIT STUDIES

BECAUSE NON-MATURITY DEPOSITS COMPRISE A SUBSTANTIAL PERCENTAGE OF BANK DEPOSITS, ESTIMATES OF THEIR INTEREST RATE RISK CHARACTERISTICS MAY BE THE SINGLE MOST IMPORTANT DETERMINANT OF THE BANK'S INTEREST RATE RISK PROFILE. TREPP WILL ESTIMATE THE INTEREST RATE RISK CHARACTERISTICS OF YOUR NON-MATURITY DEPOSITS TO SUPPORT MORE RELIABLE RISK MANAGEMENT.

DELIVERABLES

SEPARATE ESTIMATES FOR EACH ACCOUNT TYPE:
- Average life
- Average annual decay rate
- Historical sensitivity of the yield to changes in market yields
- Effective duration
- Yield sensitivity parameters for simulation models
- Fair value of the accounts

RESULTS ARE TESTED FOR CHANGES IN CRITICAL ASSUMPTIONS SUCH AS:
- Account decay rates
- Responsiveness of deposit yields to changes in market yields
- Operating costs
- Discount rates
- Average account life

BENEFITS

More Profitable Risk Management. Failure to properly understand risk characteristics can result in higher risk or costly and unnecessary hedging.

Higher Asset Yields. If non-maturity deposits have longer rate sensitivity, then a matched loan and investment would be further out on the yield curve and provide a higher yield.

Investment Depreciation. Bank regulators may consider the appreciation of economic value of non-maturity deposits as an offset to unrealized securities losses, but only if there is adequate documentation of their value.

Documentation for Regulators. New examination guidelines require examiners to review documentation that supports the assumptions on which interest rate risk is measured.

Imagine
This Scenario

- ▶ You spend a lot of time and a lot of money to hire the wrong executive, manager, financial specialist

- ▶ Your corporate strategy is based on erroneous decision information because of your hiring decision

- ▶ Critical objectives are badly missed

Now Imagine
This Scenario

- ▶ **DDJ MYERS finds the right people for you**

- ▶ Excellent process for candidate screening, selection, background checks, interviewing, provides the hiring information you should have had

Proven track record
in specialty executive recruitment
for financial institutions,
domestic and international

Chief Executive Officer	A/L Manager
Chief Financial Officer	Senior A/L Strategist
Treasurer	Funding/Hedging Manager
Marketing Executive	Investment Manager
Credit Card Executive	Interest Rate Risk Manager

Specialists in:
*Derivatives, Funds Transfer Pricing, Data Warehousing,
Performance Analysis, Balance Scoreboard, RAROC*

Financial Services Representatives in:
Asset-Based Lending, Full Service Leasing, Account Managers

Complimentary Client Services:
*Career Development Portfolios,
Behavioral and Team Effectiveness Assessments*

Specialists in locating and placing asset/liability
and treasury management personnel.

For information on how we work, contact:

Deedee Myers, President

DDJ MYERS, LTD.   2303 North 44th Street #14-400   Phoenix, AZ 85008

Telephone 602.840.9595   Fax 602.840.6486   800.574.8877

Boston   Phoenix   New York

CONTROL

YOUR INVESTMENT SKILL COMBINED WITH BARRA TOOLS AND SERVICES FORM A WINNING PARTNERSHIP.

Fixed income management has become increasingly complex. BARRA's fixed income analytics enable you to manage the risk of your fixed income portfolio by providing insight into interest rate, sector and quality risk factors and the correlation among them. We have over a decade of experience in building rigorous and practical software tools for fixed income analysis. Our expert client support staff understands portfolio strategy and the realities of today's market.

Situation

You want a profile of a portfolio's duration and curve-reshaping bets. You also want to know how closely your portfolio will track its benchmark.

Solution

BARRA's Portfolio Risk Characterization Program. The report shows:

- Term structure shift exposures and option adjusted cash flows along the yield curve
- Yield curve, shift, twist and butterfly exposures
- Portfolio tracking error

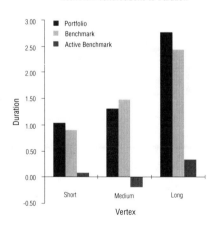

Cash Flow Contributions to Duration

Shift, Twist and Butterfly Risk Structure

	1% Change		
	Port	Bench	Active
Shift	(5.13)	(5.02)	(0.11)
Twist	(0.88)	(1.03)	0.15
Butterfly	(0.87)	(0.88)	0.02
Tracking Error			0.35

The BARRA shift, twist and butterfly report details the potential price change of the portfolio and benchmark for an equal magnitude parallel shift, flattening/steepening or reshaping of the curve.

 BARRA

BERKELEY MONTREAL NEW YORK • LONDON PARIS FRANKFURT • YOKOHAMA HONG KONG SYDNEY

INSIGHT

BARRA'S FIXED INCOME ANALYTICS ASSIST INVESTMENT PROFESSIONALS BY PROVIDING INSIGHT INTO RETURN AS WELL AS RISK.

Situation

You want to assess the risk/return tradeoffs over a six month horizon based upon your forecast of future market conditions.

Solution

BARRA's scenario analytics will perform a total return analysis on your portfolio and benchmark based on the "what if" scenarios you have created. The scenarios can include yield curve movements, sector and quality spread changes.

Situation

Your marketing department and clients want to understand how you outperformed the benchmark.

Solution

Analyze your portfolio with the BARRA performance attribution module. Performance attribution decomposes returns into components like duration and yield curve reshaping bets, sector and quality spreads, and specific issue selection. The performance analysis incorporates transactions and tabulates returns on both an absolute basis and relative to your benchmark.

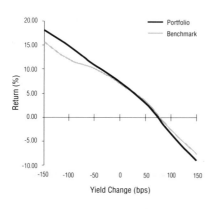

Annualized Return (6 Month Horizon)

Return %			
	Portfolio	Benchmark	Active
Rolldown	0.46	0.46	0.00
Interest Rate			
Shift	1.30	1.15	0.15
Twist	0.10	0.13	-0.03
Other	-0.07	-0.09	0.02
Sector	-0.14	-0.21	0.07
Quality Rating	-0.02	-0.02	0.00
Specific	0.02	0.00	0.02

BondEdge®
FOR WINDOWS®

Fixed Income Portfolio Analytics for Risk Management & Strategic Planning

CMS' focus is exclusively bond portfolio analytics so you have everything you need to respond to changing market conditions. •Option-adjusted risk measures that capture changes in interest rates, volatility estimates and prepayment speeds. •Specialized compliance reports with up-to-the-minute review of your investment guidelines. •Regulatory reports that help you respond quickly to increased demands. •Portfolio comparisons to any of the over 140 Salomon, Lehman, and Merrill indices maintained and fully replicated in BondEdge. •Price bonds individually and at the portfolio level including everything from corporates with embedded options to all types of mortgage backed securities and municipal bonds.

In terms of completeness and impartiality, nothing beats BondEdge. We've made the system easy-to-use with full control in your hands.

Get on the Leader Board.

Why use a putter in a sand trap?

With GAT Decision™, even the longest shots get legs. Callable corporates? Birdie. Floating rate notes? Eagle. Swaptions? Hole in one. Analyzing re-REMICs is a chip shot. Because of our extensive database of everything from treasuries to asset-backed securities, you don't need extra strokes to analyze your entire portfolio.

With Decision, you'll drive farther off the tee than you ever thought possible. Analyze portfolio risk using OAS duration and convexity. Perform scenario analysis with your viewpoint on rates, spreads and volatilities. Structure portfolios using immunization, enhanced index strategies, cash flow analysis. Windows-based analytics make it easy, so you'll produce down the stretch like a seasoned pro.

Don't risk slicing or hooking with inferior models. GAT's research is rigorous, consistent and accurate. We have an ongoing effort to examine, refine and enhance our work. Whether it's interest rate lattice generation, term structure modeling, path sampling, prepayment modeling, advanced risk measures like Key Rate Durations, or performance attribution, you'll always be pin high.

GAT's technology allows you to shape your shots to the circumstances. Integrate Decision with your own database and run it on your own hardware; it's ODBC-compliant and runs on multiple platforms. The flexible architecture of our object-oriented design ensures that you'll keep pace with the financial markets as new innovations appear. With our commitment to leading edge technology, you'll never find yourself facing an unplayable lie.